Advance Praise for *Ready, Set, Dominate*

"Mike Kennedy continues our journey through a major industrial company in its struggles to maintain competitiveness through its product development process. Our adventure began in his first book, *Product Development for the Lean Enterprise,* as our hero Jon Stevens sets out to prepare his company for an adventure through the jungle of corporate resistance to change. Now Jon is back for an even more dangerous mission to implement significant paradigm shifts beyond a department and throughout the entire company. Many other bold managers have never returned from this swamp. Through his creative style and hero, Mike shows us the way based on actual experiences of the author and his associates as they help real companies make real change and experience the rewards."

Rick Jarman
President & CEO
National Center for Manufacturing Sciences (NCMS)

"We at Fisher & Paykel Appliances Ltd. are very proud of the innovative products that we have introduced to the appliance world. Our only frustration has been the time that it takes to develop these products using conventional product development methods. We were looking for a better way and upon reading Michael Kennedy's first book the answer became obvious — 'Learning First Product Development.' The simple conceptual change from 'design and test' to 'test and design' was the clincher. We introduced LFPD to our engineering team and after seeing the benefits of knowledge capture and reuse in this area we are looking to extend the practice throughout our organization."

John Bongard
CEO,
Fisher & Paykel Appliances, Ltd.

“We at Teledyne Benthos would like to thank Mike Kennedy and his team for showing us how to replace fear with knowledge in our product development process. Our engineers have moved away from a ‘fear of the unknown’ development environment, to one that is based on firsthand knowledge of true customer interests directly coupled to the technical knowledge required to successfully develop the product. Thanks to Mike we now know: only start a product design when both forms of knowledge are well in hand.”

Ron Marsiglio
President
Teledyne Benthos, Inc.

"Michael Kennedy and his team have done what many thought to be impossible. They have provided an answer to what companies have been trying to achieve for years: achievable and significant product development improvements presented in a way anyone can understand."

Thane Hathaway
President, CEO
EAC Product Development Solutions

Ready, Set, Dominate

Implement Toyota's Set-Based Learning for Developing Products and Nobody Can Catch You

by

Michael Kennedy
Kent Harmon
Ed Minnock

RICHMOND, VIRGINIA

If your bookseller does not have this book in stock,
it can be ordered directly from the publisher.
More information can be found at the
Web site shown below,
or give us a call.

The Oaklea Press
6912 Three Chopt Road, Suite B
Richmond, Virginia 23226

Voice: 1-804-218-2394
Email: shmartin@shmartin.com

Web site: http://www.OakleaPress.com

Contents

Foreword

The earliest work on what is now being known as Lean Product Development was done by the International Motor Vehicle Program at M.I.T. in the late 1980's. The people involved uncovered two unique and potentially transforming concepts for product developers — the chief engineer system and black-box outsourcing of subsystem design to suppliers — and reported on these finding in the landmark publication, *The Machine that Changed the World.*[1] Soon thereafter, Kim Clark and Takahiro Fujimoto elaborated on these and other new concepts in their influential volume, *Product Development Performance.*[2] In it they showed how much better the Japanese automotive companies performed in engineering and design than their US and European counterparts.

At the same time, a young Army sergeant-turned-academic had recently completed his Ph.D. in Mechanical Engineering at M.I.T., and was working as an assistant professor at The University of Michigan. When he read about the engineering practices documented by Clark and Fujimoto in particular, he was convinced that these Japanese automotive companies must be using a different paradigm for product development. So he and Jeffrey Liker traveled to Japan with some graduate students to investigate whether this was true. I was fortunate to be one of those graduate students.

It turned out that Allen Ward was right — sort of. We did find a different paradigm at work in Japan, but it wasn't apparent in many of the companies we visited. In fact, we found this new paradigm at work at only one company — Toyota. Later we found out that much of the data from Japan in those early studies was heavily skewed by one company — you guessed it! We wrote about that study mission in an article that appeared in the *Sloan Management Review,* and introduced the idea of Set-Based Concurrent Engineering.

I decided to study Japanese and returned to Japan for a longer, more in-depth investigation of Toyota's product development practices. In my Ph.D. dissertation,[3] I attempted to describe Toyota's system as a set of principles that encompasses development project leadership, product development planning, communication and decision-making, the role of manufacturing engineering, and set-based concurrent engineering. As we dug deeper into Toyota, we found that the different paradigm seemed to go beyond the set-based and chief engineer ideas, extending to other areas of engineering practice.

Jim Morgan continued this work with more in-depth investigation of Toyota's practices, and together with Jeffrey Liker published a comprehensive description of its system through a set of thirteen development principles.[5] Once again, the Toyota paradigm seemed to extend even further — into the daily routines of development work and into flow of work and information.

In the midst of Morgan's and my studies, Allen Ward left the University to start a company doing engineering and consulting work. He stayed in touch with the research and even did some informal research on his own. More so than any of the authors noted so far, Al had unique insight into the Toyota practices. It went beyond simply describing them, and he began formulating a theory and framework for an entirely new way of developing products. He also experimented with his ideas in other companies to test and refine them, not always with success, but always with a great deal of learning.

Michael Kennedy met Al at a meeting at the National Center for Manufacturing Sciences (NCMS) where Al was brought in to describe Toyota's unique practices as part of a benchmarking study. The two did not hit it off at first. In fact, Mike with his three decades of engineering and engineering management experience in one of America's most successful engineering companies thought Al's ideas were crazy. But the more they argued about their ideas, the more convinced Mike became that this new paradigm was far superior to the conventional one ingrained in most US product development organizations. Soon they were working together and hatched a plan for Al to write a book that would lay out the theory and tools in a textbook-like manner, while in parallel Mike would write a business novel about a company whose key people — or at least some of them — would go through a transformation in thinking similar to the one Mike had experienced personally. Mike finished his book first.[6] Al, sadly, did not get to finish his. He died tragically in a plane crash before it was completed.

While Al's departure was a tragic loss for the product development community and lean thinkers worldwide, his work continues. The unfinished manuscript[7] was published posthumously in 2007, and a cadre has continued to develop and evolve his ideas. This sequel presents in unique form, the development of several foundational concepts while adding in a few of Al's original ideas that had not yet been incorporated into prior publications.

The book you hold in your hands continues and builds on the story of the first, but does so with an eye towards practically implementing the concepts presented in the first. The key to implementing the four cornerstones of lean product development is to recognize the mortar that holds all the pieces together. Without the mortar, the pieces just don't hold together, and improvement is modest. Michael Kennedy's second novel rivals the first, and inspires companies to not just copy Toyota and match its performance, but to surpass Toyota's capabilities and dominate their own industry. Through the novel form, Mike further paints a vivid picture of how and why the transformation is, and must be, much broader than just engineering; yet, that it can be far simpler than one might imagine at the outset. He does so in such a realistic fashion, the reader can put him or herself right in the conference room with the team. To add icing to an already delicious cake, as a kind of epilogue, the author adds two case studies of actual companies that have started their lean journeys with astounding success.

As I visit product development organizations around the country, I'm often told, "We've read the blue book," referring to Michael's first novel. "That's great," I say. Then they say, "But, how do we get started?" This book is intended to help answer that question, and you will not be disappointed. So find a chair and good cup a coffee, and start your journey. Make sure the chair is comfortable, though, because you won't want to put it down until you're through! When you're done, don't put it on the bookshelf just so that you can tell visitors that you've read it. Start (or continue) your lean journey by putting the ideas into action, and help your organization achieve industry dominating performance.

Durward K. Sobek II
Bozeman, Montana

---

1 Womack, James P., Jones, Daniel T., and Roos, Daniel, *The Machine that Changed the World*, New York: HarperCollins, 1990.

2 Clark, Kim B. and Fujimot, Takahiro, *Product Development Performance: Strategy, Organization, and Management in the World Auto Industry*, Boston, MA: Harvard Business School Press, 1991.

3 Ward, Allen C., Liker, Jeffrey, Cristiano, John. J., Sobek II, Durward K., "The Second Toyota Paradox: How Delaying Decisions Can Make Better Cars Faster," *Sloan Management Review*, Vol. 36, No. 3, Spring 1995; pp. 43-61.

4 Sobek II, Durward K., *Principles that Shape Product Development Systems: A Toyota-Chrysler Comparison*, Ph.D. dissertation, The University of Michigan, Ann Arbor, 1997.

5 Morgan, James M., and Liker, Jeffrey K., *The Toyota Product Development System: Integrating People, Process, and Technology*, New York: Productivity Press, 2006.

6 Kennedy, Michael N., *Product Development for the Lean Enterprise*, Richmond, VA: The Oaklea Press, 2003.

7 Ward, Allen C., *Lean Product and Process Development*, Cambridge, MA: The Lean Enterprise Institute, 2007.

Part I
Finding *Your* Path to Domination

Introduction
The Transformation Journey

Toyota's history of domination is well chronicled in the business sections of newspapers and in national business publications. And much of what Toyota does differently is thoroughly documented in the predecessor to this book, *Product Development for the Lean Enterprise* (Oaklea Press, 2003) as well as in several others that have been published over the last few years. It's interesting to speculate why, with all this information available, other companies have not reached the same level of domination in their fields. Few have even come close to what Toyota has been able to accomplish. This book is intended to show why.

As with the preceding book, rather than tell you about Toyota, we decided to show the Toyota story in the form of a novel, which allows you to see how the Toyota development practices and underlying thinking can be applied to a company outside of the automotive industry, and outside of the Toyota culture. Furthermore, it is the journey to achieve huge productivity gains that is important, and this involves people and their personal commitment and involvement.

We have been pleased that, although all the characters and the environment in the first book were fictitious, readers have recognized the environment as similar to their own, and the characters in the book seem very familiar to them as well. It never occurred to us, for example, there were so many Doyles in the world. In fact, one leader in a company introduced himself that way. We have also been surprised to see how well the Toyota message resonates in areas beyond the physical hardware development environment. Interest has been keen from such industries as chemicals, consumer packaged goods, medical products, and building construction.

Why this book? What has changed?

The change is that the Toyota Product Development System is no longer a mystery. It may not be as well documented as the Toyota Production System that has fostered an entire industry of consulting and improvement under the Lean umbrella, but more and more companies are realizing the amazing potential for productivity improvements and are trying to extend Lean thinking into product development.

However, despite that growing realization, successful implementation does not seem to be materializing. A common saying is that you don't learn a lot from what works — you learn a lot from what doesn't work. Based on that, a good deal of learning must be happening! Realistically, we haven't seen any company approaching Toyota's level of continued domination of an industry.

As a result, this book is not more knowledge about Toyota practices. These are well documented and, although we admire Toyota, we really don't care to know more about the company from an academic standpoint. What we are all vitally interested in is how the thinking that has led to Toyota's success can be applied in other industries, as well as in automobile manufacturing, to quickly advance product development and hopefully surpass Toyota's high level of performance. That is the purpose of this book and the need we wish to fill.

The preceding book documented the capabilities of Toyota by focusing on the company's four cornerstones: Set-Based Concurrent Engineering, the Entrepreneurial System Designer (chief engineer), the Expert Engineering Workforce, and Responsibility Based Planning.

We were introduced to Toyota Product Development many years ago at a collaborative project led by the National Center for Manufacturing Sciences (NCMS). NCMS hired Dr. Allen Ward to present Toyota's product development practices. Michael Kennedy then spent eight years learning and collaborating with Allen Ward until Allen's untimely death in 2004. Since then, additional publications from James Morgan and Jeff Liker, Allen Ward (posthumously), and Durward Sobek have continued to describe Toyota's capabilities and characteristics from each of their perspectives.

More recently, a simple statement dramatically shaped our current thinking and helped determine the emphasis of this book. The president of Toyota North America, when asked at a conference why nobody at Toyota had written a book on Toyota, responded that it would only be one or two pages long. Then, after a pause, he added that there were only three things someone needed to do to emulate Toyota: "Keep everything simple, make it visual, and trust your people to do the right thing."

His comments raise an interesting question. Is there a simpler way to see, understand, and apply the Toyota message? We think so. The focus of this book is to build on this and to trace what has been learned through trial and error by leaders who are applying the principles in their businesses. This does not in any way change what Toyota does to dominate its industry, but it does allow for new interpretations concerning why Toyota executives do what they do. This can result in better and more effective application of the principles, and it also allows us to consider how best to apply them to a variety of industries.

The preceding book proposed a different way of approaching the change journey based on proven principles for participative change and full-scale change methodologies. Now the question must be raised, is that the best way for making the change? Will the approach even work for most companies? It was all conjecture since no one, not even Toyota, has ever made such a transformation. Toyota evolved to its current capability over the course of decades. Most of us would prefer a somewhat shorter path.

The first book ended where it did because it had to. To carry the story further would have required wishful thinking and conjecture since no evidence existed at that time to prove the desired level of transformation could be accomplished. We know much more now. Not only have companies learned about the Toyota development system, they are evolving their practices to emulate them, and we have been observing the practices and results. We have included at the end of this book case studies of two companies we feel have made great strides in understanding and applying the Toyota principles.

So let us continue the journey of the Infrared Technologies Corporation (IRT) one year later. The company and the people are still fictitious. The difference from the preceding book is that the adventures of the company are based on the real experiences of a number of companies who are on the journey.

Background

The prequel to this book took place in a fictitious company called Infrared Technologies Corporation (IRT). It opened in a meeting, the main purpose of which was to review proposed changes to the standard product development process, known as PDSP (Product Development Standard Process). Doyle Mattingly, a close-minded and fastidious individual, was presiding. Doyle had led the development of the standard process over the past several years and was a strong believer in it.

On the agenda that day was an intelligent and vivacious young engineer named Jan Morris. She reported on her involvement in a project sponsored by the National Center for Manufacturing Science (NCMS) that involved studying the Toyota product development system which, as she explained to the group, had been found to be much more efficient than the method used by IRT and other western companies. Toyota's development engineers were said to spend 80% of their time adding value for customers, while the typical North American company's engineers spent only 20% of their time doing so. The response to Jan came swiftly and rudely, as it became clear that Doyle wanted to hear none of this.

In a subsequent meeting of the engineering leadership it was learned that Jack Holder had been reassigned from the position of Executive Vice President over Operations to that of Executive Vice President over Engineering. Jack was a short, wiry, outspoken ex-marine who sported a flattop even though he was balding. He was a hard-nosed individual known for taking on a problem and getting it solved. As the meeting unfolded, it became apparent he had just been handed a big problem. IRT was facing serious challenges. Market share was shrinking, overhead costs were increasing, and profits were deteriorating. The company was not keeping pace in the area of new products. And now it was Jack's responsibility to turn the situation around.

Jack turned for help to Jon Stevens, an accomplished engineer who was about to take early retirement. Early in Jon's career, Jack had used Jon as his primary troubleshooter, and later, Jack was largely responsible for Jon's election as Senior Fellow. Jon held Jack in high regard and so he agreed to take on the assignment to study the situation and then define a turnaround strategy.

Jon assembled a team to identify and think through options. During the meetings, he learned that the company already had investigated a system for developing products that was much superior to IRT's. He heard about the presentation Jan Morris had made to Doyle's group about the Toyota development system, which she had studied while representing IRT as part of a consortium sponsored by NCMS. She made her presentation to Jon's team and this time it was well received. It quickly had become apparent that Toyota's product development system was diametrically opposed to IRT development initiatives and beliefs.

At IRT, as in most western companies, project teams quickly evaluated several alternatives and decided on specifications and a primary system design or architecture. A detailed task schedule was created, responsibilities were petitioned, and detailed design begins.

The plan was followed until it failed for any number of reasons. Systems test often revealed a wave of problems and builds by Manufacturing usually revealed another wave. Each time, the product specification, product design, and manufacturing process were iterated through unplanned loop backs. Additional people were brought in until the product finally got out the door. Customer shipments regularly revealed yet more problems. These unplanned loop backs were non-productive, confusing, and costly waste.

The capabilities and characteristics of the Toyota system were hard for Jon's group to ignore against those of IRT. This stark contrast was clearly illustrated by the following table.

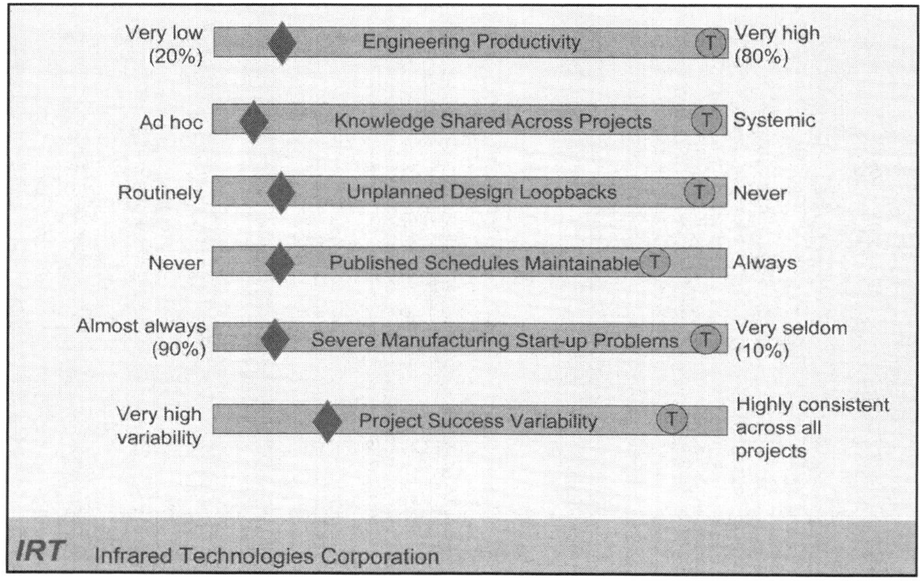

Development Environment Attributes

Attribute	IRT	Toyota
Operational Focus	Planning and Control	Learning and Doing
Progress Evaluation	Task Completeness	Knowledge Completeness
Basis for Personal Reward	Compliance	Knowledge / Expertise
Improvement Focus	Task Efficiency	Learning Efficiency

IRT Infrared Technologies Corporation

As Jan described how the Toyota system worked, it sounded completely backward to everything IRT had learned was a best practice. Even IRT's coveted National Quality Award was won because IRT excelled at compliance to its processes including its Product Development Standard Process. Toyota was the opposite — loose on structure and tight on knowledge. Yet, Toyota was achieving far superior results. Everything at Toyota seemed to revolve around creating, capturing, and reusing knowledge for decision-making.

Jan had succeeded in convincing Jon's team of two things: first that product development at IRT was all messed up, and second, there didn't appear to be much they could do about it. Jon's team searched for alternatives, particularly ones that could leverage IRT's process strength but to no avail. Jan explained that the NCMS project spent many months searching for a company with a product development methodology that approached Toyota's success, also to no avail.

Jon's team again turned to Jan to describe four key principles of the Toyota system that she called the four cornerstones. She started with Set-Based Concurrent Engineering. She described the IRT process as "point-based" because a single design approach was selected early, fully designed, and then tested. If that "point" in the design space failed to satisfy the specifications, then a new approach was selected, the designs were revised accordingly, and then tested. If that second "point" failed, then the iterations continued until a point finally satisfied the specifications . . . or time simply ran out. The truth is, Point-Based Product Development perpetually results in unplanned loop backs that weave through subsystems and cause all kinds of firefighting, confusion, and costly waste. Products are often late, over-budget, and less than desirable to the customers.

In Set-Based Concurrent Engineering, sets of possibilities are tested early, before design decisions are made. The alternatives are systematically narrowed by eliminating weaker designs relative to broad targets. Interfaces stay loose to allow flexibility. A known feasible solution is always one of the possibilities. Learning and testing continues on the designs that are not known to be feasible.

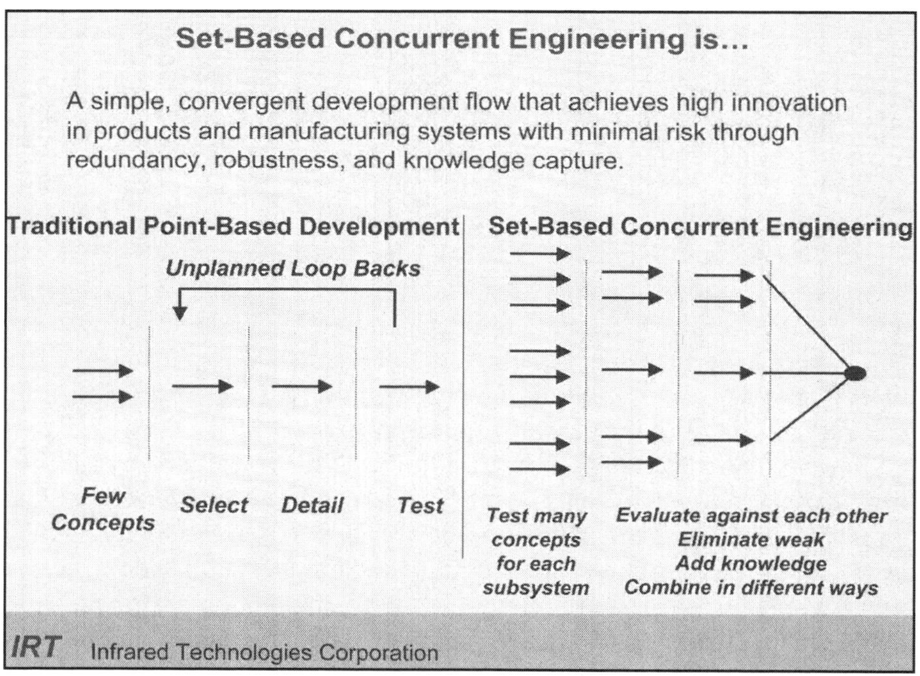

Jan was asked how Toyota could possibly afford to evaluate so many design possibilities up front. She explained that Set-Based Concurrent Engineering is a lot cheaper than unplanned loopbacks because engineers are performing tests designed to provide results for the whole range of possibilities, rather than doing a full detailed design for each iteration. And the evaluation of multiple sets of possibilities early almost ensures that more optimal product and process designs will be found.

Jan then explained that it is the knowledge of the Expert Engineering Workforce that makes Set-Based Concurrent Engineering even cheaper. She contrasted IRT's system of rapid promotions from engineer to manager with Toyota's system of clear responsibility for each part of the system.

At Toyota, functional managers are the teachers and mentors so managers tend to be the most technically competent engineers with the most experience. And managers continue to learn because they are mentoring all their engineers, and thus seeing all of the design challenges and resulting innovations firsthand.

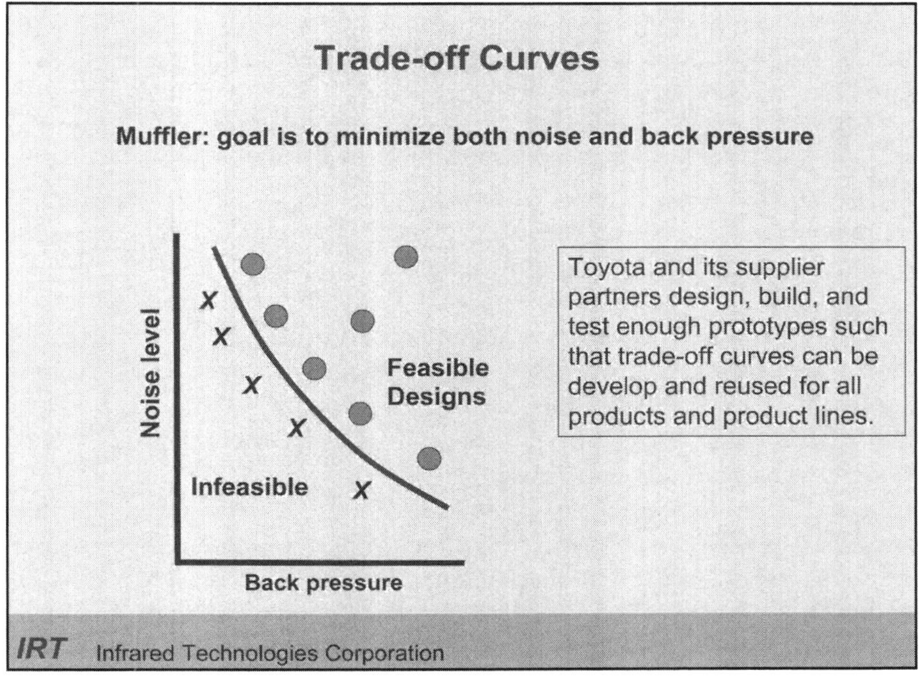

Jan introduced trade-off curves as the language of set-based design. Trade-off curves define the relationship between two or more design decisions within a subsystem like transmissions or chassis or mufflers. Trade-off curves are the subsystem knowledge from which design alternatives are evaluated and narrowed until the optimal design is chosen. As such, trade-off curves provide reusable knowledge for future product designs. Toyota establishes short and long-range targets for all their subsystems including those designed in-house and those designed by suppliers.

If a particular design doesn't make it into a specific car, perhaps because it was not proven in time, the knowledge is retained along with knowledge from other past projects, both in terms of what worked and what didn't. As a result sets of subsystem possibilities from prior projects are always waiting for the next project. Toyota does this for all their subsystems. Jon and his team were intrigued by the power of Toyota's knowledge base, and began to understand why set-based design can be so cheap and so powerful at Toyota.

Jan then introduced the Entrepreneurial System Designer or Chief Engineer. Toyota Chief Engineers have little formal authority; none of the functional engineers, who do the actual design work, work for the Chief Engineers. Their credibility as the best engineers in the company and as the designated voice of the customer, combined with strong personalities, allow them to be very persuasive.

Like project managers at IRT, they are responsible for the schedule, cost, and quality; however, at IRT, achieving two out of those three was usually considered a success. At Toyota, Chief Engineers are expected to achieve all three, plus deliver strong profit and market share growth, and mentor the functional engineers along the way.

Chief Engineers prepare a product concept, gain approval to develop the product from top management, and then establish the dates for the key Integrating Events. Chief Engineers use these key Integrating Events to manage the decisions as they converge to the optimal solution from the sets of possibilities. Ultimately, they approve every design decision and every drawing.

Finally, Jan explained Responsibility-Based Planning. She pointed out that it is the nature of product development to have variation, and there has to be variation if there is going to be innovation. Therefore the notion that a group of individuals can accurately lay out all the tasks for an entire product development project is the height of wishful thinking.

At IRT, a small group of managers did exactly that for each project. They defined all the tasks for all the engineers, their start and end dates, and their duration. The schedule deteriorated over time so it had to be constantly reworked, which was wasteful and costly.

At Toyota it is the responsibility of the functional engineering teams to prepare plans to meet the key Integrating Event dates defined by

Chief Engineers, and these dates are never missed. Planning and execution are done by the same people. Some alternatives may miss but there is always a known feasible backup.

At IRT, task-based reviews focused on percent completion metrics such as the percentage of drawings completed. At Toyota, Integrating Events are hands-on technical reviews of the results of prototypes testing, design alternatives, the latest tradeoff curves, and actual prototype demonstrations. Integrating Events are used to narrow the design alternatives.

After much discussion, Jon's team recommended that IRT adopt the Toyota methodology by implementing the four cornerstones. Moreover, it was to be done quickly and with broad participation.

Jack was faced with a serious risk-reward situation. The current product development philosophy was well directed and well supported internally but seemed to have little chance of producing the dramatic improvements he wanted and felt the company needed. But the Toyota system emanated from a different culture. Other than the obvious success of Toyota and its main supplier Denso, no other evidence of its effectiveness existed. Nevertheless, the system made sense to Jack, and his decision was to move ahead aggressively. He felt he had nothing to lose as there was no evidence that any of the current improvement initiatives could double or triple productivity, and this was what was needed in order to reach the desired improvement goals.

Jack supported the change publically and with a strong vision for the future. His goals were:

- To be the market leader in all four business segments within two years
- To dominate the four segments within four years.

Jack and Jon held a large group session to launch the change and this was quite effective in gaining engineering commitment. However, as opposed to continuing the recommended whole scale approach to change, each of the four business divisions — Military Products, Automotive Products, Civilian Avionics, Security Systems — took one of the cornerstones to develop and pilot independently. The plan was that the results from each pilot would expand naturally into all the others.

Jon Stevens deferred retirement and continued to chair on a part-time basis the Knowledge-Based Development Steering Team that guided the timing and integration of the cornerstones across all the businesses. Since Jack had decided each of the business leaders should be held responsible for their cornerstone implementations, Jon took on other technical responsibilities, reporting directly to Jack.

To Jon's great disappointment Jan Morris left the company and took a position with a high-tech engineering company in Massachusetts.

That's the summary except for one thing — as we pick up the story, the Board of Directors has run out of patience with IRT's poor financial performance and has made it clear that the profit picture needs to improve fast.

Now let's continue the journey.

Chapter 1
The Profit Imperative

Monday Morning: Infrared Technologies Corporation
(One year later)

As IRT nears the end of another disappointing year from a financial perspective, the Board of Directors wants change. Change has arrived in the form of a new Chief Financial Officer, the ambitious and industry-renowned turnaround expert, Brenda Caine. Her mission is to improve profit fast.

"Welcome to IRT," Brenda Caine said as she invited Al Frank into her posh, executive office complete with dark-stained hardwood floor and antique Oriental carpet. "Have a seat."

Brenda walked smartly around her desk and sat in her black leather upholstered swivel chair. She was a picture of today's modern rock star executive in her perfectly-fitted jet black Armani suit. Her blood red lipstick glistened.

"Thank you," Al said. "It was hard to leave Consumer Technologies but I'm here so let me know how I can help." Al was a clean-cut product of one of America's finest business schools.

"The Board of Directors hired me to do the same thing for IRT that I did for Consumer Technologies," she said.

"Good," Al said. "So you've got the full support of the executive team?"

"Almost," she answered. "There's always one guy — his name is Jack Holder. He's quite a character — a salt of the earth type who doesn't understand global economics. He was probably good in his day. You see, he has a crazy idea about transforming product development. I've run into a hundred Jack Holders and they are all the same — long on passion and short on results."

"Can he stop us?"

"No. I have full support of the Board. They want me to improve profit right away and double the stock price — just like I did at Consumer Technologies."

"I read that many of the Board members are new," Al said.

"Right," Brenda said "And they're tired of pathetic earnings and an embarrassing stock price."

"What's the timing?" Al asked.

"Within weeks we'll start cutting the fat out of the organization and start looking for buyers for the unprofitable Automotive Products business."

"Sounds serious," Al said.

"I am serious. Also in a couple of months Ray, the current CEO, is going to step down and I'll be named CEO."

"I knew it," Al exclaimed. "That's why you left Consumer Technologies. Congratulations."

"I'd have had to wait five years for this opportunity at Consumer Technologies, and you know me. I see no value in waiting to do what is obviously needed."

"What can I do?"

"As my right-hand man, I need you to lead the cost reduction effort, which includes finding a buyer for the Automotive Products business, figuring out how to consolidate into one site, and finding a buyer for the other site. Then we'll have money to spend, so I need you to find acquisition targets with high growth and high profit potential."

"Sounds like IRT is ripe with opportunity," Al said.

Brenda stood. "It definitely is. Look, I've got to run. I'm in a meeting with the executives all day today. Let's talk tomorrow."

Al rose. "I look forward to it." He turned to the expansive window. "Looks like a storm is rolling in," he said, gazing at dark clouds covering the Rocky Mountains.

Brenda nodded. "Sure does, and you know what? The CEO's office has an even better view."

"I'll see you tomorrow."

"By the way, don't mention the CEO succession to anyone," Brenda said.

Chapter 2
Assessing Progress Toward Achieving the Lean Enterprise

PDCA is the problem solving and continuous improvement cycle used at Toyota and LAMDA (Look, Ask, Model, Discuss, and Act) is how Dr. Allen Ward described Toyota's learning cycle that occurs within PDCA. We will introduce LAMDA during the course of this book and convey its power in problem solving, collaborative learning, decision-making, and communication.

Same Monday Morning: Infrared Technologies Corporation

I glanced at my watch as I briskly walked along the hallway on the front side of the building overlooking the parking lot. When I reached the open doorway, I slowed down and hung a right, mildly surprised that most of the seats around the conference table had already been taken.

Carl looked up from a stack of notes.

"Good Morning, Jon," he said.

I nodded to him. "Appears Donna booked the same room we used last year to work out this program." Then I said to the rest of the room, "Good Morning, all. I hope everyone had a nice weekend."

I took the open seat at the head of the table. "This may be a first. Looks like everybody's here on time."

This was the regularly scheduled meeting of the Knowledge-Based Development (KBD) Steering team, which normally met monthly to help me assess progress. Several members of the original team were in attendance:

- Carl Garcia: a systems engineer working in Civilian Avionics
- Greg Drucker: a Six-Sigma Master Black Belt that led the extensive Six Sigma improvement initiatives at IRT. He now worked for me and was coordinating all the lean and Six-Sigma activities across product development.
- Dick Beasley: a program manager in Military Products
- Tim Ashcroft: a program manager in Security Systems

- Vijay Suran: a program manager in Automotive Products
- Jay Gooding: a CAD/CAM technologist working in Engineering Services.
- Dennis Goodson: representing Purchasing

Also attending were:

- Robin Leibermann: from the change department in HR
- Sandra Palmer: from Marketing
- George Rogers: from Production Operations

These three had been added after Jack had committed to the change.

As I looked around, I was keenly aware that the makeup of the team had shifted. It had migrated from a problem-solving group, as originally chartered, to a steering committee that represented various organizational perspectives.

"So Jon," Greg said, "you normally send out an agenda. What's our plan today?"

It was true, I normally did send out an agenda for this meeting. It had been a year since I'd deferred retirement in order to lead the transformation to what we called the Knowledge Based Development process.

"Reflection," I said. "Is everyone aware it's been exactly one year, today, that Jack had committed to this change?"

A low murmur indicated the group was unaware it had been that long.

Sandra flashed one of her winning smiles. "I had no clue — I was just assigned to the team a couple of months ago. Had I known, I'd have brought a cake."

I smiled back, and then addressed the room. "I do want to discuss our progress today, but first, let me refresh all our memories about the plan. First, Jack established a performance vision and time goals."

I went to the flip chart and wrote Jack's vision statements:

- **To be the market leader in each of our four businesses in two years**
- **To dominate in four years**

I turned to the group. "Each of our businesses took the lead on one of the cornerstones to pilot the concepts. Our plan was to train, monitor and guide the pilots, then, when ready, integrate all of them into a system.

I turned to the flip chart and wrote on a second page:

- **Expert Engineering Workforce — Civilian Avionics**
- **Entrepreneurial System Designer — Automotive Products**
- **Set-Based Concurrent Engineering — Security Systems**
- **Responsibility-Based Planning & Control — Military Products**

"Each of these business units took the lead on piloting a cornerstone." I pointed to the flip chart. "Each of you representing the various businesses and functions were to act as a catalyst for training and sharing best practices. Right?"

I glanced around the room but did not wait for visible responses. "We've made a lot of presentations. We've bought a lot of books and read them. We've contracted with people to teach A3-based problem solving, and a lot of people have been taught. We've provided funding to groups so they can develop trade-off curves and try set-based concepts."

"So where are we today?"

I walked to the board and started writing:

- **Lots of awareness, acceptance of principles, involvement**

"It seems everyone has accepted the knowledge based principles. And they've done it under the name of Lean Product Development, which is something we should discuss at some point. Does everyone agree?"

"Absolutely, I agree," Jay said. "I think almost everyone in engineering has read at least one book on it. It seems to be very well received."

Robin piped up. "I also agree, but I have to say there's not a general consensus that anything will ever really change at the management level."

Discussion went on for a time. The upshot was we all agreed with my comments, and that overall this was a positive and lasting result.

I wrote a second item that I thought we'd achieved on the board:

- **Our problem solving has improved dramatically**

I faced the group. "I think Wayne (Wayne Tillotson was business vice president over Civilian Avionics) has done a great job here. He has trained most of his engineers on the LAMDA-based problem solving methodology, and on documenting using A3s, and he is staying on top of them. He brought Allen Ward in to teach these principles, and it has made a big difference. LAMDA has really taken off in his Civilian Avionics business and is spreading into Christine's business (Christine Dumas was business vice president over Security Systems). Both Jack and I have had the opportunity to personally review the A3s. It's good stuff."

Vijay interrupted. "Jon, can you talk some about this LAMDA process, and also how it relates to A3s? I get a lot of questions on it and I am never sure I explain it correctly. This LAMDA thinking and the importance of the A3s are things Allen emphasized after he taught Jan. What I have heard is that this is succeeding by forcing engineers to solve problems by getting to the root cause, instead of our normal approach of jumping to the solution and hoping it works."

I said, "I don't want to spend much time on LAMDA and A3s right now, but I will make a few comments. We all know that PDCA is the fundamental way that Toyota solves problems, and A3s are used for documenting the results. Allen observed, while at Toyota, that the developers always **looked** at the problem personally, got to the root cause by **asking** why repeatedly, made simple **models** for the solution, **discussed** it with all involved, and then **acted** to resolve the problems. He called it LAMDA. That is the learning process. The A3 is an essential part of the LAMDA process as it does four critical things. First, it tells the LAMDA story simply and visibly through the A3 standard structured format. Second, it documents the results for communication and discussion. Third, it allows mentoring from those who understand to those that don't. And finally, the standard format pulls the LAMDA process. Allen believed, as do we, it is the LAMDA learning cycle that makes Toyota's PDCA problem-solving so much more effective."

There was general consensus on our improved problem solving and we would discuss LAMDA in more detail later. We patted ourselves on the back a little.

I stepped back to the board and added a third positive achievement:

- **Lots of set-based activity**

I turned back to the group. "The principles of Set-Based Concurrent

Engineering have really caught on. Most of the work here has been in Christine's Security Systems business. Christine has encouraged many more early alternatives and is asking where the trade-offs are. This does not seem to be as widespread as LAMDA but it does appear to have good traction on specific projects. Christine has presented some really nice trade-off studies to Jack and me."

Tim raised his hand. "I agree partially here, but realistically, I have not seen us approaching the level of set-based systemic design that I understand exists at Toyota. We are still feeling our way, but it does have a solid foothold, conceptually, which is positive."

This sparked discussion. The group largely agreed that getting where we'd like to be was going to take time, but we were on the right track.

"Here's what's last on my list." I wrote on the board:

- **Significant waste removal activities via value stream mapping**

I turned around. "As we all know, removing waste from the operational value stream is always good. Doing so in production continuously for more than a decade has delivered excellent results and fostered many new techniques. During the past year, we've seen these techniques increasingly applied to product development — with good results. But I worry whether it will ever resolve the root causes of our product development issues. The Toyota system is really a different paradigm for development, not based on a series of prescribed tasks but rather on the continuous flow of knowledge. The strength of VSM is primarily removing the waste from defined processes, not on changing fundamental operating philosophies."

Greg had been leading these types of activities — in production, and now in product development. I turned to him for an answer.

"I understand your concern," Greg said. "You worry that we may be working to make process tasks more efficient when the truth is the entire process may need to be rethought. Let me think about it awhile."

"Yes, that is the bulk of my concern," I said.

Dick put in, "Or is your real problem that this is where Doyle's now putting all his emphasis, with a fair degree of success if the truth be known." A wry smile appeared on his face. "And you still blame him for Jan leaving, don'tcha?"

I laughed and nodded. "Yes, there could be some of that."

Greg said, "Actually Jon, I don't share your concern. As long as we understand what we're doing, I think we will get where we need to go. There's more to product development than just developing knowledge — all the documentation that goes with it has to be generated, too — customer reports, regulatory reports, process planning documents and on and on. Those are task-based activities and they should be leaned out. They can be standardized for efficiency pretty well. The trick, I think, is to always recognize there are two types of waste — process waste and knowledge waste. The key is not to confuse the two."

Carl said, "That makes sense to me. Allen Ward made that distinction quite visible as he defined three categories of knowledge waste — scatter, handoffs, and wishful thinking were the names I think he gave them. And he had one level below that."

"Okay," I said. "What I think you're saying is that, although the primary goal of product development is to generate product knowledge, there are and always will be process steps for generating the documentation required to produce and sell a product. Therefore, using traditional lean techniques for making these process steps waste-free is good. And this can be valuable in identifying where the process is actually hampering the creation of knowledge, and vice versa. A process with knowledge handoffs should be challenged from that perspective, and a process that's based on wishful thinking probably shouldn't even exist. Certainly no one ought to waste time trying to improve it."

"Is this right? Are we looking at this the right way?" I asked.

Greg said, "I have no idea. Why don't you ask Doyle?"

"I may do that," I said. "Anyway, if we are doing it the right way, then what I wrote on the board about value stream mapping is positive, okay?"

There were general nods of agreement, so I moved on. "What else are we doing?" I said as I turned to the board.

Vijay said, "In Automotive, we're looking at the role of the Chief Engineer and system design techniques. For several projects, including mine, we have started using Obeya room setups for visual planning and communication. I think it is positive and working. Not a paradigm buster, but a nice aid."

I wrote on the board:

- **Use of Obeya rooms for visual planning and communication**

"Does everyone agree?"

"Sure," Tim responded. "I went into Vijay's war room. I still like that term better, by the way. Anyway, it was really well laid out and organized. It strongly supports the two cornerstones of Responsibility-Based Planning and the role of the System Designer and keeps everything visible — both the plan and the developing product."

Everyone agreed it was an idea that reinforced the cornerstones and it should be continued and broadened.

"Okay, I have just listed five positive elements of our Lean product development environment as it is in progress. We seem to be in agreement that we are moving in the right direction. Is there more? And is this enough?"

I waited for comments as the group fidgeted.

Carl broke the silence. "On the one hand, I think we're making good progress on the cornerstones. Our project leaders are trying to be more like true Entrepreneurial System Designers. Our engineers are being allowed more freedom for learning, planning, and following good engineering principles. We certainly have some set-based activities — at least we're not throwing away all the alternatives as quickly as we used to. Probably the best news is that the engineering community as a whole has embraced the ideas. They don't look at the program as the crazy idea of the year syndrome."

"On the other hand," he continued, "do we really think this is going to take us to the Promised Land — at least in my lifetime? And I'm 48." He pointed at Jack's goal of domination in four years. "That's only three years from now."

Carl did have a way of bringing us back to Earth. What he said made sense. The truth was I'd been uncomfortable for a while — the same lingering thought on my mind.

George Rogers from production services chimed in. "I'll tell you what's bothering me. I know I'm a newcomer to this steering group. I see all this stuff going on. I read all the Toyota books about how they really focus on manufacturing know-how in product development. And I don't see anything that's any different than before. Engineers still make the same stupid design decisions that cost us time and money. That hasn't changed, and I don't see anything here that will change it."

Sandra Palmer from marketing, also a relatively new member of the group, said, "In Marketing, we don't know what our role is going to be. Some of the new project leaders, now Chief Engineers, say they're taking our role — because that's what Toyota is doing. I'd have to say we are confused."

Dick added fuel to a growing fire. "I was talking to Doyle the other day, and he made the comment that this was actually going okay. Let me tell you, guys, if Doyle thinks this is going okay, we must be missing something, don't you think?"

Dick may have made this comment half in jest, but it hit home. Jack had stopped the PDSP initiative that had focused on a detailed standardization of process steps, but we all knew Doyle still believed in it strongly.

I said, "We haven't talked too much about Military Products. What are they up to, Dick?"

"Well, they've been slow to do much in the main projects," Dick responded. "As you know, I'm primarily on concept projects that have less oversight and progress deliverables. Doyle and Nathan have developed what they call the 'Lean Phase Gate System.' It focuses only on the main project reviews, supposedly as dictated by the Department of Defense. They're doing a lot of value stream mapping to make the process for creating the deliverables more efficient." He shrugged. "Sorry, I can't tell you more. I haven't had time or the willpower to get too involved."

Robin said, "Let me raise another issue."

"Sheeze, a few minutes ago we were patting ourselves on the back, and now the sky is falling," I said.

"Sorry." Robin forced a sheepish grin. "But you did ask, and I meant to bring this up earlier. This discussion has been good background for this information." She turned to the others. "I assume we all remember that we developed a productivity assessment of 20 questions so we could monitor our progress. It was designed to be very difficult to score well. Even Toyota, according to our projections, was only at about 80%. The thought was that the productivity numbers should mirror Jack's goals that we needed to double our productivity in two years and triple it in four to reach his market numbers. If you remember, Jan had developed this right after our go-ahead. We had several group meetings for assessing ourselves. Our score was 19, which as you recall seemed in line with what we expected. Jan had also worked through NCMS and got similar numbers from several companies. Well, a few weeks ago, we sent the forms out to the same people, about a hundred of them, to get their feedback as to how they saw it now. We just finished calibrating them yesterday. May I have a drum roll please?"

She beat an imaginary drum, and then said, "The average was 23. There is no way that I can tell you whether this really means anything; but, no matter how you look at it, it certainly didn't take a huge leap — nor do I believe Jack will look at this as encouraging."

Greg held up a number on his cell phone screen. "That's a 21% improvement. I'd take that any year in the stock market."

"Let's take a twenty minute break," I said." But before we leave, has anyone heard from Jan. I really miss her — and her knowledge, too."

Vijay said, "I received a Christmas card from her. She really likes her job — small high tech company. She really hated to leave, but the opportunity was just too juicy for her not to take it. "

"I'll bet Doyle got a nice card from her," Greg said.

"A last thought before break," Carl said as he stood up. "Jon, no offense to you or to any of us, but do we know enough? Jan was our bridge to knowledge. Allen Ward was our guide. Jan left. Allen was killed in the plane crash — can you imagine where we might be if we still had his guidance. What we have left is a lot of books on the theory of Toyota, but no guiding principles for putting it into practice." He shrugged. "Let's not be too hard on ourselves. At least we're trying and making some progress."

During the break, I went back through my files and found an initial metric chart Jan had used as a part of the NCMS project. She'd used that as a general guide to develop the assessment that Robin referred to.

I decided to use it after break. I didn't think anyone here had seen it. I wasn't sure whether it would add value, but it seemed to me we needed to get above the details for at least a few minutes.

As everyone dragged themselves back in, I made an observation. "It seems to me that if we were on a continuous improvement journey, we'd be satisfied with our progress. A 20% improvement of our metrics is really not that bad. However, at 20% improvement per year, assuming we can maintain that the way we are going, it will take a really long time to get to 2x improvement, let alone 3x or the 4x that seems to be possible.

"I think Carl made a really good point before the break. We don't know enough to do anything differently. The big question is, of course — is it enough? And if it isn't, what the heck do we do about it?

"Here is a simple assessment chart that Jan had developed, or I think revised from the original NCMS project." I projected the slide onto the screen.

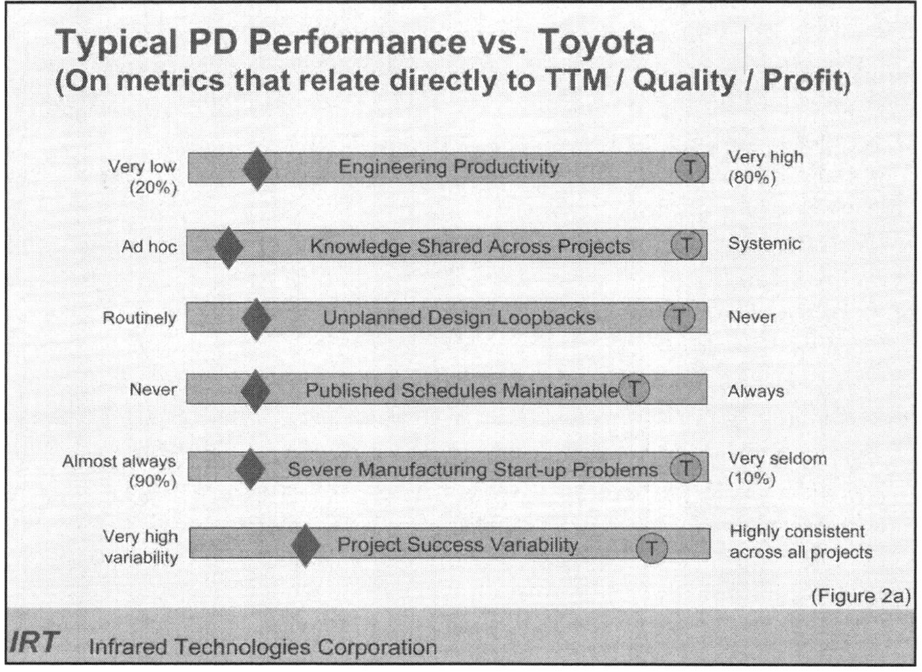

(Figure 2a)

"Just when I thought we might actually get through a meeting without a slide," Vijay said, laughing.

I gave him a nasty stare, then continued. "Think of this as a sliding bar scale of key capabilities. Our 20-question assessment form digs deeper and tries to be more exacting, but the diamonds are where most companies are. The circles are Toyota. Jan used this for a presentation at a lean product development forum. This seemed to be a pretty accurate picture of the capabilities of the companies represented there. Does everyone agree that we are similar to the diamonds when we started and where we are today? A 20% change is pretty insignificant."

Carl answered for everyone. "Sure, we are on the left side. We have all those problems."

I said, "Will implementing any or all of the improvements we just listed ever get us to the other side?"

"Not without some sort of miracle," Tim said with a chuckle.

George Rogers said, "If you want some good news, tell Jack that Security Systems had better manufacturing ramps than the other businesses and better than they've had in the past. So if we can replicate that success in all the businesses we should be able to reduce serious manufacturing problems."

After some discussion, we all agreed that if continuous improvement was the goal, we were doing quite well. But no one thought our current pace of progress would ever be enough to reach Jack's goals.

I said, "Who wants to volunteer to tell Jack we're really doing well, but not nearly well enough?" After few moments of silence, I answered my own question. "No takers."

I drummed my fingers on the table. "Any last comments before we close for today? I'll try and see Jack this afternoon — I think he's in town. We need some direction on next steps. I'm sure it won't be long before we regroup to figure something out. I seriously doubt Jack will revise his goals — not at this point, anyway."

Everyone got up to leave. Robin stopped in front of me. "You do know that a 20% improvement path per year is not bad at all."

I appreciated Robin's attempt at offering solace, and reflected on her comment as I walked to the other side of the building and the corner offices affectionately known as "Mahogany Row." Jack and I go way back. I still remember his first words to me when I started working for him. "I know you will screw up at times. Just make sure I hear it from you first."

There was no doubt about it. I felt a real sense of failure and direct responsibility for the lack of progress. My gut was telling me things weren't coming together at all the way they should. Each of the business leaders had convinced Jack that they were on board and would do their part — and seemingly, they were and had.

For no particular reason — except maybe to postpone what I was certain would be a difficult discussion — I took a detour through the cafeteria and stopped for coffee. I smiled to myself as I looked over at the corner Troy had occupied during most of the days leading up to his retirement. He had left and I had decided to stay on. We still played golf regularly; the difference was he now beat me more often than not.

With coffee in hand, I continued my walk through the manufacturing side of the building. I had achieved my rank of Senior Fellow through developing manufacturing technology and still felt manufacturing was home. It made me feel proud when I realized I was the first ever from manufacturing to achieve that level. Delaying retirement had given me a chance to work across engineering and manufacturing to help integrate some new technologies, independent of the knowledge based efforts. It concerned me that I'd spent way too much time focused on that during the last year.

I entered the executive offices and was greeted with a smiling face.

"Hi, Jon. Haven't seen you for a while. Normally, you'd have needed my advice on something long before now," Donna said in her characteristically wry matter-of-fact tone.

"Hi, Donna," I said as I walked to her desk. She'd been my secretary for years in my early manufacturing management days. Then she'd become our group administrative assistant. Even so, I think she always thought she really worked just for me.

Donna had a rare presence about her. She always seemed a step ahead of everyone, which, along with her in-your-face bluntness, made her great at her job. I guessed her to be forty-something. She'd become Jack's administrative assistant about six months ago.

"So, you finally came all the way over here — just to see me, right?"

"Absolutely," I said. "But since I'm here, I might as well schedule a meeting with Jack as soon as you can fit me in. It will take about an hour."

Just then Jack came rushing into the offices with an all too familiar I'm-gonna-kill-someone look. He saw me and pulled up.

"Jon, good, I need to talk to you." He tramped into his office without waiting for me to follow.

Donna winked at me. "Fast enough for you, Jon? Tell me I'm not good."

With a helpless shrug, I walked in and closed the door — not wanting the entire office to hear me getting verbally thrashed by the old Marine. I assumed Jack had already figured out what I was here to tell him.

"We have a lot to talk about," Jack said. He looked tired but full of nervous energy, as always. "I've been spending significant time with Brenda Caine, our new CFO. She was hired to bring this place back to profitability and has prepared an extremely aggressive plan. She just briefed Ray and the execs — I just came from the meeting."

I said, "I haven't met her but I have heard she was very successful at her previous company—"

Jack interrupted. "Our financial performance is not acceptable. Revenue's flat, market share's declining. Profit is down to three percent. We've missed our earnings commitment three quarters in a row."

"We've been missing our commitments for years," I said. "That's why you came from production into engineering to implement a new vision."

"The difference is — at least from Brenda's point of view — we're out of time. The way she explained it, our investors would be better off pulling their money out of IRT and putting it in a mutual fund they pick by throwing a dart."

What else is new? I said to myself. That's why I'd pulled IRT stock out of my retirement account.

Jack said, "Brenda has a four point plan. Before I tell it, you have to understand this conversation is confidential. I don't want rumors flying around."

Jack stared at me.

Strange. It wasn't like Jack to act paranoid. "You know you can count on me," I said.

"First, she wants to sell the Automotive business. She can't fathom how we can ever make an acceptable profit given the demise of the U.S. auto business. She points out that our customers are American, not Toyota."

I clenched my jaw to keep it from dropping.

"Second, she wants to outsource manufacturing for the Security Systems business. She is sure that will save millions. Third, she wants an across-the-board workforce reduction and to consolidate into the main building. Finally, she wants to use the profits generated to buy what she calls can't-miss cash cow companies."

"Whoa," I said. "Is she trying to destroy the company?"

"Jon, Brenda was hired to help this company achieve an acceptable level of profit and she is recommending exactly what a lot of companies have done. She has done this a number of times already and guarantees it will work."

"But what about our vision — your vision?"

"I told Brenda and Ray that my plan is to improve profit by being faster to market than the competition with superior quality."

"How does Brenda feel about this?"

"She asked me when profit would start to improve and I stuck my neck out and promised we'd pull up half our schedules by a month and eliminate most of our quality problems on next year's new products." Jack looked me straight in the eye. "Jon, you really need to come through for me."

I must admit I squirmed in my chair. "I've got bad news," I said.

"We've made good continuous improvement but we haven't made the transformation we need."

"Cut through the crap," Jack snapped. "What can we do in the next year?"

I wasn't ready for this. I needed some sort of answer. Then it came to me that George had mentioned the potential for reduced manufacturing problems. "We should be able to reduce severe manufacturing problems, uh, maybe by twenty percent, maybe more, but unfortunately, I doubt if anyone is going to commit to pulling up their schedules."

Jack's face flushed red. "Jon, you sold me on this Knowledge-Based Toyota Product Development you said is four hundred percent better than we are! And all you've got after a year is 20% fewer manufacturing problems!" Jack sat back and rubbed his eyes. "Next year this company will deliver acceptable profit, and we will do it one of two ways. Either we introduce many of our new products early with much better quality, or Brenda is going to get her way and IRT will be carved into pieces." He thumped his fist on the desk. "I don't want my legacy to be layoffs! Brenda is focused on profits and she has Ray's attention. Just today Ray reminded me that it has been a year since we launched KBD and there is little if anything to show for it."

I was stunned. This had changed the stakes greatly; Jack was making these promises that looked impossible to keep. Of course, I could see how he would since I'd told him many times that the benefits of Knowledge-Based Product Development were faster-to-market and better quality. Jack had been counting on me and I had let him down.

Reeling, I said, "How big a workforce reduction is Brenda recommending?"

"Twenty percent."

"Why 20%?" I asked.

"Simple math — a 20% workforce reduction will reduce costs by enough to improve profit from three percent to seven percent. It's highly predictable because the amount of profit improvement is dialed in. Costs are reduced by a known amount and profit increases by a known amount. A one percent increase in profit requires a five percent workforce reduction."

"Man," I said. "I had no idea layoffs were an exact science."

"Well, we hired an expert," Jack added.

"When does she want to do it?"

"In six weeks, after all the new products are shipping. As you know we have a couple of late military products."

"Yes, I've been spending all my time on those late products," I said. "Why so soon?"

"Brenda has done this many times and she says workforce reductions can be quite disruptive so the best time is right after new products start shipping to customers."

"I agree workforce reductions are disruptive," I said, "but how does doing it right after new products ship help?"

"Two reasons," Jack said. "First because the company will have a revenue stream from the new products so people can be cut with minimum impact on revenue, and second it provides the survivors time to figure out how to get next year's products out with fewer people. Obviously we would have to outsource a lot of what we do now."

"What about the following year?" I asked, trying to imagine how we would compete with 20% fewer people.

"Brenda insists we need a minimum of seven percent profit, and each year has to deliver ten percent more profit dollars than the previous year. If we speed up time-to-market each year with good and improving quality, we easily increase revenue fast enough to deliver the profit dollars."

"No, I meant 20% of the workforce is two hundred people. How are we going to compete in the marketplace the following year if we lose 20% of the company's capabilities and expertise?"

"We're supposed to be smart enough to deliver an acceptable level of profit."

"What if we lay off a bunch of people and profit gets worse?"

"Then Ray will hire somebody who is smart enough to deliver an acceptable level of profit!"

I was speechless.

Jack swung around in his chair and gazed out the window. I looked down and could hardly breathe. I felt as though I'd just been hit in the chest by a Roger Clemens fast ball.

Jack turned around. For the first time, I saw a weary look on his face I'd never seen before. My initial thought was that the time to retire had come and I ought to convince Jack to join me. He was 63 and deserved some rest and relaxation.

Then it came to me that Jack had few hobbies. The company was his life. Would it be possible to teach him golf?

Jack leaned forward and said, "Jon, we know Toyota dominates the automobile industry, right? And we know we don't dominate our business. But we do have the best people and the best technology. From my viewpoint, Brenda's position is defeatist. It shortchanges our people and our people are the true strength of this company."

So much for Jack's moment of despair. He was now fully energized. He stood and began to pace. "Jon, we screwed up." He stopped. "No, I screwed up. I let all the business leaders take parts of the Toyota cornerstones and develop the pieces assuming they would come together naturally. I filled your plate with other assignments." Jack shoved a fist into his hand. "Darn it all, we've been poking at this change — not making the change. I absolutely believe in the metrics that we came up with — market domination in four years. But it's wishful thinking that it can happen through natural migration of Toyota-style thinking. Brenda has delivered a rather rude wake up call — but perhaps it's one we needed. Either we're on the road to domination, or we submit to profits through cost reduction."

He stood for a moment, apparently in thought. Then he said, "We need to take the project back. We need to give it the emphasis that making it happen will require. Jon, drop everything else I've asked you to do. We're going to fix this!"

I stared at him, speechless.

"Do you disagree?" he asked.

I have worked for Jack for many years. He did not want discussion. He wanted recommitment. Jack might blame himself, but I knew darn well I deserved a lot of blame as well. We'd been too doggone complacent.

I shook my head and asked, "What about Brenda?"

"We'll discuss that in a moment. How can we reenergize this project? I'm still dead serious about my vision." Jack looked up at the ceiling. "Hope we haven't wasted a whole blasted year."

Luckily, I had been thinking about that following this morning's meeting.

"Jack. Do you remember when Allen Ward was teaching us about LAMDA and the Toyota way of solving problems? He invented the term while he watched what went on in product development. He admitted that Toyota would say that they just do PDCA as taught by Deming, but Toyota's implementation was more powerful than what he had seen in other companies that implemented PDCA.

"'Look' is the first step in LAMDA. Go see for yourself. We haven't done that — neither of us. We really don't know what's going on. We just hear that things are going well — but from whose perspective? I've even heard that Doyle is happy."

A little smile appeared on Jack's face that made me feel a bit better.

I continued. "We've also ignored the second letter. We also haven't asked 'why' enough to understand the root cause. We have a model, the four cornerstones, that is great for understanding Toyota, but is it the right model for implementation? Jack, we have a problem and we really don't understand what it is or the root cause. My plan tomorrow is to start the Look process. I'm going to see for myself what's going on. Just me, nobody else. Then let's you and I talk again."

Jack stared at me. I think he wanted to come out swinging at something. "Good idea and talk to Brian Hawkins (VP of Marketing and Sales). Find out how product development is doing from the perspective of the sales force. Let me see what you have before you make any final conclusions or recommendations."

"How about Brenda?" I asked, again.

He leaned back and frowned. Then he stood up. "Come with me," he said.

The two of us walked out of his office, down the wood-paneled hallway and straight into Brenda's office. Jack was not one to be held back by protocol.

Brenda was thin and attractive, in her early forties. Her immaculate appearance was in sharp contrast to Jack's — in his wrinkled blue shirt and loose-fitting slacks.

Brenda looked up, obviously surprised at the sudden, unannounced entry. To her credit, she waited for Jack to speak.

"Brenda, this is Jon Stevens. Jon's leading the efforts I briefly described to you regarding the implementation of Toyota's principles for excellence. It's no secret you and I have some disagreements, and I want to make sure you give Jon the time to understand your position."

I stepped to her desk and extended my hand.

She shook it graciously, but not surprising, seemed a little taken aback. "Nice to meet you, Jon. I've heard a lot about you."

I had no idea where Jack was going with this discussion, so I said little beyond the usual pleasantries.

Jack went to Brenda's white board and wrote:

- **Market leadership in two years**
- **Market domination in four**

He turned to Brenda and asked, "Is this my vision or our vision? If it is mine only, then I want to list yours below. Jon is responsible for meeting this one. If you have a different one, then we need to reconcile them. Also, I want one of your most experienced financial people to be on Jon's team. Assume fifty percent of their time will be required, and that they can speak for you. If that's not possible, it needs to be you."

Brenda seemed to squirm, I suspect because she was not in control, did not know the game, did not know how to answer, and had a really intimidating set of eyes staring straight at her, awaiting a response.

She said, "I'd prefer to let Jon's team do its work. I'll be glad to review his findings in detail."

Jack said, "Nonsense! We all work for the same company. Your recommendations for cost reduction will have a significant impact on Jon's team. I refuse to waste their time. You can think about the vision statement. But have your person ready to go when Jon is ready. That will probably be in a day or two."

Brenda blinked. Then she slowly turned her head to look at me. "All right, I'll give you someone to work with your team and to refine the vision statement."

Jack said, "Also, Jon, give Brenda and her analyst copies of all the Toyota books and articles we have read." He turned to Brenda. "Thank you," he said.

Jack and I left her office and walked back to Jack's. He closed his door.

"I just integrated the two projects, Brenda's cost reduction project and our KBD project. You take it from here."

He seemed to think for a moment, then said, "We've been given a wake up call. Continuous improvement will not make the changes required to make this company the way it needs to be. We've poked around at this long enough. It's got to be done right from here on out."

"No question about it," I said. I gave Jack a nod and left his office, closing the door behind me.

Donna looked up from her work. "So, how did it go?"

"Better than I expected," I said. "It wasn't me he was really mad at."

"Uh-huh. Somehow I guessed that when you two marched into her office," Donna said with special emphasis on, "her." Donna can say more with only a few words than anyone I know.

"Donna, can you commandeer one of the four corner team rooms for me. I want to put things on a wall where they won't be disturbed." The executive office area had four team rooms, one in each corner, that were hardly ever used since the individual offices were just as big.

"Sure," she said. "How about this one right here? It's between Jack's office and Brenda's, and close enough that I can observe. I'll put a note on the door and have a couple of flip charts brought in."

"Thank you, Donna. We'll start using it — probably on Thursday. One more thing — I need to meet with Brian Hawkins soon," I said as I walked away.

"What about?" Donna said. "I try to include a topic for the meetings I schedule with executives, if it's not too much trouble."

"Fine," I said as I walked back to Donna's desk. "Product development metrics from Sales Perspective. Tell him I'd like to see any metrics he has."

"Brian is in today but out the out the rest of the week. I can squeeze you in at 5:00."

"Great. I'll be back at five o'clock."

I returned to my office and called Carl Garcia, Dick Beasley, Tim Ashcroft, and Vijay Suran and asked them to schedule time with the people who are actually implementing the four cornerstones. I had to drop Jack's name to get people's schedules cleared tomorrow and Wednesday. I needed to get a handle on what is going on before the end of this week because I would be in Tampa all next week at a Lean conference.

I reentered Mahogany Row a little before 5:00 and arrived at Donna's desk. Brenda's door was closed. Jack's was open although he wasn't there and Donna was typing at her computer.

"Brian's in his office," Donna said without looking up. "He's on the phone but he's expecting you, so go on in."

"How did you know it was me?" I said.

"I can smell coffee on your breath a mile away."

"Then I'll grab another cup so you'll know I got home safely," I said as I refilled my mug.

Donna smiled and shook her head as she typed away.

I entered Brian's office. He was a heavy-set man, reclining in his chair with his feet on his desk and talking on his cell phone. He raised a finger, quickly wrapped up his call, and motioned me in.

"You know," he said, "the rallying cry that this quarter is the most important of your life loses meaning after you've heard it every quarter for five years." He shook his head, put his feet down and leaned forward. "Let's see, you're here to talk about product development metrics, right? Weren't you going to retire?"

I said, "Yes, I was going to retire but Jack talked me out of it. And yes, I'm here to talk about product development metrics from the perspective of the sales force."

"To tell you the truth, the only thing I care about is, 'did the customer get what we promised?' Say, what ever happened to the project you were leading — the one about using Toyota product development principles to gain market leadership? That started with a bunch of fanfare, but I don't hear much about it anymore."

"We made good progress but no where near the amount Jack was counting on, and now we're under the gun for more profit, so Jack wants me to combine both goals into our effort."

Brian said, "You realize, of course, that we are moving in the opposite direction in both market share and profit?"

"Yes," I said. "I just talked to Jack and he made that crystal clear. Now the goals are to achieve Jack's vision of market leadership in each business in two years and market domination in four and increase profit to at least seven percent."

Brian pursed his lips. "If I were you, I'd reconsider retirement," he quipped.

"My golf game could use the help," I said. "The reason I'm here is to get your thoughts on how we could do it. I did a little math, and if we increase annual revenue from five to six hundred million we would deliver seven percent profit with our current cost structure. How close would we be to market leadership with six hundred million in revenue?"

"That depends upon how the additional revenue is distributed," Brian said. "We don't push Automotive too hard because we lose money, but the irony is we just moved back to market leadership in Automotive Products because the market leader filed for bankruptcy protection and cut back sales. Give me a second to find the latest market share report."

Brian turned to his computer, quickly searched and found the file and printed it on his laser printer.

"We're number one in Automotive," he said, "number two in Security Systems and Civilian Avionics, and we're number three in Military. If the additional $100 million is evenly split between those last three we might be number one in Security Systems and Civilian Avionics too. The Military Products business would have to increase revenue by $100 million itself to regain market leadership, and that will take a while because of the qualification process. But the Military business is high profit, so I'll take all I can get."

"Number one in three of four businesses isn't bad," I said.

"We might be able to achieve something else," Brian paused to punch numbers into his calculator. "I'd want to talk to my staff before making any commitments. But before I do, help me understand what miracle is going to deliver six hundred million in revenue at seven percent profit?"

"I don't know yet," I said. "Right now I'm trying to figure out what metrics we would have to achieve in order to deliver it, so that I can set the right goals. Jack told me he wants to pull up schedules on half of next year's products and reduce most manufacturing problems. What do you think it would take to achieve six hundred million?"

Brian fumbled through a couple of folders on his desk and retrieved a spreadsheet. "I give this report to Jack every month," he said, "but I don't know what good it does other than raise his blood pressure. It tells me and my team which products and businesses we can count on, at least relative to each other."

He placed it in front of me and pointed to the rows with his pen. "These are all twenty products from our four businesses. The first column is on-time delivery status and we met about seventy percent of our schedules, which doesn't sound too bad. But the problem is we usually don't find out about delays until we've already made commitments to customers, so customers think we're completely out of control. Military and Automotive habitually find major problems right before we're scheduled to ship, and in some cases after. We're still not shipping a couple of Military Products."

"I know," I said. "I've been working on those."

"The next column is cost, meaning cost-of-sales, and we achieve our cost targets on sixty percent of our products, which isn't too bad except for warranty costs. Our warranty costs are increasing as a percentage of revenue because our prices have decreased, but our warranty costs have not, which leads me to the biggest problem — quality."

I'd figured he would be screaming for cheaper products released sooner.

"This is our quality metric," Brian said pointing to the third column, "the total annual failure rate and it includes everything that goes wrong with our products in the customers' eyes — recalls, customer returns, and rework at the customers' site. We're currently running over four percent of the total product shipped, actually 4.3% which is typical for us. But we have more competition than ever before, so our customers have more choices and there is no patience for quality problems. In addition to the cost of warranty failures, these problems are costing us sales every day. All our customers have at least two qualified suppliers, so if we slip up they simply buy more from a competitor."

"How good do we have to be?" I asked.

"Our products have to be the best in the eyes of the customer. We need to be under two and a half percent."

"Whoa," I said. "That's aggressive. We've been running in the four to five percent range for years, sometimes higher."

"I know it's aggressive," Brian said. "But the competition has changed the game. If we want to win, meaning market leadership and profit leadership, we have to have the best quality in the industry — no exceptions, no excuses. It's that simple."

"Well it makes sense," I said. "I just don't know if it's achievable."

Brian continued with a tone of frustration. "Jack's organization has to understand that quality problems prevent my sales force from selling. When quality problems occur, we stop selling and spend all our time recommitting deliveries, coordinating rework, and doing damage control. I can cite five examples of where we lost big multi-million dollar deals because of our quality problems."

I continued looking at the spreadsheet. "Only two of twenty new products this year met all three criteria."

"And they are both in Security Systems," Brian added. "If you group the products by business you'll see that Security Systems performs the best and Military Products the worst."

I said, "Six hundred million in sales in two years is largely dependant upon the products we release this year. The annual total failure rate has to be under two and a half percent. What about schedule and cost? What metrics do we need there?"

"When do you need to know?" Brian asked. "The reason I ask is I'm meeting with my sales force tomorrow night and I would like their input — although, to be honest, I'd hate to get their hopes up if this is just an academic exercise we're going through before we start selling businesses and cutting the workforce."

"In my view this is our last hope of avoiding what Brenda is recommending."

"Okay, I'll talk with my sales team and shoot you an e-mail Tuesday night or Wednesday morning. Besides, I don't want to be the object of Jack's rage."

"Thanks," I said. "Can I have this?"

"Sure," Brian said. "If you want, I'll put you on the distribution list."

"Please do," I replied, "and can you send me the last five years of reports, so I can see the trends?"

"I'll send you the annual roll-ups that I show the Board of Directors."

"Great. Thanks again."

DISCUSSION

We've tried to make IRT, our fictional company, reflect in many ways the manufacturing companies we see and visit regularly. IRT has taken a top-down approach to the change, and we believe top-level managers should be driving this change. Many companies do not have that top-level commitment. Instead, what they have are internal believers in this way of development. These believers have been inspired by Mike's first book and by the excellent books from Jeffrey Liker, James Morgan and Allen Ward, as well as other sources that espouse this 'Toyota way' of developing products. These believers are usually mid-level managers who have a good understanding of their companies' practices and are well respected. Their approach to change is more of a guerrilla warfare approach: keep putting in the right practices across the company and let the system grow from there. We will comment in the Discussions sections on how the messages in this book reflect on their efforts.

IRT is clearly an unsettled company from a management and business perspective. Management knows they are in trouble, and they are determined, one way or another, to make dramatic changes. Their problem is meeting promised expectations against aggressive business goals. We have illustrated a second alternative to business change: the cost cutting, acquisition model, based on a financial rather than an engineering model for achieving dramatic improvement. An interesting question is whether these are mutually exclusive strategies. These issues will play out through the rest of the book.

Another message in this chapter is that management became complacent and assumed that the system would develop naturally. In reality, there was no serious recognition that this was a completely new business system, rather than simply a collection of parts. There was no real ownership of the system. To use Toyota's words, there was no Chief

Engineer for the new product development system.

What about the companies that don't have a burning business reason to change, or don't perceive that they do because they are delivering acceptable customer satisfaction and a good return on investment? We would argue that if a company is indeed operating at low levels of engineering productivity, as we believe most are, then they actually do have a burning business reason to change — even if it has not been recognized. Therefore even if a company is successful with low engineering productivity, it is short-changing its customers, employees, and investors by not improving. Why be content with a 20 to 25% percent yearly improvement from the implementation of various Toyota practices, given that a 4X productivity gain is actually possible?

Chapter 3
Looking at the Realities Firsthand

The first step of the LAMDA model is to 'Look', which does not mean at reports or e-mails; it means going physically to the source and seeing for yourself.

Tuesday Morning: Infrared Technologies Corporation

The drive to work took longer than usual as the roads were extremely congested. The good news: it gave me more time to reflect. In spite of yesterday's bad news, I felt strangely energized. Perhaps this was because everyone on the team had realized we'd lost momentum. Now we were motivated to regain it. We had no choice.

To be honest, I wasn't sure how we'd lost our focus, or whether we actually had. Somehow, we'd managed to convince ourselves we hadn't made much progress in our discussions yesterday. Maybe we hadn't been fair to ourselves. Whatever the case actually was, I was resolved to use this opportunity to refocus on Jack's vision.

I spent some time reflecting on the time line. I wanted to get a better handle on where we'd gone off track. I suppose there was also some rationalization involved. After all, I did have primary responsibility for the project.

The brake lights of the car in front of me flashed red, and I took my foot off the gas. Seconds later we were crawling along.

We'd actually gotten off to a good start a year ago. Jack had communicated his vision and his expectations, and we'd organized a large, two-day meeting to kick things off. This seemed to have been successful. Each of the four businesses had taken one of the cornerstones to pilot and to grow the capability within the business. One member from my team was responsible for communicating the results across the businesses.

Originally, our plan was to have another large group session after about three months to review, discuss and integrate the cornerstones. The business managers had balked and convinced Jack to allow the practices to naturally evolve. I had disagreed, but Jack had decided to go along — probably because he was under overhead cost pressures. And reports indicated things were going well. Of course, Allen Ward had told me not to rely upon reports but to go see for myself. Today was the day.

Thanks to Carl, Vijay, Tim, and Dick, my plan was to spend today with Civilian Avionics and Automotive Products and tomorrow at the main site with Security Systems and Military Products. I'd left it up to them to decide how to get me debriefed on what was actually happening.

I arrived in the parking lot at about eight o'clock — a few minutes after the time I'd set with Carl. I found a spot near the door, a nice perk for all technical fellows, and decided to go by the little cafeteria to get a large cup of coffee.

Carl was in his office when I arrived. He stood and came around his desk.

"Good morning, Jon," he said as he stuck out his hand.

After a few minutes of small talk, Carl asked whether I had gotten to see Jack.

"Yes, I'm afraid so," I said. "I learned he's under huge pressure from the new CFO to bring costs down. The fact that we seemingly are not making the progress planned was definitely not what he wanted to hear." I looked Carl in the eye. "We were pretty hard on ourselves yesterday about our lack of progress. My goal today is to see for myself. It'd be nice to go back to Jack and tell him that it's not as bad as I reported. That's why I called you. What's the best way to show me, so I will see what's really going on? You guys in Civilian Avionics have been focused on developing the **Expert Workforce** cornerstone, right?"

Carl said, "That's correct. To be specific, as Allen Ward taught us, we focused on problem solving using the LAMDA process and documenting the results on A3s. After I learned you were coming, I sent a note to all the engineers who've been trained, inviting them to join us. I'm not sure how many will show, but this seemed to be a good way for you to get a good feel for what's going on. The meeting starts at 8:30, so we better get moving."

"Sounds good," I said.

When we arrived, the small conference room was almost full with about 25 engineers present. I took a seat at the front of the room along with Carl.

While we waited for stragglers, I introduced myself to the few designers I didn't know and caught up with some of those I did. After a few minutes, Carl described the meeting as one meant for open information sharing and turned the meeting over to me.

I gave some background and then got down to business. "I want to understand what you guys really think about what we've been asking you to do — follow the LAMDA-based problem solving process and document the learning on A3s as progress is made. The floor is open — I want the good, the bad, and the ugly."

After a few awkward moments, Bill Starks, a well-respected design engineer, opened the discussion. "While I understood and liked the logic, I will admit that when I first took the training class, I really didn't understand the power of this simple, repetitive approach. I have done about eight A3s and have to say this is a really powerful problem solving approach. I can present more essential facts on one side of an 11 x 17 than I can in a thirty-slide PowerPoint or a ten-page report. The 'Ask' part of the LAMDA process prevents us from skipping the root cause and jumping directly to the solution. When you follow the process, the problem is solved robustly and permanently."

I could see a lot of nods around the room as Bill talked. Several others added similar comments. Bill handed me his A3s and they were impressive. There was no doubt that they saw the power of LAMDA and A3 thinking. The group estimated that about one hundred A3s had been completed and at least several had solved long-standing problems.

Then Scott Palmer, one of the design managers, changed the tone somewhat. "While I generally agree with the comments thus far, I do have a few concerns. First, only about half of the engineers who have taken the training are actively creating A3s. Also, I see the number of A3s being developed dropping off. Does anyone disagree with me on this?"

I could see from the faces that everyone reluctantly agreed.

Scott continued. "Also, the purpose of the conciseness of the A3 was to ensure clear communication and that mentoring would occur. I know that we have all been diligent on creating really great A3s. But does it matter if no one else ever looks at them? So, of you here, and you are the most proficient, how many have used other's A3s to guide your design decisions? How many have seen A3s used as a part of a design review?"

After some discussion, the general consensus was that Scott was right. Except in a few cases, the A3s had largely become personal problem solving documentation.

"Now, don't get me wrong. I think LAMDA and A3s are great but I don't see this becoming a core part of our product development process."

"Should it?" I asked.

"Certainly, it should," Scott said. "But it has to be ingrained into the design discipline, and it's not at the moment. And I don't see that happening. We still have all our same design pressures, our same deliverables, many of which are not useful, and we all have too much to do. Proper problem solving does not add much more time, maybe 20%, but I will guarantee that slowly we will fall back to our old ways."

Bill jumped back in. "Jon, we all hope you can work through these problems. We, the engineers, really like solving problems the right way. That's why we became engineers. But it shouldn't just be an extra duty that has limited value because the additional work produced never sees the light of day."

A really young man with long black hair named Jason, sitting in the back of the room, cleared his throat. "I'd like some help on an A3," he said.

"Sure," I said wondering whether this kid was twenty years old yet.

Jason said, "I took the training a year ago while I was an intern. I was going to show you some of the pretty A3s I've already completed, you know to suck up like my cohorts here, but instead, I thought I'd show you this one because it ain't working." Jason looked around at his unimpressed colleagues and laughed.

"Okay," I said. "What's the problem?"

"Exactly," Jason said. "As you know, our customers put our products in small airplanes so they want IR systems that are small, light, cheap, and last forever or at least thirty years. My boss tells me he wants an accelerated life test that correlates with the field results"

"Is your boss here?" I asked.

"No. He's visiting customers, making promises we can't keep."

This guy has quite an attitude, but then I guess I had some attitude when I was his age.

He placed his A3 in front of me entitled, "Accelerated Life Test that Correlates with Customer Experience."

I took a good look at the Problem Description.

Problem Description

- Current accelerated life test does not correlate to field experience.
- Test produces false failures, consequently many test failures are waived and products are shipped.
- Product specification is 20,000 cycles: ground conditions to flight conditions (temperature, humidity, pressure) and back to ground conditions.
- Test plan can be found at: \\Quality\Test\CivilAvionics\Environmental\Life

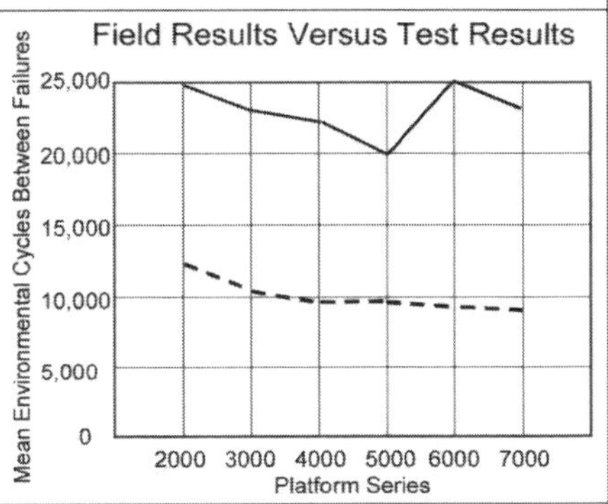

Objective: Develop a test that correlates to customer experience that can be confidently used to evaluate new designs and technologies. (table 3a)

I said, "Your problem description looks okay."

"Except it's wishful thinking," Jason said. "I talked to my buddy in Quality and he said correlation can be improved by slowing down the test so the product has more time to stabilize before the next environmental stress, but we'll never be able to create a short test that correlates with what happens in an airplane when it takes off from high temperature in high humidity places like Miami or Singapore and reaches 40,000 feet and 50 below zero in twenty minutes."

"Is anyone working on this with you?" I asked.

"No."

"Do you consider this project worthwhile?" I asked, trying to be Socratic.

"Sure. There would be benefit if such a test existed, but I don't know how to create one."

Dawn Lindsey had entered while Scott and Jason were talking, and began studying Jason's A3 from behind us. Dawn was recognized as one of the top managers in Civilian Avionics and reported directly to Wayne Tillotson, the VP of Civilian Avionics.

"Why do you assume the test doesn't correlate?" Dawn asked.

"Look at it," Jason said. "All the platform series results are higher than the spec of twenty thousand environmental cycles but the test results are about half of that."

"How many data points are represented in each platform series? Dawn asked."

"Some have six and some have twenty," Jason answered.

"Do me a favor," Dawn said. "Go back and calculate the correlation coefficient between field results and test results using the raw data within each platform series. Call me when you're done and show me what you found. Then we'll figure out what the problem is and define a plan for Root Cause Analysis and figure out who you should work with."

"Thanks," Jason said, surprised.

Dawn addressed the room. "Wayne and his staff have discussed this in detail. Wayne recognizes that we have made progress, but we need to fully implement LAMDA and A3s in Civilian Avionics, meaning everyone needs to do it with effective collaboration and mentoring, and we need to make sure the knowledge is used in design decisions. Wayne has decided to make LAMDA and A3s standard operating procedure in Civilian Avionics, and you will find that Wayne has started sending his monthly status reports in A3 rather than PowerPoint format. The first was sent out this morning."

This meeting confirmed what we had discussed yesterday. If continuous improvement is the goal, then we were doing pretty well. But dramatic improvement was what was needed. The good news was that the engineers liked LAMDA and A3 and wanted the program to be successful. The bad news was we were not yet an Expert Workforce.

I spent the rest of the morning reviewing a number of the A3s the engineers had completed and was quite impressed with the quality. They seemed to relish that someone was actually reading them other than themselves.

I jotted down a few notes:

- 100 A3s
- Improved personal problem solving
- Little reuse
- Not used for design decisions
- Little mentoring, collaboration, or peer review
- Training in root cause analysis techniques needed for new hires
- A long way left to go to become an Expert Workforce

Carl and I met for lunch. I asked him if he could meet with Greg and me on Thursday and probably Friday.

"I want to debrief on what I learned, but would like to do so to a smaller group. I think you mentioned that you had some time available. Someone appointed by Brenda Caine, the new CFO, will probably join us."

"Sure, I can," he said. "I'm supposed to be working 20% for you, anyway. But tell me, do I have to be civil to the bean counter?" Carl also told me what was going on with A3s across all the businesses. He guessed there were about 75 engineers trained and another 50 or so that had picked it up on their own. Next, at one o'clock, I went to find Vijay to discuss the Chief Engineer cornerstone, which was being piloted in the Automotive Products division. When I got to his office, he was with Brad Wolfson and Susan Jackson, both program managers in Automotive Systems.

I greeted them when I entered.

After a few minutes of catch-up discussions, Vijay explained what he planned to do to bring me up to speed on where his unit was on piloting the Chief Engineer.

"I invited Susan and Brad because they've actually tried to be Chief Engineers and apply the principles," he said. "Let me give them the floor to talk of their experiences."

Susan and Brad exchanged looks.

Susan took the lead. "I'm glad we are having this meeting, Jon, because this has been a very frustrating experience for us. We know it makes sense, we've read all the Toyota books, but there's something fundamentally missing. The concept of a Chief Engineer, or an Entrepreneurial System Designer — to keep it more generic — is perfectly logical. Having one person who really understands the customer, and has responsibility for all the integrating decisions, makes sense. The problem—" she paused as though searching for the right words. "The problem is we don't know how to actually make it work. We know the image of the CE is of an almost godlike figure who is able to know all, see all, and make perfect decisions. Well, we are not that smart, and while Toyota Chief Engineers may be well trained and highly experienced, we don't think they are perfect either. We believe Toyota must have some sort of collaborative ecosystem."

Brad picked up on what was being said, somewhat as if this had been scripted. The two of them must have discussed this ahead of time.

"Let's look at our current structure for decision making," he said. "Before we became all-knowing Chief Engineers, we had, and we still have a boatload of administrative responsibilities. Just managing all our phase gate deliverables is a full time job. We had technical system designers that worked for us who were responsible for the technical system architecture and for managing all the technical specifications. We don't have them anymore — *them is us.*"

Susan jumped back in. "Then there's marketing. They think managing customer requirements including schedules and spec changes is their birthright. Engineering somehow needs to solve all problems on cue. We, as Chief Engineers, have to orchestrate all this. Not only that, we need to look at trade-offs from multiple perspectives with multiple alternatives, and at the same time not miss any schedules. I remember Allen Ward saying that Toyota Chief Engineers choose between feasible trade-offs. We trade off best guesses!"

I felt my brow furrow as Susan drew a breath. Brad took the ball.

"Realistically, Jon, what we have been given is a new title. We've removed the administrative burden from some engineers since they work for their discipline managers, but other than that, nothing has changed. The role of a Chief Engineer cannot be implemented as an island. It's not hurting anything, I guess, and maybe the title is important, but we believe that the way the Chief Engineer Cornerstone actually should work needs to be thought through from a much broader perspective."

I shook my head. "I don't understand," I said. "Jack continues to get good feedback from Charles Osgood that the CE role is working well." Charles was VP over Automotive products.

With a half grimace and a partial smile, Susan said, "You might say that from Charles' perspective, it is. You realize, of course, he actually never wanted to do this in the first place. He will certainly embellish whatever he needs to in order to keep Jack focused elsewhere. Brad and I believe very much in what you are doing, so we volunteered to be the guinea pigs. His reported successes come from us."

Susan drew a breath and then continued. "What we've just discussed is what we think you need to know. On the other hand, let me describe what has worked. One of the things we understood and liked from the material on Chief Engineers was that they start with a high-level concept paper. On our projects, we insisted the customer requirements would not be written as specs, but rather be targets and ranges. In effect, we delayed detailed specifications by one phase gate — about six weeks. This allowed some additional conceptualization before design freeze. While this didn't seem like much to Brad and me, we both saw a small reduction in problems and stayed on schedule longer. This has been enough to make Charles happy. The bottom line is that we both believe that this really feels right, but we don't yet know how to make it work."

"I'm curious," I said, "do you use A3s and LAMDA in your role as Chief Engineer?"

"Yes," they both answered enthusiastically and then looked at each other.

Susan went first. "The good news is that we both use A3s to communicate project status and expect everyone to read it before our weekly meeting, and I'll bet we save fifteen minutes a week, minimum."

Brad added, "The bad news is that Charles hasn't shown any interest in A3s. He still requires status reports and presentations be in PowerPoint."

Susan shook her head in agreement. "I send him every A3 but he has never made a single comment."

"This is what we mean by additional work," Brad said.

I jotted down a few notes:

- Concept paper of targets and ranges is delaying final design decisions, which has reduced downstream problems.
- A3s save meeting time.
- Eco-system is not in place to support Chief Engineers:
  o Don't know the feasible alternatives
  o Marketing role is unclear
  o Need relief from administrative responsibilities
  o Training needed?
- Lack of management support from Charles

After a few more minutes of discussion, I headed back to the main plant and my office. I needed to contemplate all I had heard. Although I'd verified we were clearly not on the fast track to meeting Jack's goals, there were some positive signs.

Wednesday Morning, IRT Corporation

I arrived at the main site at eight o'clock. Today, I meet with Security Systems and Military Products, the best and the worst. Could Christine Dumas, Security Systems Vice President have successfully implemented Set-Based Concurrent Engineering? I'd find out later this morning, but first I'd meet with Military Products and my expectations were quite low. I knew Nathan Jorgenson, along with Charles Osgood in Automotive, were the two vice presidents who wanted no part of Knowledge-Based Development.

Military Products was the foundation business of the company. It was still the largest business, although growth was slightly negative. But it always turned a good, solid profit year after year — even with a declining market share. And we had spun off some great technology while reducing costs and weight for the commercial businesses.

I grabbed a quick breakfast and a cup of coffee and headed straight to Dick Beasley's office to talk about how Responsibility-Based Planning was implemented in Military Products. Dick had been on my original team. Unfortunately, his aligning with me had not been career enhancing for him, but he was too near retirement to care.

As I approached his office, I heard two familiar voices in a rather heated argument. It was Dick and Doyle Mattingly. I felt my blood pressure rise and my face flush as I approached the office door. I paused when I heard Doyle say he didn't want me wandering around talking to people. I must admit I really disliked the man for a lot of reasons. For one, he played a big role in Jan Morris leaving the company. No doubt he blamed me for his demotion from czar of the IRT process to Nathan's lean production coordinator.

I walked through the door. "Hello, Dick. Hi, Doyle. So, did I understand correctly, I'm not allowed to walk around and talk to people about what's going on. Really!?" I stared straight at Doyle. "Tell me. Is this unit still part of IRT?"

"All I was telling Dick is that I know what's going on. You can talk to me."

"Fine, I'll talk to you," I said. "But like it or not, I'm still going to talk as well to whomever I want. Got a problem with that?"

He shrugged, and I thought I saw a puff of smoke rise from his ears.

"So what is your role, Doyle?" I asked. "I thought you were Nathan's lean production coordinator?"

"I am, but we rolled all of this knowledge based stuff under that umbrella."

It looked to me like this was going to be a waste of time.

I said, "You're supposed to be piloting **Responsibility-Based Plan-**

ning. Tell me, what are you doing?"

"As you well know, we canceled the PDSP (Product Development Standard Process) in favor of this Toyota knowledge based approach," He said. "We adopted this phase gate system instead. Nathan approved it last week. We're in the process of defining all the tasks to be reviewed at each gate. Each engineer will be required to prepare a plan to achieve the gate requirements."

He took out a sheet that defined the projected phase gates and laid it out on the table in front of me.

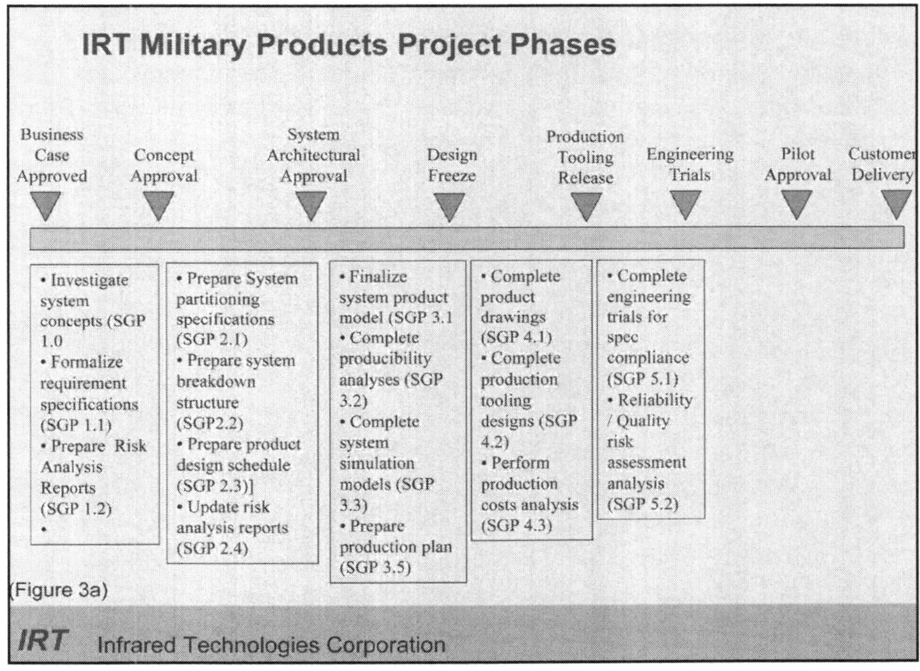

(Figure 3a)

"In addition," he said, "we've defined a number of important processes that need to be leaned out. I've assigned these processes to some of my Lean coordinators for value stream mapping. These are our initial targets:

- The drawing release process
- The ECN process
- Final testing / qualification process

"These don't go away and they need to be efficient. That's our mission."

"Are you using A3s for anything?" I asked.

Dick glanced at Doyle. "A few engineers are but it really hasn't caught on," Dick said with disappointment.

"We're focusing on value stream mapping right now," Doyle said.

"My view," Dick said, "is value stream mapping can be improved by using A3s and LAMDA to track progress and solve the problems uncovered during the VSM process. I converted a PowerPoint VSM presentation to an A3 to prove my point."

Dick handed me an A3.

I looked at it and handed it to Doyle. "What do you think Doyle?" I asked. "You're the efficiency expert."

Doyle looked it over. "It looks okay. I'll think about trying it."

Yeah, right, I thought sarcastically as Doyle gathered his things and left. Then Dick and I wandered around talking to people.

I was not surprised to find that Military Products was clearly focused on process efficiency as the means for implementing lean.

I made a few notes:

- Military Products regressed into a highly structured stage gate process and required engineers to meet pre-defined tasks — missing the whole point of KBD
- Little use of A3s
- Management was undermining the effort.
- Value stream mapping parts of the PD process should help

I met Tim Ashcroft on the way to the cafeteria for a coffee refill. He told me that Christine Dumas, the Vice President of Security Systems, wanted to meet with me herself. She had been reporting good progress every month on understanding and applying **Set-Based Concurrent Engineering.**

We arrived at Christine's office at about 10:30 in the morning. She'd been a supporter of this effort from the beginning. I was curious to hear her reaction.

Tim had briefed her on my mission and concerns. Then I related some of what I'd learned so far. Now it was time for her to relate the progress her unit had made on Set-Based Concurrent Engineering.

"Jon, do you remember the bicycle example you used when you were describing the Toyota system?"

I nodded and she continued. "That idea really made sense to me and that is what we have been doing. All of our security systems break down into at least four standard components: the housing, the IR sensor assembly, the display, and the electronics module. Our approach has been to establish a geometric interface standard and a standard spreadsheet analysis tool for decision trade-offs. Or you might call it scoring, really. Every project is required to have three geometric alternatives for each subsystem. The plan is for every alternative to be developed until our 'System Architectural Approval' gate is reached. The ones that don't get approved go on the shelf ready for the next project.

"I wish I could give you some really positive results, but the jury is still out on how much this will buy us in quality and cycle time. We're several months away from finishing our first project using this approach. However, I have to say, I am sure it is going to be successful to some degree — if for no other reason than it has forced us to really think through levels of potential standardization. With that said, I don't see this as the real driver to reach Jack's goals. It presents well. Everybody likes it. But it seems too rigid and limited to be the real driver of quadruple productivity."

I urged her to express her concerns in more detail.

"Okay," she said. "But these are just my gut feelings."

"Fair enough," I said.

She took a deep breath as she appeared to collect her thoughts. "How we see different types of trade-offs is only geometrically focused, and a lot of effort is required to get to multiple solution sets at the geometry level. Can we afford that on an ongoing basis? A spreadsheet standard analysis form seems way too simple for meaningful trade-offs. Forcing ourselves into interface standards would seem to inhibit innovation. In a nutshell, I feel we've taken too simplistic a view of the power of set-based design. I think in the end it will be very good at show and tells, but not all that meaningful as a driver for quadrupling productivity — or even doubling it, and I'd be extremely happy with doubling it." With a slight grimace, she added, "I don't think we really understand the nature of Set-Based Concurrent Engineering. We're making it into a tool, but I think there's more. Am I making any sense?"

She was. I was impressed with what they were doing, but her concerns seemed compelling. I said, "Interesting points, Christine. I had the same thoughts yesterday when we were discussing A3s — that we were seeing the obvious but missing the really important message. By the way, I've heard good things about your recent product releases from both George Rogers from Production Operations and Brian Hawkins from Marketing and Sales. Was there anything you did differently?"

"Actually there was," she said. "Early on, I began receiving A3s on the Set-Based Concurrent Engineering project. Initially I thought they were just more desk clutter but I started reading them and making comments and passing them back to the authors who would quickly respond and return them. Then it occurred to me that I was able to understand A3s much faster than normal e-mail, and I've got to tell you, I am inundated with e-mail and many have mind-numbing attachments. I spend every weekend guzzling coffee and catching up on e-mail."

She paused to sip her coffee.

She continued. "So about three months ago, I asked my staff to communicate important problems and proposals on A3s using LAMDA and it caught on. Before I knew it, I was receiving a dozen A3s a day dealing with design and manufacturing problems on the new products. With A3s, my managers and I could understand the problems in minutes, and I mean a shared understanding — as opposed to ongoing confusion and arguing about what the problem really is because everyone has different data. We were able to quickly take the appropriate action, and we did it without long drawn out meetings."

"Are you saying that A3s are the reason why your new products have performed better?" I asked.

"Better is relative," she said. "We had a lot of problems but we were able to quickly figure out which people needed to be assigned to each problem and new people could be rapidly brought up to speed by reading the A3s."

"Interesting," I said.

Christine continued. "But the truth is, most of them are closer to A4s. I receive status reports all the time on 8 1/2 x 11 inch paper, and we use the same format and LAMDA all the time. Here are some that I was just working on."

She handed me three. Each had the same format: title, problem / proposal description, root cause analysis, alternatives, recommendation, implementation plan, and follow-up plan. They were all work-in-progress and each had several comments from Christine.

"These look good," I said.

"I was marking them up when you arrived. I'm sold on them."

"Have you prepared any?" I asked.

"Probably a dozen," Christine answered. "The first few were challenging but now I've gotten pretty good at. I just write up what I know and show them to the experts, who provide tremendous insight. Circulating these documents is what we do now in Security Systems."

"Do you file them anywhere?" I asked.

"We place them on a shared drive so people can find them."

"Does Jack know this?" I asked.

"Yes. I told Jack we were using A3s and LAMDA to tackle problems on our new products. At the time it seemed like we had more problems than usual and the A3s and LAMDA helped us fix the problems faster. Competitive pressure has forced us to shorten our product development schedules so we just don't have the time to perform as many design and test iterations as we used to, which results in more problems."

"Have you seen this," I asked, handing her my copy of the spreadsheet Brian gave me.

"Jack sends those out once a month," she said glancing at it.

"Your business did the best of the four."

"True, but three of our five new products missed one or more key metrics, and we lost market share for the third year in a row, and we're barely profitable. That's why I believe we are still missing the big picture."

Christine had a knack for hitting problems right on the head.

"I'll be meeting with the team starting tomorrow," I said. "We will think it through. I think you're right, we are missing something."

I made some notes:

- A3s as a collaborative problem solving and communication tool results in faster and better decisions.
- Concurrent engineering focused on geometries
- Missing the big picture

As I headed back to my office I started thinking about what I'd learned and it was a lot. We were definitely not on a path to meet Jack's metrics. Our problem was we just didn't see the big picture. Or maybe, we wouldn't recognize it if we saw it. We also suffered because people like Doyle, Charles and Nathan were at best just pretending to understand and cooperate in the effort.

Meanwhile, I had two problems to solve: how could I achieve Jack and Brenda's combined goals and why wasn't the KBD implementation accomplishing more?

The first thing I needed was the e-mail Brian Hawkins promised with the cost, schedule, and quality metrics that the sales force needed to reach six hundred million in revenue at seven percent profit. I checked e-mail and voice messages — nothing. I sent him a reminder e-mail and grabbed a quick lunch and went outside for a walk.

It was beautiful fall day in Colorado — clear and cool, but warm enough to walk around the building a couple of times to collect my thoughts.

My cell phone rang. It was Donna.

Where are you?" she asked. "I called you, e-mailed you, and stopped by your office."

"Jack's keeping me pretty busy. I'm taking a short walk outside right now."

"You don't sound busy. Look, Brian just called me and he wants you to call him right away. He's stuck in an airport in Chicago and didn't know how to reach you."

Donna gave me his cell phone number and I quickly returned to my office.

"Hello Jon," Brian said, as he must have seen my name on his cell phone.

"I hear you're stuck in Chicago," I said.

"I'm at O'Hare and you know their motto, 'Clouds in the sky, we don't fly.' Anyway I wanted to talk to you about my meeting with my sales team last night."

"I want to hear it," I said and waited for the airport public address system to announce a flight cancellation.

Brian continued. "The good news is six-hundred million revenue should give us market leadership as a company as well as leadership in every business except Military Products."

"What do you mean by market leadership as a company?" I asked.

He said, "Last year I bought a Honda Pilot and the Honda sales guy told me that Honda sells the most internal combustion engines in the world when you total their automotive business, their motorcycle business, plus boats and All-Terrain-Vehicles, and so forth. If our sales are six hundred million we should sell more infrared systems than any other company. We'll be number one in every business except Military products. You'll have to talk to Jack and see if he will accept that."

"What will it take to be the market leader in every business?" I asked.

"Like I told you the other day, Military will have to add a hundred million in revenue so start there."

"Okay," I said. "What about metrics to achieve six hundred million?"

"My team agrees with me on the metrics," Brian replied. "If product development can meet seventy percent of the schedules as they exist today with no late surprises and meet over half of the cost metrics and reduce the annual quality failure rate to 2.5%, we should be able to sell six hundred million year after next."

"What do you mean by no late surprises?" I asked.

"I have to have at least four months notice on any schedule slip. That means when we get within four months of shipments to customers, the schedules have to be absolutely locked down — no exceptions. Otherwise I have to push out ship dates causing customers to lose confidence. That often means they will buy from our competition."

"Makes sense," I said. "I really appreciate you pulling this together."

"Now my sales team is wondering exactly how you're going to pull this off," Brian said.

"I will let you know as soon as I know," I said. "Thanks again.

DISCUSSION

There is no denying that many companies are seeing positive results from piloting various parts of the Toyota system. The use of A3s for problem solving documentation probably has the longest history of success. While working with Allen Ward, we had a number of companies actively using A3 methodologies. The efforts always appeared to be successful, initially. But when we revisited most of those companies, we found the efforts had waned or been completely stopped. The efforts never really got out of the pilot stage and became ingrained in the system. The question was, why not?

Many companies also focused on emulating the role of the Chief Engineer in their companies. We have not seen much evidence of success from following this route. Generally, it has simply defined more engineering responsibilities for the job title but it never relieved the administrative focus of the job, or most importantly, built the eco-system required for success.

More recently, Set-Based Concurrent Engineering has become a pilot focus for many companies and we have seen many innovative ways to inject more early options into design. It does appear that there are some good localized success stories. Most of these efforts have focused on keeping more options open longer into the detailed design part of the process. Our worry is whether it is sustainable and will become a part of the long-term system. This will largely be based on the cost tradeoffs between more effort up front versus real benefits at the end of the project due to reduced iterative loopbacks and a better product. The benefits are rather easy to project in pilots but will they obviously play out as a part of the system when fully implemented. As you will understand as you read ahead, the Toyota view of Set-Based Concurrent Engineering is more about exploring design options with a broader focus much earlier in the development process.

More and more of late, Obeya rooms are being established for visual planning and communicating project status. Again, we have seen some very impressive activity on projects when this is done. We believe Obeya-type setups will be a useful part of the visualization and communication, which make it an effective complement to a knowledge-based system.

Most companies with active Lean production initiatives are also applying the same principles for leaning out the product development processes using traditional value stream mapping techniques and projects. We have seen this approached from two perspectives.

The first is using these techniques to find wasteful tasks within current processes, and then to refine the processes to eliminate wasteful activities. While this leads to more efficient task productivity — much more in some cases — it is unlikely to create the paradigm shift required to dominate. The reason is that while waste removal helps companies develop products faster, the products can still be sub-optimized. Waste removal simply doesn't create the vital new knowledge about customers and technologies required to develop more optimized products. We work with several companies who excel at process efficiency but these same companies experience excessive post-release product design and manufacturing problems.

The other way we have seen value stream mapping used is to build the as-is map to show how amazingly wasteful the current development system is — to the point of recognizing the futility of trying to fix it. In other words, VSM showed the company really needed to start from scratch and rethink. This was Allen Ward's approach when he worked with a new company. He spent sufficient time to build a detailed process map to highlight all the knowledge wastes. He would then discuss the Toyota principles and challenge the company to refine the process to achieve the Toyota results. They would quickly determine they needed to rethink the entire system.

Are we suggesting that all companies implementing bits and pieces of the Toyota system should stop? Absolutely not. But they need to worry about long term sustainability and how all the bits and pieces will become a complete product development system. We absolutely admire all of the guerrilla warriors out there weaving their way through their system bureaucracies to pull all this together. They deserve promotions. Unfortunately, the reality is that over time the guerrilla leaders retire, get transferred, get tired, or lose whatever management support they may have had. Hopefully, the remaining chapters will help bring to light what needs to be done in that regard.

Chapter 4
Digging to the Root Cause

The second step in LAMDA is Ask which means to get to the root cause of the problem. This is probably the most important step and the one most often short-changed. Why? Because it takes time, and most of us want a solution now – so we can do it over again next year.

Thursday Morning: Infrared Technologies Corporation

Traffic was moving along much better this morning. It may sound strange, but I was almost disappointed. Somehow, reflecting on the task before me seemed much safer at five miles per hour than at sixty.

Even so, I came to the conclusion that I now understood the problem and the opportunity. The only difficulty was that I was not sure at all how to tackle it and make things work out right. But there was no question in my mind about one thing — we had to change direction, that was clear. And I certainly now understood the value of seeing for myself as opposed to relying on reports from others.

My meeting this morning was with Greg, Carl, and the new financial manager assigned to my team. It appeared Brenda had decided to play seriously. She had assigned her right hand man, Al Frank. Al had just joined IRT from Brenda's previous company. Jack sent me a note saying she had complete confidence in him. I'd been able to spend a couple of hours with him late yesterday and he'd seemed pleasant enough — and smart enough. But then, anybody would have appeared bright after my encounter with Doyle earlier that day. Al had been on a crash reading frenzy on Toyota since he'd learned of his assignment and that impressed me.

I arrived at the plant about seven-thirty, opened up my office, and hustled down to the cafeteria for coffee. Then I went straight to Mahogany Row to the executive team room Donna had commandeered for me. As I entered into the office area, Donna waved me over to her desk. She was on the phone but covered the mouthpiece.

"I know you are addicted to coffee," she said. "So I had it brought in. There's also a white board and two flip charts. Good luck."

As she had promised, she had put a "Reserved until Further Notice

— Donna" sign on the door. That her name was there instead of Jack's made me smile. There was no doubt who was in charge when it came to office logistics.

Greg and Carl were already there. Al came out of Brenda's office as I was leaving Donna's desk. Probably there'd been some last minute strategizing going on. He walked in behind me and took the opposite side of the table from Greg and Carl in this ample, eight person conference room.

I introduced Al to Greg and Carl.

"Welcome aboard, Al," Greg offered. "Jon mentioned that he briefed you on our project. Any first impressions?"

"It's certainly very interesting and it makes a lot of sense, intuitively."

"How do you like the idea of the Chief Engineer running the whole project and being responsible for profit?" Carl asked with his arms folded tightly across his chest.

Al said, "Jon mentioned that the Automotive Products business has been piloting the Chief Engineer, but that there were some problems because it was mostly a change in title, so the product development system was essentially the same."

It occurred to me that Al had skillfully avoided the question.

I said, "Before we get into any details, I'd like Al to bring us up to speed on the financial situation."

"Sure," Al said clearing his throat. "As you probably know, IRT has been missing its financial commitments fairly regularly for years. In the past year, several people on the Board of Directors have been replaced. The new Board has made it quite clear to the executive team that IRT must consistently meet its financial goals and earn an acceptable profit."

Carl kept his arms folded, his teeth almost clenched. "I suppose that means you start laying off the people who built this company and sell whatever you can to make a quick buck."

"Well, I wouldn't put it that way," Al said.

Carl fired back. "Then how do you greedy bean-counters justify firing people that build companies? Is it to receive bigger bonuses?"

"All right, that's enough!" I said. Carl was a brilliant systems engineer and had a reputation for being opinionated, but I hadn't expected him to attack Al. "I think we need to begin by reviewing the ground rules. Carl, you've been on this team for a year. We're not here to criticize or to attack one another. How do we handle disagreements? Let me ask you, what does Toyota do?"

Carl said, "Toyota makes a ton of profit by harnessing the collective wisdom and creativity of its employees, not through knee-jerk layoffs."

"I know that, Carl," I replied. "And we're not Toyota. We're IRT and we have serious problems to solve. So let me repeat the question, how does Toyota resolve disagreements?"

Carl sat silently with his arms still folded.

"Carl?" I repeated.

Carl spoke softly and quickly. "When people disagree it's because a gap exists in their knowledge. Toyota uses the LAMDA learning process to find and remove such gaps."

"And that's what we're here to do," I added. "Jack wants us to integrate the financial requirements with our Knowledge-Based Development project and find a solution that meets all of IRT's needs. We have gaps in our knowledge and we need to fill them. Let's take a short break. Al, I'll buy you a cup of coffee from one of these thermoses."

Greg and Carl headed out to the coke machine. I took the opportunity to apologize for Carl's behavior. The last thing I wanted was for Al to tell Brenda that we were using him as a punching bag.

Al accepted my apology. Then he shook his head. "Engineers are so sheltered from the realities of business. IRT exists because investors believe they will get their money back and make an acceptable return on their investment. This company's investors have run out of patience. Hiring Brenda is more likely the first executive replacement than the last."

"What do you mean?" I asked.

"Isn't it obvious?" Al said. "Jack has bet the farm on you and this Toyota thing, and if you deliver, great. But if you don't, guess who's going to be held responsible. And it won't be you."

"You're saying Jack's job is on the line?"

"Hell, what Jack has committed to has never been done. Most of the executives including Ray, Brenda, and the entire Board of Directors think Jack is peddling East Asian mystical smoke and mirrors."

"You're right about one thing," I said. "What we're trying to implement has not been proven."

The magnitude of Jack's expectations finally hit me.

Al said, "Look, I don't like layoffs and selling businesses and outsourcing. I know people will have to uproot their families and move. But let's face it. IRT's financial results stink. Three years ago IRT made six percent profit on five hundred million in sales. This year IRT will make three percent profit on the same five hundred million in sales and most of our markets — Security Systems, Military, and Civilian Avionics are growing. In fact the Security market is exploding. IRT has missed a golden opportunity to grow its business and increase profit. Instead things are headed the other way. Profit dollars are half what they were three years ago."

All I could think about was Jack, and that he had trusted me to make this transformation happen and I'd let him down.

"What Brenda is advocating," Al continued, "is no different than what most successful companies are doing. First, you decide what businesses you should be in. Second, you globalize, and third you reduce costs. Then you do it again to continually refresh the company. It's a proven formula."

I was not sure I wanted to know the answer but I asked anyway. "How much trouble is Jack in?"

Al leaned forward to make sure no one else could hear. "Word is there's already an executive search underway to replace him."

I saw Carl and Greg coming and indicated this by nodding toward the door. We all retook our seats.

Carl said, "Al, I'm sorry I lost it earlier. My big-spender younger brother was laid off from the only job he's ever had and couldn't make his house payments. So last month he, his wife, and his five kids moved into my house. The tension level in my household has gone through the roof. I guess that's why I'm a little sensitive to layoffs."

"No problem," Al said.

"Carl, aren't your kids in college?" I asked.

"My two girls have graduated and both have jobs. Now I have five kids under ten in my house. It's a zoo. My girls won't even visit unless I pay them because they know they will have to babysit." He shrugged. "Anyway, I don't want to bore you with my troubles."

Greg gave me a wink, indicating he'd talked to Carl during the break.

"All right, then," I said. "Let's get started. Everyone has seen Jack's vision — market leader in two years and domination in four. Any questions or comments?"

"As a matter of fact, yes," Al said. "That speaks to market success but not to profit success."

"What kind of profit success do we need?" I asked.

"We need to deliver a minimum of seven percent profit next year,"

Al answered. "Then we need to increase profit dollars by ten percent each year, and we need to meet or beat our profit and earnings-per-share commitments each quarter."

"This is where I get hung up and confused," Greg said. "Three months is a short period of time. One unfortunate event can blow us out of the water."

"It's not as hard as you think," Al said. "In the 1990s, Microsoft met or beat their quarterly commitments every quarter for ten years. The trick is to always be ahead of the financial plan made public to the investment community. For example, we announce that we will increase profit dollars and earnings per share by ten percent, but in reality we have an internal plan to increase by 15%. Even if something goes wrong we will still achieve ten percent. And if we're ahead of our internal 15% plan, then we can work with customers to take some shipments after the end of the quarter. That way we save some profit for the next quarter."

"Which is why our new product schedule slips and quality problems are killing us," I added.

"Exactly," Al said. "If shipments of new products are delayed for any reason, then revenue is pushed out, often into the next quarter. So the sales team has to scramble to fill the revenue shortage for the current quarter, and they do it by offering deep discounts to customers on whatever they have to sell, which robs revenue from the next quarter. So profit takes a double hit — you lose the sales of new products — which usually have a good profit margin — and you sell existing product at lower prices. That's what IRT has been doing. And it's the exact opposite of what we need to do."

Greg said, "If I understand what you're saying, Al, we mitigate quarterly risk by having a plan that should deliver higher profit than is communicated externally."

"Right. That's basically it."

"But that's really hard to do," I said, "when we're missing schedules, quality goals, and cost targets on most of the new products."

Carl thumped the table with his fist. "That's the beauty of our Knowledge-Based Development. We will significantly reduce both schedule risk and manufacturing startup problems. But it won't work — can't happen — if you outsource manufacturing. Because we need manufacturing knowledge."

Al looked at me.

I understood that Al wanted a response from me. "Carl," I said, "we'll get into that later. First, let's finish the discussion on profit. Jack's vision says we become the market leader in every business in two years and dominate in four. What should that mean for profit? Al, your call."

"In two years, we earn at least seven percent profit in each business and in four years we earn the highest profit percent in the industry — or seven percent — whichever is greater."

"Why industry-leading," Carl asked. "Isn't seven percent enough?"

"It would be hard to claim we're the leader in the industry if we don't earn the most profit," Al said. "A competitor with higher profit percent could reduce prices, bring their profit down, and take our market share."

Carl nodded in agreement.

"How will we know we're in position to dominate?" Al asked. "GM, Sears, Xerox, and Kodak once dominated their industries, but they don't any more."

"Good question," I replied. "I'm confident Toyota will continue to dominate because they've implemented a learning system that encourages their employees to learn more about their customers than the competition does. And it also encourages employees to learn more about the ability of product and manufacturing technology to meet customer needs than the competition. Equally important, Toyota has implemented a cadence or rhythm of innovation for each major subsystem – – engines, transmissions, and so forth, that removes peaks and valleys from workloads and results in faster implementation of game-changing features."

I stood and wrote on the white board:

- **Two years:**
  - o **Market leadership in each of our four businesses**
  - o **At least 7% operating profit in each business.**
- **Four years:**
  - o **Market leadership in each of our four businesses**
  - o **Industry-leading profit percent or at least 7%, whichever is higher**
  - o **Establish fastest cadence in the industry for introducing game-changing technology**

"Everyone okay with that?" I asked.

They all nodded.

"I'm curious," Greg said to Al. "What reaction do you expect from Brenda?

"She'll like the profit goals," Al said.

"What about market leadership and fastest cadence?" Greg asked.

"She'll like market leadership because it generates momentum for more profit. Cadence is a means to that end."

"Typical MBA," Carl said. "What about customer satisfaction and employee satisfaction?"

"We leave them out for now," I said, even though I knew this would not be popular with a lot of people, including Greg and Carl.

"We've always had metrics for customer and employee satisfaction," Greg said.

"Toyota says that if they lead in customer quality, market success will follow," Carl added.

"Okay," I said. "We'll say these two metrics — market leadership and profit leadership are results and speak to what the company will achieve. Customer and employee satisfaction metrics speak to how results are achieved, and we've not yet answered that question. Okay. Next, I want Al to explain Brenda's plan."

Al hooked up the projector to his laptop and brought up a slide.

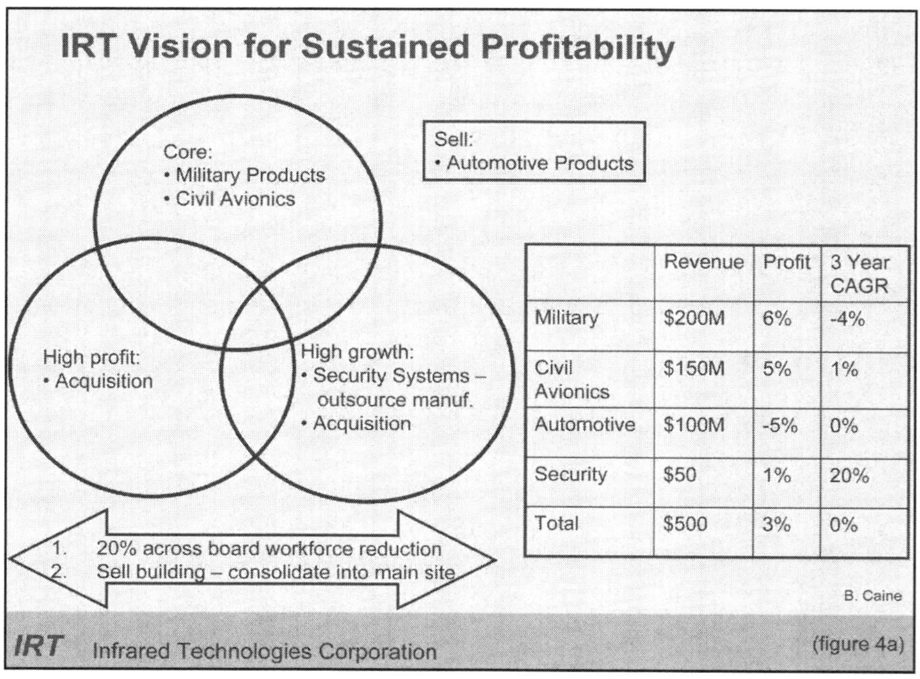
IRT Vision for Sustained Profitability
Core:
• Military Products
• Civil Avionics
Sell:
• Automotive Products
High profit:
• Acquisition
High growth:
• Security Systems – outsource manuf.
• Acquisition
1. 20% across board workforce reduction
2. Sell building – consolidate into main site
B. Caine
IRT Infrared Technologies Corporation

	Revenue	Profit	3 Year CAGR
Military	$200M	6%	-4%
Civil Avionics	$150M	5%	1%
Automotive	$100M	-5%	0%
Security	$50	1%	20%
Total	$500	3%	0%

(figure 4a)

I looked around. Carl had folded his arms across his chest again. Greg had slumped back in his chair.

"Brenda's vision has three types of businesses," Al said. "Our core businesses are Military Production and Civil Avionics. These are cash cows. Both these businesses deliver pretty decent profit but aren't growing very fast. In fact Military Products has negative growth. We want to milk them for everything they are worth. Any questions?"

"What is three year CAGR?" Carl asked.

"Three year compounded annual growth rate," Al replied.

"So the only business that has really grown in the last three years is Security Systems, right?" Greg asked.

"Correct," Al said, "but profit is too low so we recommend that Manufacturing be outsourced in Security Systems. Lastly, we need to acquire some high growth and high profit businesses. Any questions?"

"Why isn't Automotive Products in one of the three circles?" I asked.

"Because the Automotive Products Business is losing money, and if you look at the entire automobile industry, it is one the worst performing industries in the country. Last I checked, the return on assets for the entire industry was negative so we can't imagine how the Automotive Products business will consistently earn an acceptable profit. Many automotive companies are either in bankruptcy or on the verge of bankruptcy. It's just a bad industry to be in."

"That's interesting because Toyota is enormously profitable," Greg said. "Honda is doing very well too."

"That very well may be," Al countered, "but our customers are not Toyota and Honda and the industry as a whole is performing poorly, and it's likely to get worse with China and India investing a fortune to establish their auto industries. Consequently, Brenda is recommending that we sell Automotive, outsource manufacturing for Security Systems, reduce cost through an across the board workforce reduction, consolidate into the main site, and use the profits to buy high growth and high profit companies."

Al wrote on the board:

Four point plan for sustained profitability:
- **Sell Automotive business**
- **Outsource manufacturing (Security Systems)**
- **Across-the-board workforce reduction / consolidate into main site**
- **Use profit to buy high growth, high profit companies**

"If you're an investor," Al said, "where do you want to put your money?"

"If you understand what Toyota is doing, you'd put your money in Toyota," Greg said. "You can't ignore the differences between companies within an industry."

Carl added, "If it's all about return on investment, let's sell everything and buy Chinese growth stocks. We'll be a bank."

"Carl, we're not a bank," I said. "We're a manufacturing company. I asked Al to present Brenda's plan so we understand it — not so we can criticize it. Brenda's approach is no different than what most successful companies are doing these days. Al, have you identified companies that you want to acquire?"

"I've identified some candidates," he replied. "Some look very promising."

"Who decides which companies to buy?" I asked.

"Brenda will make a proposal to Ray and Ray will make the final call."

"Sounds like we're a bank," Carl said.

Al said, "Look, over the past few years IRT's markets have grown very rapidly, but IRT has missed a great opportunity to grow revenue and deliver strong profit. IRT is stuck at five-hundred million in revenue with declining market share and profit. The question we've been asking ourselves in Finance is 'how should IRT position itself for profitable growth?'"

Al stopped and looked at each of us. Then he continued. "We've been asking ourselves three questions. The first is what businesses should IRT be in to have a balanced portfolio of core, high growth, and high profit businesses? Are there businesses that should be sold or shut down? Are there companies or businesses that should be acquired? The second question is, 'How can we take better advantage of global economies?' Are there activities that other companies can do cheaper and better than IRT? If so, those activities should be offloaded. Third, 'Are there opportunities to reduce costs?'"

"Those questions seem fair to me," I said.

"Sounds reasonable," Greg added.

"I don't have any problem with the questions," Carl said, "but I struggle a whole lot with your answers. We're in these four businesses because there is leverage across them. Advancements in each business help the other three, and we manufacture right here so Product Design Engineering can understand what is going on in Manufacturing."

I stood, went to the flip chart and wrote Al's questions:

1. **How should IRT position itself for profitable growth?**
2. **What businesses should IRT be in?**
3. **How can we take better advantage of global economies?**
4. **Are there opportunities to reduce costs?**

I said, "Let's look at the first question. How should IRT position itself for profitable growth? We're counting on Knowledge-Based Development to speed up product development, improve schedule compliance, reduce manufacturing startup problems, and accelerate innovation. Is it enough? What do you think, Al?"

"At the risk of getting thrown out the window, my answer is no, it's not enough. Based upon how the implementation is going, there's no evidence it can be implemented here in a reasonable timeframe."

Carl shook his head in disgust. "Typical MBA response to anything other than cost reduction."

"Wait, Carl," I said. "Let's hear Al out."

"Let's talk about accountabilities and responsibilities for a minute," Al said. He brought up a new slide. "I've only been here a few days but

	IRT Today	KBD
Marketing	• Responsible for market share. • Voice of the Customer to Product Development Team. • Prepares product specifications based upon customers needs and competitive landscape	Under development
Finance	• Responsible for profit percent and profit dollars.	
Product Design Engineering	• Design products that meet specifications and cost targets on-time and on-budget	
Manufacturing	• Manufacturing Eng. reviews product design alternatives and provides feedback to Product Design Engineering. • Develops new processes concurrently with product design. • Deliver products to customers on-schedule, at or below cost targets with acceptable quality	
Quality	• Ensure customer satisfaction goals are met. • Execute product performance and reliability testing.	
Top Management	• Make strategic decisions that position company for short and long term success. • Assist as necessary to ensure each functional area meets their accountabilities.	(Fig. 4b)

here's a list of what appear to be the key accountabilities by functional area." Al quickly ticked off the accountabilities in each functional area in the middle column. "Does this represent the accountabilities at IRT today?" We studied it for a moment.

"Close enough," Greg said.

"Based upon what I've learned about Toyota," Al said, "we are going to have to make extensive changes in all these responsibilities. We haven't even talked about management systems, business planning, and training and development."

"What's your point?" Carl said.

"Here's my point. It appears that every job in the company changes. No American company has ever accomplished this. The only guy who knows how to do it is dead. But you guys think you can pull this off in a year or two working in the trenches with a handful of engineers. What you are proposing is perhaps the greatest example of wishful thinking in the history of business."

"The engineers are highly motivated to make this happen," Carl said.

"I don't care how much the engineers like it!" Al shot back. "This is a business, not a pep rally. You guys talk about feasibility. Where's your feasible plan?"

"Okay, I want to stop this here," I said. "We'll pick it up later."

Carl and Al looked at each other. I think both of them wanted to defend their positions.

"Why stop now?" Carl said. "I'd like to discuss this in more detail."

Al nodded. I imagine he was happy to continue educating engineers on the financial aspects of running a business.

I said, "I'm stopping now because what we're looking at here is an alternative plan for meeting the goals. We're not ready yet for alternatives. In fact, I am pretty sure we weren't ready when we launched our cornerstone in each business strategy. "

I looked at Al. "One thing I do know, Al. There is no way — absolutely no way — that you and Brenda know this company well enough to be making the proposal you're making. We're just getting started here. I hope you will participate on this team with an absolutely open mind." I turned to Carl and Greg. "And that goes for all of us, including me. We need to re-look at everything with an open mind."

The room was quiet as they considered my words, uncertainty on their faces.

I continued, "IRT has a problem, right? What is our problem solving process — as taught to us by Allen Ward? LAMDA, right?"

Seeing recognition on Greg and Carl's faces, I concluded. "That's my plan for this meeting — for as long as it takes."

Al said, "Two questions, Jon. I read about LAMDA in the material you gave me, but would you mind elaborating on it? Does Toyota call it that — is it the same as PDCA? And second, I don't quite understand why we're switching gears."

"We're switching gears because we don't know enough to come to any conclusions on your recommendation, or on our approach of one cornerstone per business. Can you name any company that has achieved long-term sustained growth with your strategy, much less reached the domination goal that we have agreed to?

Al responded quickly, "GE under Jack Welch was extremely successful with a strategy of mergers and acquisitions and cost reduction, and GE is very successful today. Welch sold companies that didn't fit into his growth strategy and reinvested the proceeds in businesses that would deliver high growth or high profit or both such as medical and financial services. Welch decreed that GE would be first or second in market share in every business and profitable or be fixed — meaning new management, sold, or closed. In four years he sold 125 businesses. Then he bought RCA — the biggest non-oil deal as of that date in time — as well as Thompson's medical diagnostics business, and Kidder, Peabody — one of Wall Street's oldest investment banking companies. He did that partly to avoid paying banks a fee every time he bought or sold a company. GE Capital produced 40% of GE's record profit in the late 1990s."

"Didn't he also get rid of a hundred thousand employees and earn the nickname, 'Neutron Jack?'" Carl quipped.

"GE had a lot of waste when Welch took over," Al said. "Many companies have produced great results using this strategy. Look at some of the high-flying medical companies and health insurance companies. Heck, most mid-sized and large American companies use a similar approach."

"Is layoffs and mergers what they teach in business school?" Carl groused, "Did they mention that some medical companies are protected from foreign competition by the FDA and make ridiculously high profit. Insurance companies are buying each other so they can charge monopoly prices. Regulators are letting all mergers go forward, even if competition is reduced and thousands of people lose their jobs, because regulators are bankers and bankers make money on mergers."

Al shook his head. "Just listen to yourselves! You guys are rationalizing why certain industries are successful. Why not follow their lead and use what they've shown will work? Let's acquire some of these companies that have an unfair advantage and dump losers like Automotive that are never going to earn a decent profit. There are entire industries that earn 15% profit."

Why had I opened this can of worms?

"Thanks, Al," I said. "Now to your questions — why LAMDA, and why now? PDCA, Plan-Do-Check-Act, is Toyota's standard problem solving and knowledge generating process. Dr. Deming taught them that and that's what most Toyota experts recognize as what put them over the top. Their quality became renowned and they've never looked back. Realistically, PDCA has two cycles, one for PD which solves the problem, and one for CA which validates the solution and standardizes it, so that that problem will never occur again. Too often, companies don't recognize the critical role of CA and short change the process. Following LAMDA as pulled by a Problem A3 helps to avoid that because the A3 pulls two full LAMDA cycles, one for PD and one for CA.The two LAMDA cycles constitute a complete PDCA cycle." I paused for a second to see if this had sunk in. "Let's take a fifteen-minute break and I'll print my A3 problem description. I just updated it with what we decided this morning."

After a quick trip to the printer I returned to find Carl and Al at it again.

"Then go work for a company that doesn't need to make a profit," Al snapped.

"I'm certainly not going stick around here to watch you and your boss play balance sheet bingo with my livelihood," Carl retorted.

"All right. That's enough," I said as I passed out copies. "Some of this data and some of the goals came from a discussion with Brian Hawkins from Marketing and Sales. I asked Brian what it would take to regain market leadership and deliver six hundred million and seven percent profit. He said that it could be done if we can reduce quality failures to below 2.5% while maintaining our cost and schedule performance, as long as we can give reliable schedules four months out. I also looked at IRT's annual report to see our financial history."

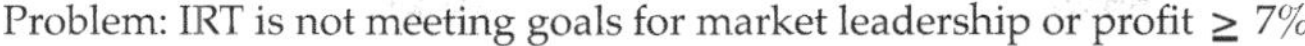

Problem: IRT is not meeting goals for market leadership or profit ≥ 7%

Problem Description

- IRT market share and profit have both declined over the last 5 years.

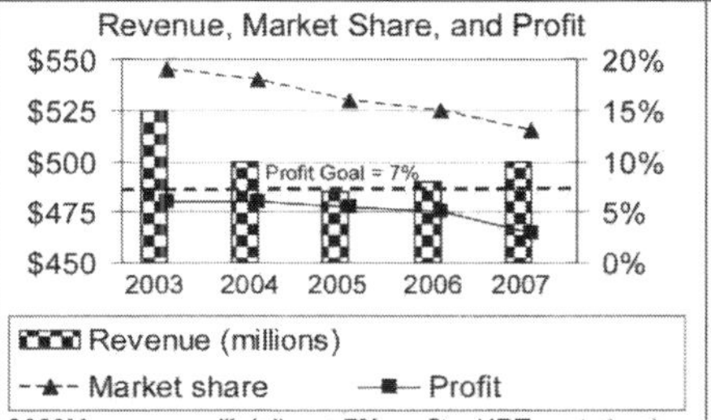

Revenue, Market Share, and Profit

$550 $525 $500 $475 $450

20% 15% 10% 5% 0%

2003 2004 2005 2006 2007

Profit Goal = 7%

Revenue (millions)
Market share
Profit

$600M revenue will deliver >7% profit w/ IRT cost structure:
- Gross margin = 30%
- Fixed expenses = $135M

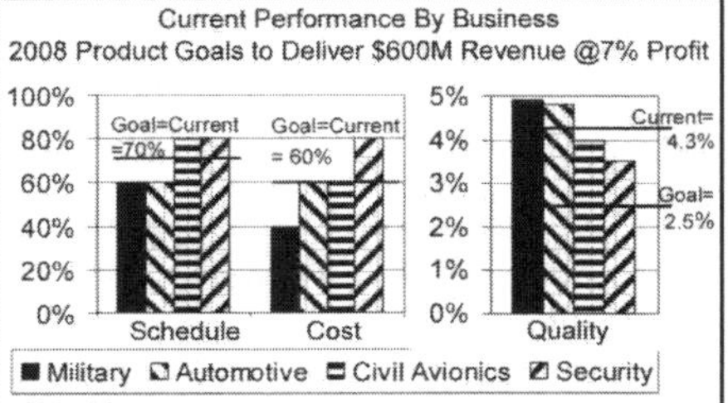

Current Performance By Business
2008 Product Goals to Deliver $600M Revenue @7% Profit

100% 80% 60% 40% 20% 0%

Goal=Current =70%
Goal=Current = 60%

Schedule Cost

5% 4% 3% 2% 1% 0%

Current= 4.3%
Goal= 2.5%

Quality

Military Automotive Civil Avionics Security

- Schedule:
  - % of products that delivered quantity by committed date.
  - No slips within 4 months of first customer shipments.
- Cost – % of products that met cost-of-sales target.
- Quality – total annual failure rate: returns, recalls, rework, etc.

- 2009 Goals:
  - $600 million in revenue @ 7% profit by adding roughly $33M to Military, Civilian Avionics, and Security each.
  - Highest IR company market share
  - Leadership in 3 of 4 businesses, all but Military Products
- 2008 new products reduce quality failure from 4.3% to ≤ 2.5% while achieving 2007 level of schedule & cost.

- 2011 Goals:
  - WW market leadership in all businesses
  - $??? million in revenue @ ???% profit (7% or higher if a competitor is higher).
- 2010 new product metrics:
  - Schedule - TBD
  - Quality - TBD
  - Cost – TBD

(table 4a)

"Can we ask questions now?" Al asked punching numbers into his calculator.

"Please do," I answered.

"Your statement is true," Al said. "If we generate six hundred million in sales with our current cost structure and do it by adding 33 million dollars each to Military, Civilian Avionics, and Security, then we will deliver over seven percent profit. However, I think you mean direct expenses, not fixed expenses. There are some fixed costs in cost-of-sales and some variable costs in direct expenses. If you change the wording to direct expenses equal 135 million dollars you would be accurate."

"Easy fix," I said.

"Your revenue, market share, and profit graph sure doesn't paint a pretty picture," Greg said.

"No, it doesn't" I said.

"Our business performance is dropping like a rock," Carl added.

"How confident is Brian that he can generate six hundred million in revenue if those metrics are reached?" Al asked.

"He is confident," I answered.

"You mind if I follow up with him?" Al said.

"Be my guest," I said. "My main question is how will Brenda react to the time frame? This goal statement has profit at seven percent in the year after next, not next year."

"There are two problems with this," Al replied. "First, the profit increase is a year late and second, do you have any idea how you would achieve the schedule and quality goals?"

"What happened to market leadership in every business?" Greg asked before I had a chance to respond to Al's question.

"I'll answer Greg's question first." I said. "Brian said he would have to add a hundred million in sales to Military Products to achieve market leadership, and given the time required to qualify new products, there just doesn't seem to be any way to achieve market leadership in Military Products year after next. I'll have to see if Jack buys into this new objective, which of course now includes seven percent profit."

"Five years ago, we were the market leader in Military Products," Carl said. "Where did we go wrong?"

I replied, "Two answers — Nathan and Doyle. Al, regarding profit, obviously there is no way new products can improve profit as fast as a workforce reduction. How do you think Brenda would respond to this?"

Al said, "She might consider waiting for profit if the plan to achieve it year after next is rock solid and profit dollars increase continually from there."

"Why are profit dollars so important?" Greg asked.

"Profit dollars drive the numerator in earnings per share, which is the most watched metric by investors."

"At the risk of agreeing with Al," Carl added, "the schedule goal is challenging but the quality goal is very aggressive. If we could do that we would certainly lead the industry, but we're even not close."

"That's the message Brian is sending," I said. "The competition is just too intense to win with anything less than industry-leading quality."

"Are there any more questions on the Problem Description?"

"How many products were delayed within the four month window?" Carl asked.

I retrieved Brian's spreadsheet from my folder. "Let's see," I said. "A total of four — two in Military and two in Automotive Products."

"You might add that to your graph," Carl suggested.

"Good idea," I said, as I made a note on my copy.

"Just a comment," Greg added. "It appears that Security Systems is doing the best and Military Products the worst. Is there anything that Security is doing that the rest can benefit from?"

"Yes and no," I replied. "I asked Christine Dumas that same question yesterday, and while Security is doing better than the other businesses, she was quick to point out that three of their five products missed one or more important metric, they have lost market share three years in a row, and they are barely profitable. She thinks we are failing to see the big picture, and I agree with her."

Greg added, "It's interesting that we beat ourselves up over schedule and cost, while the biggest problem and opportunity is in quality."

"Thanks for reminding me," I said. "Brian went on and on about how quality problems paralyze his sales force and cause customers to lose confidence in IRT. Today customers have so many choices that they can easily switch from us to a competitor, and they do."

"Can't say I blame them," Greg said.

"Al," I said, "this is how LAMDA is applied to a problem description."

"I like the use of visual models," Al said.

"That's what Allen Ward used to call visible knowledge."

"Where do we go from here?" Al asked.

"We do the Root Cause Analysis section," I answered. "Here's a start."

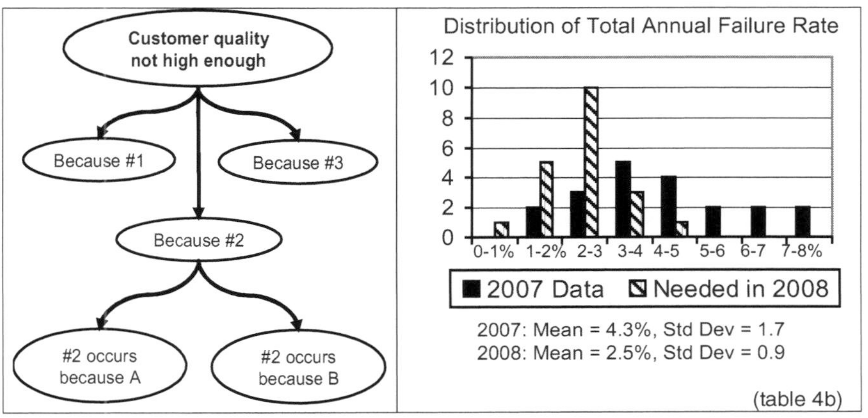

(table 4b)

"I've been in this industry twenty-five years," Carl said, "and never has any company made such dramatic improvement in quality in one year. Besides we only have ten months until year after next's products release and most designs are frozen."

"I know it's not going to be easy," I said, "but let's follow LAMDA and see if we can find a solution. Next are the Root Cause and the five-why approach."

"Why is the five-why approach so special?" Al asked.

"It's easy to learn and promotes good root cause analysis," Greg explained. "It forces people to keep asking 'why' until all the root causes are identified and understood, which is important when you're trying to solve complex problems. It's better than merely asking for root causes because people often jump to conclusions or, if put on the spot, even guess."

"We know the problem is loopbacks," Carl stated. "Quality problems exist because we got the design or manufacturing process wrong, and we shipped bad product and had to fix it. We knew that a year ago."

"A year ago we jumped to the conclusion that implementing one cornerstone in each business would help a lot and it didn't," I replied. "So I want to take a different approach this time. I want to investigate every quality problem on last year's new products and find out exactly what went wrong."

Everyone was silent.

"Look," I said, "we can't afford to be wrong this time."

"What do you want us to do?" Greg asked.

"It's 10:45," I answered. "I'd like you and Carl to review whatever information exists on these customer problems including design and process changes and failure analysis reports, and identify the root cause as best you can. We will meet again tomorrow at noon. Greg, can you take Security Systems and Military Products and Carl, Civilian Avionics and Automotive? And talk to the engineers if you can. Tell them you're on a mission from Jack but make sure they know this is not a witch hunt, just data gathering."

Carl looked at me and said, "What are you going to do?"

"I'm going to do two things. First, I'm going to prepare another A3 on why implementing one cornerstone in each business didn't work and second, I'm going to buy you lunch tomorrow."

"Make it good," Carl said.

"What can I do?" Al asked.

"A couple of things," I replied. "First, figure out the revenue and profit goals for four years out. Second, set up a meeting with your old company next week while I'm in Tampa at a Lean Conference. I'd like Carl and Greg to understand exactly what happened there."

"Sure thing," Al said.

"Tampa in October," Carl quipped. "Sounds like a boondoggle to me."

Friday at Noon: Infrared Technologies Corporation

Donna bailed me out and got Carl's favorite lunch — pizza, and his favorite type of pizza — Mediterranean.

I arrived at 11:55 to find the room empty except for the pizza so I grabbed a slice and a large cup of coffee.

Al arrived precisely at Noon. "How's the pizza?" he asked.

"Grab a slice before Carl gets here or you might not get any."

"I called a colleague at Consumer Technologies Corporation where Brenda and I used to work," Al said as he filled a plate with pizza and salad and grabbed a bottle of mineral water. "We're set up for Monday. We'll meet with both finance and product development people."

"Thanks," I said. "Sorry I can't join you. I scheduled this Lean conference months ago. Have you talked to Brenda?"

"No," Al answered. "Have you talked to Jack?"

"No, but I plan to drop an updated version of my A3 on his desk before I leave today."

"Send me a copy and do the same for Brenda."

"Sure thing," I said.

"Why do you call it an A3?" Al asked.

"Because that's what Toyota calls it, based on the paper size," I replied. "We probably need a better name. Where are those guys?" I asked.

Greg and Carl entered the room. "They're eating while we're working?" Carl said as he spotted the pizza. He put his computer on the conference table next to Al.

"Jon, you remembered," Carl said and filled a plate.

"What are you waiting for Greg?" I asked, as Greg sat down next to me.

"I don't want to get between Carl and the pizza," he said. "Besides, I'm trying to watch what I eat. I'll have a salad in a minute."

"More for me!" Carl exclaimed, putting a fourth slice on his plate.

"I suggest we get started," I said. "Al, did you get a chance to update the financial goals?"

"Yes," Al said plugging in his laptop. "First, I created a spreadsheet and copied it to a slide like I've always done. Then I decided to make visible knowledge, so I made a couple of graphs and played with the scales and fonts to make them easy to read. I haven't broken it down for each business yet."

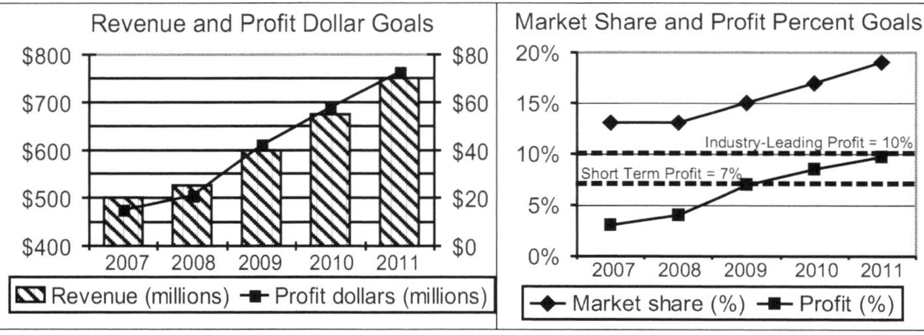

Assumptions:

- Gross margin = 30%
- Fixed costs: people incl. benefits - $100 million, buildings, etc. - $40 million:
  - Flat through 2009 = $140 million
  - 5% annual increase starting at end of 2009, only if profit goals are met.

(table 4c)

"We need ten percent profit in 2011?" Carl exclaimed.

"Yes," Al said. "I looked through the annual reports of the competition and we have two competitors that make roughly nine percent profit so we need to be around ten percent profit in 2011 to have the highest profit in the industry, and that requires 750 million in revenue, assuming fixed costs are flat through year three, and then increase at five percent annually."

"Why did you use fixed cost after telling me to use direct expenses?" I asked.

"The point I'm making," Al said, "is that fixed costs, and particularly people costs, have to be flat until we meet the seven percent profit goal."

"That means no raises," Carl grumbled.

"The workforce could get a five percent raise next year and again the following," Al replied, "if you are willing to sign up for 650 million in revenue in 2009."

"I'd rather freeze my salary and go for the six hundred million than have a layoff," Greg countered. "How does this compare with Brenda's plan?"

"I really shouldn't share the details of Brenda's," Al said.

"Al," I said. "Jack and Brenda agreed to combine the projects so we have to make the details visible. Jack already told me the details and I know you can trust these guys."

"Okay," Al said turning to Carl and Greg, "but you have to understand this information is of the highest sensitivity so you have to keep it to yourselves — understand?" Al waited until Greg and Carl nodded affirmatively.

"Okay, Brenda's plan," Al continued, "is to cut 20% of the workforce this year, which saves twenty million dollars next year and increases profit by four percent, from the current three percent to the seven percent we need."

"So, the company would make seven percent profit next year, as opposed to our plan, which reaches seven percent the year after next?" Greg asked.

"Yes," Al answered, "we will be making seven percent profit starting in the first quarter of next year. Then we sell the Automotive Products, outsource manufacturing in Security Systems, sell a building, and buy a business that makes good profit, and we should be at ten percent profit by the end of next year!"

"Really," I said. "ten percent profit by the end of next year? Jack didn't mention that."

"Yes," Al said proudly. "Brenda's plan is to improve profit from 3 to 10 percent in one year. Greg and Carl will see what I mean when we visit my old company on Monday."

"I can't wait," Carl said sarcastically.

"The big difference," Al said, obviously tiring of Carl's obstinacy, "is that Brenda's plan is high confidence. You guys don't have a clue how to achieve your plan. And even if you did, why would the Board of Directors wait three additional years to reach ten prercent profit?"

"Toyota added nearly seventy billion dollars of very profitable organic growth in five years," Greg countered.

"We know we still have to produce a plan," I said to change the subject. "Greg, what did you and Carl find?"

"Carl and I spent an hour putting this root cause analysis together based upon what we learned from going through a total of eighty different problems," Greg said as he hooked his laptop to the projector. "The first question is why customer quality is not better? The answer is because of manufacturing escapes, early life failures, and what we called excessive customer usage, which means the product broke doing something it wasn't designed to do, and products we can't find anything wrong with. You can see the distribution of failures by business in the bar chart entitled 'Categories of Customer Failures'."

"What's a 'manufacturing escape'?" Al asked.

"Manufacturing escapes are units that should have been caught by process testing or inspection but were not," Greg explained, pointing to the 'Manufacturing escape' bubble in the root cause analysis. "In my experience it is rare when a test or inspection process catches 100% of out-of-spec units. It could also be due to test variation, out-of-spec test, operator error, and so forth. If defective units are built, invariably some will escape to customers. That's why we can't afford supplier or manufacturing defects."

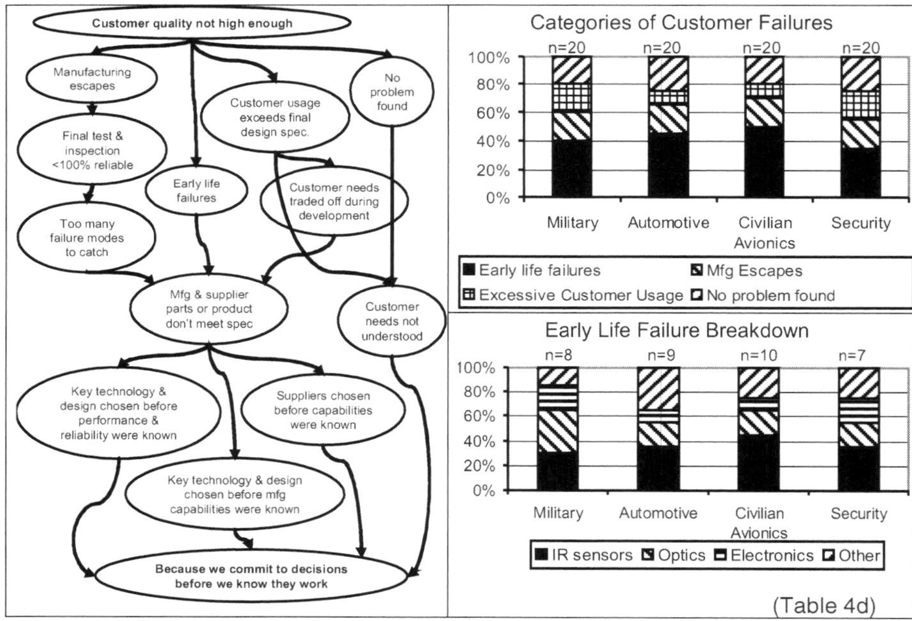

(Table 4d)

"Thanks," Al said. "Why is the 'No problem found' bubble connected to 'Customer needs' not understood'?"

Greg said, "We assume customers had some reason for returning it and we just don't know what it was. Historically, we find that customers wanted better image quality or longer range."

"So no problem found is really no knowledge found?" Al asked.

"Exactly," Greg replied, "You're catching on."

"I talked to George Rogers in Production about manufacturing escapes," Carl said, "and he said it's the same old problem — he can't hold some of the design tolerances and neither can suppliers. The last thing he wants is to tighten down all the production tests. He said his rework line can't keep up as it is. George wants the answer to be designs that work."

"We looked at test results for thirty-six early life failures," Greg added pointing to the bar chart entitled 'Early Life Failure Breakdown.' IR sensors were the top failing component followed by optics and then electronics."

"I talked to three engineers in Civilian Avionics who I've worked with closely for years," Carl said. "They said they do the best they can with the time they are given to complete their designs, but all three said they are rarely more than eighty percent confident their design will work until prototypes are built and tested. We can all do the math. If ten subsystems each have an eighty percent chance of working, the probability of the product working is ten percent."

I said, "The bottom line is that we make design decisions before we know they're going to work. Is that it?"

"Yes," Carl said, "and that's what causes these customer loopbacks."

"We have a conclusion," Carl added as Greg showed the next slide.

Analysis Conclusion

The design–then-test product development paradigm will not deliver needed quality and cost on schedule.

Carl stood and walked to the board. He talked while he drew. "We're in a constant state of unplanned loopbacks to fix what didn't work — both product design and manufacturing process design. Here's the basic problem. We have this phase gate system that has evolved over several years. We define our specs, pick a concept quickly, partition into design specifications for the subsystems. Then we begin our detailed designs.

"Then the loopbacks begin. The basic cause is lack of knowledge. Marketing, or whomever, sets specs that we don't know are possible and dates that are purely wishful thinking. In reality, long-term research is often needed for the product even to be viable. The problem is we don't know but we try. We then make early conceptual decisions so we

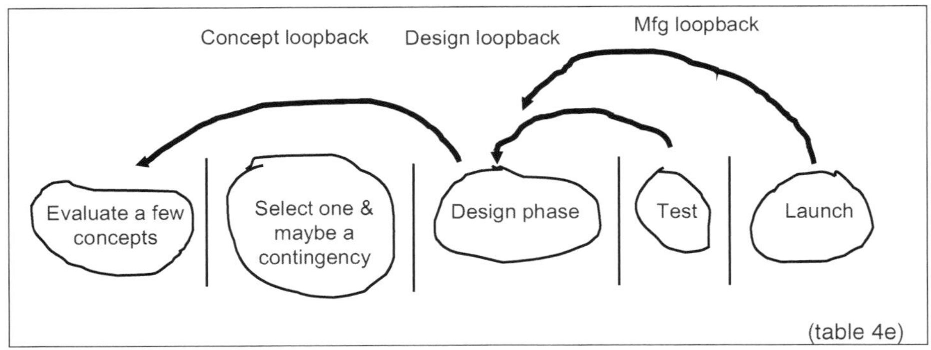

(table 4e)

can start designing. These early decisions are often made without understanding the end user ramifications, or the ramifications to service, or manufacturing. Not only that, the loopbacks drive shoddy problem solving because of a perceived need for quick solutions, rather than the right solution based on the real root cause."

Carl turned and glanced at us. "It gets worse," he said. "Because of our firefighting mentality, very little of what's learned flows forward to future projects, so wheels are constantly being reinvented." Pointing to the gates, he said, "The gates are really just administrative reviews, set as early as possible, where we check off all the process tasks that were in Doyle's old PSPD process. Loopbacks flow freely back across these gates. In my opinion, this product development environment will always yield pathetic results, and that's what is killing this company. It's inevitable, and it's that simple. "

Carl sat down.

Al looked at each one of us in turn. He seemed puzzled, but no one spoke.

"Okay," Al said. "I see the point, and it's not a pretty picture. I see a lot of detailed planning followed by expected chaos as those plans go awry. But I thought the four cornerstones of Toyota were supposed to fix all that. Isn't that what I read in the material you gave me, Jon?"

"Good segue to tackle the next problem," I said handing out A3s. "Al, remember yesterday when I said LAMDA is used again during the CA step of PDCA? That's what we're going to do now. A year ago we decided to implement one cornerstone in each of the businesses, the D of PDCA, and it didn't work as hoped, which means we didn't understand what we were doing."

"Al," I said, "we talked about the first slide that compares IRT to Toyota yesterday. Any questions?"

Problem: Cornerstone Implementation Didn't Deliver Needed Results

<table>
<tr><th colspan="2">Problem Description</th></tr>
<tr><td>Implemented one cornerstones in each business:
♦ Civilian Avionics – Expert Engineering Workforce
♦ Automotive – Chief Engineer
♦ Set-Based Concurrent Engineering – Security Systems
♦ Military – Responsibility-Based Planning</td><td> 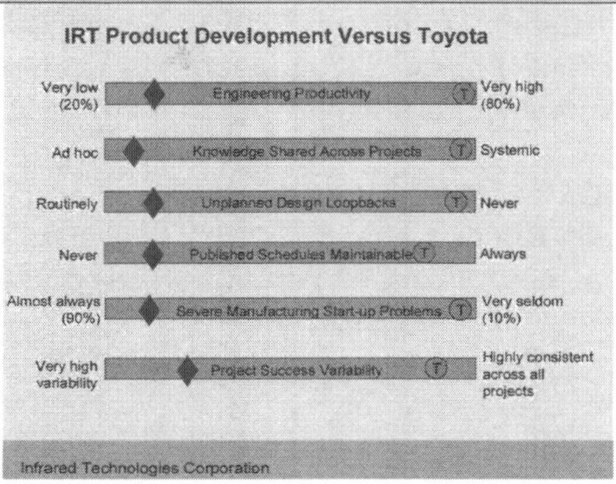IRT Product Development Versus Toyota
Very low (20%) – Engineering Productivity – Very high (80%)
Ad hoc – Knowledge Shared Across Projects – Systemic
Routinely – Unplanned Design Loopbacks – Never
Never – Published Schedules Maintainable – Always
Almost always (90%) – Severe Manufacturing Start-up Problems – Very seldom (10%)
Very high variability – Project Success Variability – Highly consistent across all projects
Infrared Technologies Corporation</td></tr>
<tr><td>♦ IRT product development performance assessment score increased from 19% to 23%.
♦ Business results correlated with the extent of LAMDA and A3 usage in problem solving, decision-making, and communication
♦ <u>Objective:</u> Identify root causes and develop plan to increase Product Development performance to 40% in 1 year.</td><td> 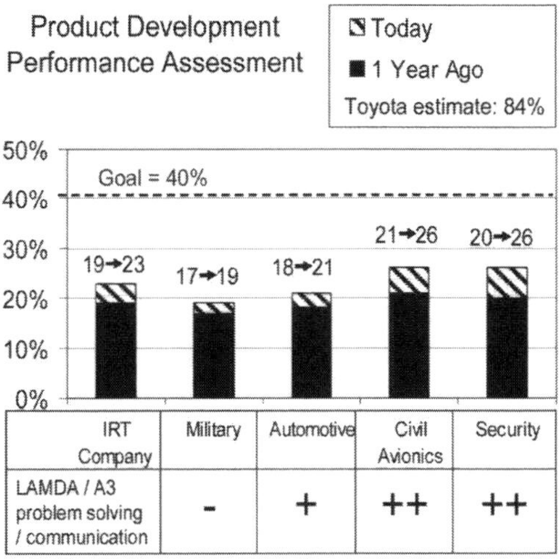Product Development Performance Assessment
Today
1 Year Ago
Toyota estimate: 84%
50%
Goal = 40%
40%
30%
20%
10%
0%
IRT Company: 19→23
Military: 17→19
Automotive: 18→21
Civil Avionics: 21→26
Security: 20→26
LAMDA / A3 problem solving / communication: IRT Company –; Military –; Automotive +; Civil Avionics ++; Security ++
(table 4f)</td></tr>
</table>

Al said, "It just boggles my mind that Toyota can be so much better than everybody else. There are a lot of smart people in western companies."

I said, "I was skeptical too until Allen Ward explained how Toyota does product development."

Al said, "I have a question on your bullet that states there is a correlation between use of LAMDA and A3s to solve problems and the amount of improvement. Where did that come from?"

"I spent two full days talking to the people who have been implementing the cornerstones in each business. Civilian Avionics trained everyone in LAMDA and A3s because they tried to implement the Expert Workforce cornerstone and it spread over to Security Systems. Both Wayne Tillotson, who heads up Civilian Avionics and particularly Christine Dumas who heads up Security Systems, are leading by example. The Chief Engineers in Automotive Products use A3s to communicate status and it has saved valuable meeting time, but Charles still wants all of his presentations in slides. Military Products hardly uses LAMDA and A3s at all."

"You're saying that using a consistent and effective method for problem solving, decision making and communication of status consistently improves productivity?"

"Particularly when there is collaboration and mentoring," I added. "That the difference between solving problems to the best of an individual's ability versus solving them to the best of the company's ability."

"Where'd you get your objective of 40% in one year?" Carl asked.

"It's just a starting point," I said. "I wanted to set it high enough to require a transformation and not just more continuous improvement. I don't know. Maybe it's not high enough. What do you think?"

"If we can improve from 23 to 40 in one year," Greg said, "we will certainly be transformed. I'd leave it."

"What went wrong?" Al asked.

"As you can see, I started a root cause analysis."

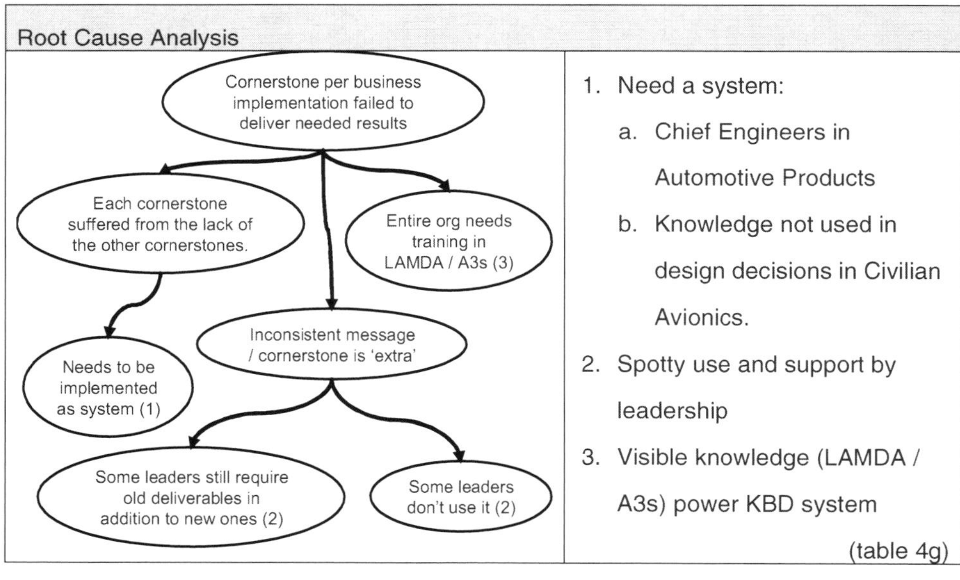

Root Cause Analysis
Cornerstone per business implementation failed to deliver needed results
Each cornerstone suffered from the lack of the other cornerstones.
Entire org needs training in LAMDA / A3s (3)
Needs to be implemented as system (1)
Inconsistent message / cornerstone is 'extra'
Some leaders still require old deliverables in addition to new ones (2)
Some leaders don't use it (2)
1. Need a system:
a. Chief Engineers in Automotive Products
b. Knowledge not used in design decisions in Civilian Avionics.
2. Spotty use and support by leadership
3. Visible knowledge (LAMDA / A3s) power KBD system

(table 4g)

I said, "Our biggest mistake was not implementing the four cornerstones as a system. We implemented things piecemeal. The Chief Engineers in Automotive Products found that really frustrating and one of the managers in Civilian Avionics pointed out that they were capturing knowledge but they weren't using it in any design decisions."

"What do you mean by spotty use and support from leadership?" Al asked.

"It's no secret that Nathan Jorgenson in Military Products and Charles Osgood in Automotive Products are less than enthusiastic in their support," I replied.

"Why does Jack put up with that?" Al asked.

"It's a mystery to me," I said.

"What does your third bullet mean," Carl asked, "the one about visible knowledge powering the KBD system?"

"It's a theory I came up with after talking with everyone over the last two days," I replied. "It occurred to me that visible knowledge, which is created through LAMDA and A3s, enables collaboration, mentoring, thorough problem solving, good decision-making, efficient communication, and reuse. Without it, the KBD system will grind to a halt. People are more likely to collaborate and mentor if they can quickly understand the problem, root causes, and alternative solutions. Knowledge is more likely to be reused if it is presented in easy-to-understand visual models like trade-off curves and free-body diagrams."

"Do you have a conclusion?" Greg asked.

"No, not yet," I said. "There are a number of issues I still don't understand. Are the four cornerstones enough? Did we implement correctly? Is there too much opposition? Realistically, all the divisions are integrating things they like into the existing process. They're not replacing the existing system, and that's what's needed. But—" I raised a finger in the air, "if we completely change the system, we'd better be right. That's why I'm rethinking this with you guys. We have to get it right."

I paused and looked at Carl, and then continued. "Isn't what Carl described the root cause? Isn't the basic problem the fundamental absence of the knowledge needed for making design decisions that won't result in loopbacks."

Greg said, "No. That can't be the root cause. If it is then we will just build an elaborate knowledge management system, and that will never work. We already have one. The knowledge is not trusted, not up to date, not findable, not applicable, or not understood as such. It has to be more than that."

"Okay, then" I said. "Why do we commit to decisions before we know they will work?"

"Well," Carl said slowly. "I'd say because we know we will figure out whether the design works in integration testing, manufacturing pilot production, volume production, and in customer usage. So, I suppose we really shouldn't be committing to decisions until after then?"

Greg disagreed, "We obviously can't delay design decisions until the product is out the door. We know Toyota delays decisions, but that's a bit extreme."

"Wait a minute," I said. "We were taught that Toyota delays decisions until they know what they need to know to make the decisions."

"If that's the case," Carl said, "then we need to somehow bring the testing from late in the process to very earlier in the process. But how can you test something you haven't yet designed?"

This conversation was giving me a headache. I walked over to the thermoses, refilled my coffee mug, and stood next to the table with the thermoses in case I needed another refill soon.

After a moment Greg said, "It takes a long time to design a product for the market, but a prototype can be whipped up pretty fast if a lot of the details are ignored. How many times has Sales and Marketing given us a hard time for taking over a year to get a product to market, after they saw us build a research prototype in no time flat?"

I nodded. "We've read about Toyota having 'test vehicles' that are designed for rapid prototyping and testing of different components and assemblies in their operating environment."

"And," Greg said, "simulation tools can allow us to very quickly generate simulated test results. I've seen the guys whip up 'throw-away designs' in no time, when they don't have to worry about all the details of a real design."

"Okay," Carl said. "The reason we commit to decisions before we know they will work is because we fail to do the necessary testing up front. Wow, that's just not how we think about the design process."

"It is somewhat of a paradigm shift," Greg said. "But we sometimes make that shift in the Six Sigma exercises we've done very early in product development when we are just exploring ideas. The focus has been the design of the experiment, rather than the design of a specific product. But to make that shift for the whole product design and development process is definitely a different way of thinking."

Carl said as he stood and took a deep breath, "So, the root problem is that we are stuck in the wrong paradigm. The way we think about product development is the way we behave. Our paradigm is 'design and then test to see if the design meets the specs.' The Toyota paradigm is fundamentally different. It is to learn first and then design based on what you know. That's basically it, in short. We need to change from a 'design-then-test' mentality to 'a 'test-then-design' mentality."

"Okay," Greg said. "We have always known that there is a fuzzy front end, and in our case, it is really fuzzy. We really 'guess then test' in many instances. Based on what we're saying, I don't think Toyota has a fuzzy front end at all. We've gotten some Toyota practices going, but we haven't come close to making this paradigm shift."

Al spoke up. "Few things are more distasteful to investors than 'fuzzy.' Replacing the 'fuzzy front end' with something that is not fuzzy sounds productive."

"Hmmm," Carl grunted, as he seemed to wince at the thought of what he was about to utter, "the engineers might actually agree with the investors on that count. Engineers like absolutes . . . math and science. It's really not fun to design by best guess when you know the penalty for being wrong is late nights fire-fighting when you get into the inevitable design loopbacks. Yes, eliminating the fuzzy sounds very appealing."

After a pause, Carl said, "But it would depend on building the system to support it. And I don't think we know how."

Greg said, "How does what we've been talking about affect the four cornerstones that are in the piloting stage in the different business units? Is this a change? How do we explain it?"

After a moment of silence, Carl said, "They're the same but different." He looked at us with an amused expression. "Perhaps the four cornerstones are Toyota's operational paradigms for implementing 'test-then-design' development. Perhaps the Expert Workforce doesn't just know a lot, but also knows how to learn quickly up front. And Set-Based isn't just about keeping design options alive longer, it's also about the up front learning you gain from exploring those sets of alternatives. And Responsibility-Based Planning would be needed to support a process that starts with testing and learning up front. The Chief Engineer — hmmm."

Greg jumped in. "The Chief Engineer is not letting the decisions be made until he sees the test results that prove there is a feasible solution for the customer and manufacturing. In a sense, the Chief Engineer is pulling the necessary testing."

I thought for a moment, and then said, "If we are right about the root cause, then we've uncovered the flaw in our implementation. And it ties in with what I heard yesterday. We have piecemealed out the parts, but the parts are not the goal. The goal is to establish a new paradigm where we learn first. By the way, 'Learning-First' sounds better to me than 'Test-First.' And 'Learning-First' requires all four of the cornerstones. With just one cornerstone in each organization, none of the organizations could ever achieve 'Learning-First'. And hence, we couldn't possibly achieve the results we were hoping for. As Al noted, those are game-changing results. We should expect to have to change the game to get there."

The discussion continued. After a while, we all realized we were worn out. But we agreed that this view of a paradigm shift felt right. We had identified the key issue.

I said, "I believe you guys know I am going to a conference next week. It's in Tampa and on 'Lean everything' including product development. I'll be leaving tomorrow. My wife has a cousin that lives on the beach nearby and we'll be visiting them over the weekend. Even so, I will certainly be thinking about this as I walk the beach in the mornings. Let's plan on meeting back here a week from Monday. We'll revisit whether we are comfortable with our analysis. Then, I believe the next step will be to define some implementation alternatives and models."

I began to gather my stuff "One more thing," I said. "Let me know what you learn from Al's former company. And let's all of us keep an open mind. I want to integrate the best of both approaches before we bring Jack and Brenda into this."

"We're driving down Monday morning," Al reminded me.

"Good, see you next Monday," I said.

DISCUSSION

You may have noticed that as soon as Jon presented his A3 with a Problem Statement everyone started working together instead of defending their individual beliefs. We see this in companies that use LAMDA and A3s effectively. The discussion changes from who is right to what is right.

Hopefully these examples show how starting with a concise problem description and performing a root cause analysis results in a deeper understanding of the problem, as opposed to beginning to think about alternative solutions too early. Further, we hope these examples illustrate the power of Discussion (D in LAMDA) to expose new ideas.

For Jon's team, discussing a problem statement and analyzing the root causes revealed a paradigm limitation — the 'design-then-test' paradigm.

'Design and test' may work well for companies in industries with little competition and little need for innovation. But in today's ultra-competitive global industries, designing and testing one or two alternatives at a time is too slow, even with today's automated design tools. And because it is too slow, there is increasing pressure to speed up decision-making, which invariably results in wishful thinking.

The need to introduce new products faster puts pressure on Product Design Engineering to freeze the design earlier and be frugal with innovation, because innovation increases the likelihood that more loop-backs occur. Marketing is under more pressure to define product specs earlier in order to provide design engineers with more time to design, test, and iterate. Program managers are under pressure to keep the program moving. Manufacturing is under pressure to accept component and assembly specifications even if processes are not capable. Once again the program bets on expert firefighters to solve the remaining problems, and some how get the products out the door.

We've met with executives of companies who tell us that in the past, they would spend considerable time in advanced development proving that new technologies and processes work before committing to product designs. Then they would schedule six or seven whole-product prototype build and integration test cycles on new platform designs. But competitive pressure has forced the elimination of most advanced development activities and reduced the number of whole-product prototype builds.

Unfortunately, many of the solutions to these problems are also based upon wishful thinking. It's likely a number of companies which have successful Lean production efforts underway have assumed those same practices would be the answers to all their product development problems. But that's jumping to a solution without really understanding that product development problems are significantly different from production problems.

How many companies decide on a financial based solution — cost cutting, outsourcing, acquisition — without really understanding the real reason for their declining ROI?

Likewise, many companies assume a more rigorous stage gate system is the cure — the assumption being that the problem is lack of engineering discipline so the more process tasks, the better the product. But in reality the opposite is true because it is the nature of product development to have variation. It is therefore impossible for a group of individuals to accurately lay out all the tasks for an entire product development project where learning is required up front.

We refer a lot to the chart below because it is simple, very revealing and has been shown to correlate nicely to business results. From our experience, we have seen very little improvement in these metrics over the past decade — in spite of an increasing emphasis on product development improvement initiatives. The fundamental reason is a lack of learning and knowledge flow across projects. Companies frankly don't know how to take advantage of what they know. Product development must be a system of continuous applied learning. Understanding that is IRT's next challenge.

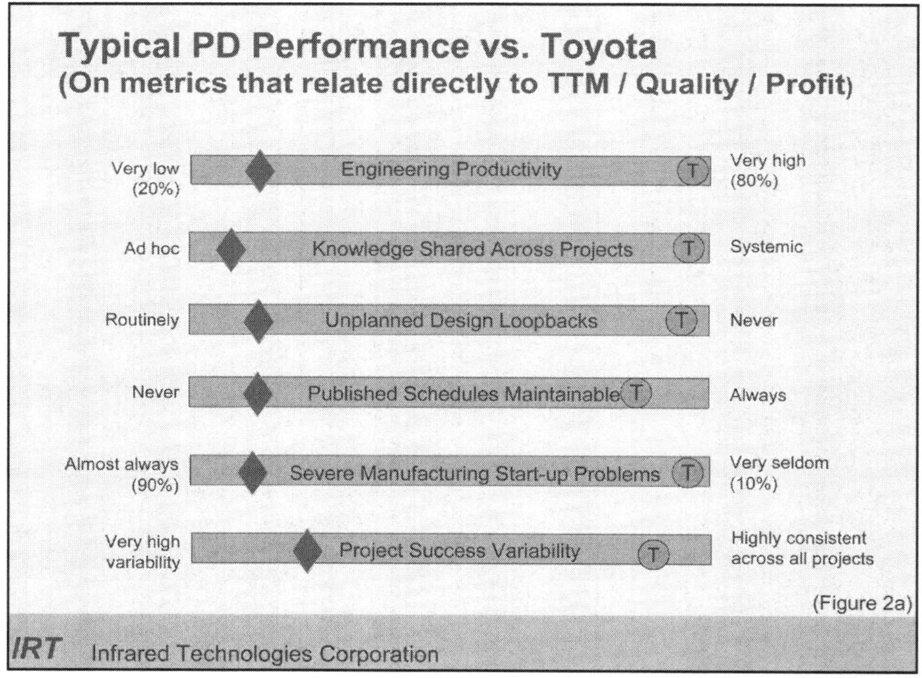

(Figure 2a)

Chapter 5
Looking at the Cost-Focused Model

A different cost model has been proposed as a solution alternative but does it resolve the root cause? It is time to look some more, and to ask some more. LAMDA is a continuing process for learning.

Monday Afternoon: Consumer Technologies Corporation

While I attended the conference as planned, Al, Carl, and Greg visited Brenda and Al's former company, Consumer Technologies Corporation, commonly known as CTC, located in Colorado Springs. Al had set up two meetings. The first was with the new Chief Financial Officer (CFO) Mark Balco, who worked with Al and was promoted after Brenda left. The second meeting was with the leaders of product development. I was later given a play-by-play description of what went on in both meetings, so I'll relate what happened as though I'd been a fly on the wall.

Mark met Al, Carl, and Greg in the lobby of CTC's large and modern glass and chrome building at about two o'clock. After the introductions were made and pleasantries exchanged, Mark led the group to the elevator and pushed the button for the fifth floor.

"Mark," Al said, "IRT faces the same challenges we faced three years ago and Brenda is recommending a similar solution. I thought it would be helpful for you to explain how it's working for CTC."

"I'll be happy to," Mark said. The elevator door opened and Mark led the group down a well lit hallway filled with cubicles and offices. At the end was another door with a card reader. Mark swiped his card, and they all entered the executive suite. The entire area had wood-paneled walls adorned by expensive oil paintings in lavish frames. They entered the executive conference room.

Carl and Greg stopped to admire the large mahogany conference table surrounded by twelve leather-rivet armchairs. A dark-stained oak bookcase graced an entire wall and tall tropical plants stood in the corners.

"Business must be booming," Carl said.

Mark said, "We are doing very well, and we wanted a nice area to host important customers, suppliers and investors."

Mark reached to the middle of the table and turned on the projector.

Al said, "Let me describe the history, first. Then Mark will present the current situation. The cell phone industry is incredibly competitive, and three years ago CTC's profit was two percent and market share was 16%, which was down from 25% three years earlier. The Board of Directors hired a new CEO who brought in Brenda as Chief Financial Officer. Brenda recommended the same three-circle strategy that she's recommending at IRT. The current cell phone business is core. CTC realized it had to purchase high growth and high profit companies, so it bought a small medical company last year and is looking at other acquisitions. CTC executed a comprehensive cost reduction plan that included a twenty percent across the board workforce reduction. That's about it, I guess. Mark, can you take it from there?"

Greg said, "We're engineers, so please use layman's terms."

"Sure," Mark said as he projected a slide from his laptop. "The bottom line is our new strategy is working extremely well. Our profit has skyrocketed, we have lots of cash, and the stock price has doubled."

"This slide shows our core business," Mark said as he walked to the front of the room. "We executed a comprehensive cost reduction program three years ago in 2004 and profit immediately quadrupled to eight percent. It has remained at that level for more than two years. Market share increased from 16 to 20 percent."

	Profit	**WW Market Share**
2004	**2%**	**16%**
2005	**8%**	**16%**
2006	**8%**	**20%**
2007 (projection)	**5%**	**18%**

Carl rubbed his eyes. "Which department lost the most people during the across-the-board layoff?"

"It was mostly Product Design Engineering and Manufacturing because that's where most of the employees were," Mark said.

Carl said, "Did the product portfolio change after the employees left?"

"Last year we introduced three mostly outsourced new products at the low-end and they have done very well," Mark replied. The high-end market isn't as strong as it once was, and as you can imagine, those products take a little longer to develop."

"So profit improved in 2005 because you received revenue from products that were developed by people who no longer work at the company," Carl said. "Is that true?"

"That is mostly true," Mark said. "We also sold a building and made other cuts."

Carl said, "Guess you can't sell a building unless you fire the people who work in it."

Greg said, "How were you able to increase market share?"

"We lowered prices and were still able to increase profit," Mark said with enthusiasm. "Our cost reduction program far exceeded its goals. In addition to selling a building, we put most employees in smaller cubicles. Brenda projected six percent profit and sixteen percent market share. We beat them both!"

"What about this year?" Carl asked. "Looks like profit is back down to five percent."

"I probably shouldn't have shown you that projection," Mark said. "Actually, it's not going to happen. We will take actions soon that will dramatically improve our financial situation."

"Are you going to have another layoff?" Carl said.

"I'm afraid I can't reveal the details right now," Mark said. "But I will say that we have learned that cost reduction has to be a continuous effort."

"Show the results from the medical company you bought last year," Al said.

Mark flipped through his slide set and put up another slide.

"The first year was awesome," he said. "15% profit, which pulled company profit to ten percent. This year it's still doing pretty well but not as well."

	Profit WW	**Market Share**
2006	**15%**	**25%**
2007 (projection)	**11%**	**22%**

Carl said, "Looks like profit and market share are dropping like rocks."

"That's new," Al exclaimed. "Last I saw the medical business was increasing profit and market share. What happened?"

"We just found out that a couple of new products slipped because we lost some key people. Our CEO said we have to be aware that sometimes the revenue from the combined company is less than the combined revenue of the individual companies. Consequently the cost reduction has to be large enough to compensate. Again, I shouldn't show you the projected numbers because we're going to take action to improve the financial picture."

"Another layoff?" Carl said.

"Help me understand," Greg said. "How will cutting people this year help this year's financial situation? Don't you have to pay severance to departing employees?"

"Let me explain," Al said, as he knew Mark didn't want to reveal his company's plans. "When we implemented a workforce reduction three years ago we took a restructuring charge in the second quarter that included all the severance charges. Profit in the third and fourth quarters jumped because the people were off the books. The whole year wasn't any more profitable but the third and fourth quarters were far more profitable. So the investors were happy and profit increased again with the acquisition of the medical company."

"And the stock price doubled," Mark added. "That's important because the stock was strong enough that we were able to purchase the medical company by issuing new stock. So our cash position remained strong, and we didn't take on any additional debt. In fact, we've had enough cash from our record profits to repurchase our stock the last two years, which keeps the price up and investors happy. "

"In the age of global competition, why would anyone use profit to buy back stock?" Carl said. "Doesn't it make far more sense to reinvest profit in the company to develop better products and beat the competition?"

Mark glanced at Al and rolled his eyes.

Al said, "Buying back stock removes shares from the marketplace and raises the price of the stock, which is exactly what people who own stock want to have happen. Fewer shares outstanding translate into higher earnings per share, which is the most watched metric by investors. Also, a stock is a financial asset. If the price is high and increasing, then it has more value, and more people want to own it. If the stock has value, it can be used to buy assets like other companies. It also inspires confidence with customers, suppliers, and investors. A stock with a high and increasing price is a sign that investors believe the company has its act together and will have it together for the foreseeable future. Now does it make sense?"

Carl said, "Makes great sense if your focus is short term."

Al said, "Mark, the company was close to announcing another acquisition when I left. Is it still going to happen?"

"That's part of what I can't talk about. But I will say that we will make a big announcement next week and you will not be surprised."

"The competitor?" Al asked.

Mark nodded affirmatively.

Al smiled. "Investors are going to love that."

Carl shook his head. "You fire people to prop up profits in the short term and when profit drops, you fire more people. You acquire a company and it performs worse than it did before you bought it, so you fire people. Then you buy another company and fire people right away because you know it's going to perform worse. Am I the only one who thinks this is insane?"

Greg jumped in. "What my straight-talking colleague is saying is this: it doesn't appear that any value is being created here."

"Think of it this way," Al replied. "Value can be created and value can be captured. Value is captured when a workforce is reduced or a building is sold or when redundant activities are eliminated during a merger. Value is created when an investment is made in a new technology, a new market, or a company. CTC is still investing in new technologies. Next week when CTC buys a top competitor in the medical market, CTC will jump to market leadership with industry-leading profit."

"Al," Mark cautioned. "It's not announced yet."

"Sorry. But I want these guys to understand that this strategy does achieve industry leadership in market share and profit."

"But for how long?" Greg said.

"Look," Mark said, "three years ago our stock was in the dumpster. We had no cash, and we were a takeover target. We have already quadrupled profit and increased market share in the ultra-competitive cell phone business. We've also established a strong balance sheet and doubled the stock price. We're buying companies. We're on the road to industry leadership. But we know we're not perfect. We know we're still learning how to do this. As we get better at it, we will make even better decisions with greater and longer term returns. I'm sure of it. Investors are very bullish on our company."

Carl shook his head and rolled his eyes.

"So you believe this strategy is working?" Greg asked.

"Absolutely," Mark declared.

Al glanced at his watch. "Thanks Mark, we appreciate your time," he said. "We have a meeting with some of the product development people."

"Right. I'll escort you over to the engineering area."

"I know the way," Al said.

"Our policy is no unescorted guests, and you are now a guest."

Mark led Al, Carl, and Greg downstairs to the third floor that housed Product Design Engineering and Marketing. Carl noticed that it was not as posh as the executive wing. Actually, it was rather drab.

"Great seeing you again Al," Mark said shaking Al's hand at the door of a large conference room. "And good luck," Mark glanced at Carl. "Let me know what you decide to do."

"Thanks for setting this up," Al replied. "I'll call you next week after your big announcement."

Mark walked back upstairs.

Al, Carl and Greg entered the conference room.

Al introduced Carl and Greg to Laura Sloan, the Vice President of Product Design Engineering, Nick Walker, Director of Engineering who worked for Laura, Sarah Gibson, Director of Marketing, and Scott Douglas, the Vice President of Operations.

"Good to see you again," Laura said to Al. "How's working at IRT?"

"So far, so good. IRT has some of the same challenges we faced here three years ago, so I wanted Carl and Greg to meet with some folks at CTC to see how things are going here. How are things in Engineering?"

"Frankly, it's been a challenge since the workforce reduction three years ago," Laura said. "We lost some of our most experienced engineers — the people who really understand the science behind our products. But my biggest concern is that attrition has steadily increased."

Al said, "Weren't you going to outsource activities and reduce the workload?"

"We did and we brought on suppliers that do pretty well on the low-end of the portfolio. But they don't have the capability to design our high-end products, which is where we make most of our profit. So we slipped schedule on a couple of high-end products that we desperately needed to replace old non-competitive designs.'

Al said, "Scott. How are things in Manufacturing?"

"Life changed dramatically for us three years ago too," Scott replied. "But there's no going back, so we have to figure out how to make it work. But it's tough because we're cutting back investment in our core business and we're being asked for more profit."

"And that profit is used to buy companies," Carl added.

"It's a huge motivational challenge," Scott said. "I lost some of my best manufacturing engineers because early retirement was offered. All that knowledge walked out the door with a severance check. Meanwhile my procurement people are on the phone with Asian suppliers every night trying to figure out what they're doing, and my travel budget has gone through the roof."

Carl nodded. "Things don't sound as rosy down here as they did up in the ivory tower."

"We've got our challenges," Nick said. "But we still have industry-leading technology in a number of areas."

"Yes," Sarah from Marketing said. "We have leading technology but our customers don't, and if we don't get the new technology into the marketplace soon, we're going to lose the high-end market. The competition is coming after us."

Carl asked, "How has Marketing fared since the big cost reduction?"

"We lost some of our most knowledgeable people, too," Sarah said. "We don't know customers like we used to, and we risk making bad product decisions as a result. Like Scott said, there's no going back so we have to figure out how to make it work."

Al said, "Is there anything you have learned now that you have been managing through these challenges for three years?"

Scott said, "For me, yes. I don't know if my colleagues agree, but a lot of people including managers hung onto the past. We should have outsourced more aggressively than we did at the low-end. Then we could have moved engineers off the low-end products onto the high-end products to help finish them on schedule. I think we would have gotten out the low-end products faster, too."

Laura said, "I can understand how you can say that now that the low-end products are shipping and the high-end products have slipped. But my engineers found and fixed some major bugs on the low-end products that would have caused serious problems for customers."

Greg glanced at his watch. "As you know we'd like you to take our product development performance assessment. It will take about an hour and we'd like you to provide two scores, your score today and your score three years ago before the workforce reduction."

"Let's do it," Laura said.

"The assessment is twenty questions and each question is scored between zero and five, five being the best. We arrive at a percentage by adding up all the scores. It assesses a company's product development capabilities relative to Toyota. Most American companies don't do very well. When we're done, I'll show you our scores and a Toyota estimate."

Greg handed out paper copies of the assessment to everyone in the room and plugged his laptop into the projector. "Okay, now. This should be spontaneous. We'll have a brief discussion and then we'll decide on a score. Any questions?"

"Let's get started," Laura said.

"First question," Greg said. "Are initial schedules met? I'm talking about new products, new platforms, and new product lines, not light-touch changes to existing products or accessories. As you can see a zero means initial schedules are almost obsolete by the end of the project. You score a five if you always meet initial schedules and you don't have to trade-off features and functionality to achieve schedules."

		0	1	2	3	4	5
1.	Are initial schedules met? New products, platforms, and product lines, not light-touch changes to existing products or accessories.	Initial schedules are almost always obsolete by end of project	Initial schedules are usually obsolete by end of project	Initial schedules are usually met. Features and functionality are regularly traded off to meet schedule.	Initial schedules are almost never missed Features and functionality are regularly traded off to meet schedule.	Initial schedules are never missed Features and functionality sometimes have to be traded off to meet schedule.	Initial schedules are never missed. Features and functionality are refined and enhanced at end of project, not traded off to meet schedule.
							(table 5a)

"I'll jump in," Nick said. "I'd say we usually meet our initial schedules. Let's see. That gives us a two. Man, tough grading system."

"Are you kidding?" Sarah said. "I can't remember ever meeting our initial schedules. I'd give us a zero."

"No," Nick countered, "we never meet your Marketing schedules."

"How do we resolve this?" Laura asked.

Greg said, "Let me ask, do you meet the initial schedules that are communicated to customers."

Laura said, "Almost never — for a lot of reasons. Competitors make moves and specifications change. New technologies don't work as hoped, and to Nick's point, sometimes Marketing communicates what I would call a soft schedule to customers to keep them interested. We never meet those."

"What are your scores today and three years ago?" Greg asked.

"Let's see. I'd give us a one three years ago but today we're closer to zero, particularly after slipping those two high-end products.

"Okay," Greg said. "Next question. Is a big resource push with fire-fighting required to complete new products? You get a zero if a large unplanned resource push is usually required and a five if unplanned resources are never required. You can read the rest."

Nick said, "If we're talking about major new products and platforms, the score is one for now and one for three years ago."

"Everybody agree with Nick?" Greg asked.

"We're probably a little less than a one but let's round up," Laura said.

		0	1	2	3	4	5
2.	Is a big resource push with firefighting required to complete new products?	Large unplanned resource push is usually required. Next generatio n projects are usually impacted	Large unplanned resource push is sometimes required. Next generation projects are sometimes impacted	Large planned resource push is usually required. Small unplanned push is also usually required Next generation projects are rarely impacted	Small planned resource push is usually required. Small unplanned push is also usually required Next generation projects are never impacted	Small planned resource push is sometimes required Unplanned resources are never required Resources are always available on schedule Next generation projects are never impacted	Unplanned resources are never required. Most resources are reallocated to next project before pilot production Resources are always available on schedule Next generation projects are never impacted
							(table 5b)

"Question #3," Greg continued. "Does Manufacturing experience serious problems with new products? Scott, what do you think?"

"We're a one," Scott said, "and it hasn't gotten any better in the last three years. If anything, we have more serious problems now, and most of them are caused by our new suppliers."

		0	1	2	3	4	5
3.	Does Manufact-uring experienc e serious problems with new products?	Almost always: Many serious manufactur ing problems occur in pilot production and during production ramp.	Usually: Many serious manufact uring problems occur in pilot productio n and several during productio n ramp.	Often: Several serious manufact uring problems occur in pilot productio n and some in productio n ramp.	Sometimes: Some serious manufactur ing problems occur in pilot production and a few in production ramp.	Very rarely: Serious manufacturing problems almost never occur in pilot production and never in production ramp.	Never: Serious manufacturi ng problems never occur in pilot production or production ramp.
							(table 5c)

Forty-five minutes later Greg had tabulated the results. CTC scored 20% three years ago and 17% today.

Laura said, "That is depressing. But I'm not surprised at the results or the fact that we've gotten a little worse since the workforce reduction. How did your company do?"

"We scored 19 a year ago," Greg said, "and we're up to 23 now that we've been trying to implement some of Toyota's best practices."

"How does Toyota score?"

"Toyota's score was estimated by Dr. Durward Sobek. Dr. Sobek has studied Toyota for nearly twenty years and lived in Toyota City, Japan where he directly observed Toyota Product Development. His estimate for Toyota is 84%."

"Eighty-four!" Laura exclaimed.

Greg continued. "Toyota scored a four on the first question, meaning that initial schedules are never missed, but features and functionality are sometimes traded off to meet schedule."

"Wow," Sarah said. "Initial schedules are never missed."

"On the second question Toyota also scored a four. Small planned resource push is sometimes required. Unplanned resources are never required."

"No way," Nick said. "You've got to be kidding."

"On the third question, Toyota also scored a four. Very rarely does Toyota experience serious manufacturing problems. I suspect that has gotten worse with Toyota's recent quality problems. Do you want me to go through all of the Toyota scores or are there any in particular you want to know?"

Laura said, "In the interest of time I'd like to know how Toyota scored a couple of questions. How did Toyota score on question nine, problem solving?"

"Let's see," Greg said as be scrolled down. "Toyota scored a three. Toyota has a consistent method for solving problems throughout the company. Problems and their root causes are always investigated deeply enough to understand the root causes. Knowledge is visible to a department. Same and similar problems never reoccur within a department. The challenge Toyota has is making knowledge visible to its design and manufacturing groups around the world. Toyota has built lots of manufacturing facilities and design centers in the last fifteen years."

"We scored a one," Laura said. "And we were being generous. We have a consistent method for problem solving throughout our company, but we often don't have the time to really understand how causal factors govern the problem. And the same problems do reoccur."

"We're trying to fix that, too," Carl said. "We call it guessing."

"What about number thirteen?" Laura asked. "Knowledge creation / Invention / Innovation? How'd Toyota score?"

"Toyota scored a four," Greg said. "New and existing technologies and processes are always tested to failure with sufficient prototypes to create trade-off curves. Trade-off curves are almost always robust enough for reuse on other and future products."

"We scored a zero," Laura said. "We usually test new and existing technologies until they pass in order to ship as soon as possible. How about the next question, number fourteen?"

"Knowledge capture and reuse across departments, platforms, product lines, and businesses," Greg said. "Again, Toyota scored a four. All departments capture knowledge needed to design products and processes and the system identifies trustworthy knowledge. Knowledge is reused across departments, platforms, product lines, and within businesses. But problems reoccur in different businesses and geographically split locations."

"We scored a zero on that one, too," Laura said. "For me these three questions explain Toyota's amazing productivity. They solve problems just once all the way to root cause, they capture the learning so it can be used on multiple products, and they reuse everything they learn."

Carl said, "What impresses me is that Toyota has the discipline to implement this at every level of the organization from the CEO to the factory worker. In American companies, tools like Six Sigma are primarily engineering tools. Top management doesn't usually bother to get actively involved."

Al said, "What impresses me most is that Toyota has added nearly seventy billion dollars of organic growth in five years. Never has a manufacturing company achieved such phenomenal growth — not against firmly entrenched competition. Equally remarkable is the fact that last year Toyota earned fourteen billion dollars of net profit, nearly half of it in the North American market — where most auto companies are losing billions."

Carl glanced at Greg and grinned. He tipped his head in Al's direction. Maybe a finance guy could actually appreciate the Toyota Product Development System.

"Any other questions?" Greg asked.

"Yes," Sarah said. "How does Toyota do on number seven?"

"Depth of Product Design Engineering — Knowledge of customers and competitors," Greg said. "Toyota scored a five."

"A five," Laura exclaimed. "How can thousands of engineers at a company the size of Toyota all be experts about the customer?"

"Toyota does it with Chief Engineers," Greg answered. "The Chief Engineer is a very experienced engineering manager who has been trained to be a customer expert. He has a very deep understanding of customer needs and competitive threats and is an expert at designing cars. He is responsible for the overall design of the car as well as schedule and cost. He makes sure designs are optimized for the target customers."

Laura looked at her watch. "I'd like to learn more about Toyota, but I'm double booked in meetings. Can you send me an e-mail of the best books and articles on Toyota?"

"Sure," Greg said. "Thanks for your time."

Greg and Carl piled into Al's car. In a few minutes they were headed back to IRT, which was located just north of Denver. As they approached the city, rush hour brought traffic to a halt.

Greg said, "Thanks for setting up the visit, Al. I learned a lot."

"Me too," Carl agreed. "What a contrast between Mark in the ivory tower and the product development people in the trenches."

"Change is hard," Al said. "But they're figuring it out."

"You must be kidding," Carl retorted. "It was apparent to me that

CTC is a disaster, and if IRT decides to go the same route, you can put my name on the top of the layoff list."

"Careful what you wish for, Carl," Greg warned.

"I'd rather go in the first round," Carl said, "than play musical chairs until I lose. And I'd rather look for a new job now when I'm forty-eight than in five years when I'm fifty-three."

"Some people do struggle with the new strategy," Al said. "The fact is it's best if they do move on. You heard what Scott said about people hanging onto the past at CTC. I agree with him one hundred percent."

"Carl is one of the engineers we don't want to lose," Greg said. "Nobody knows what Carl knows about some of our infrared technologies."

"Oh, I don't know, Greg," Carl said. "Apparently the MBAs know it all."

"Okay, then," Al snapped. "What's your plan? Is IRT supposed to wait five years for you to figure out how to increase product development productivity to thirty percent? No question about it, I'm impressed by Toyota. You may not have noticed, but I drive a Lexus. The problem is, IRT is not Toyota — and you guys and Jon don't have a plan to become Toyota!"

"What would it take for you to change your mind?" Greg asked.

"Simple," Al replied. "Come up with a can't-miss plan that delivers six hundred million at seven percent profit with next years new products and keep increasing revenue and profit from there."

Greg continued, "What would it take for you to reconsider selling the Automotive Products division?"

"Figure out how to earn at least seven percent profit," Al snapped. "Look, I would much rather have you guys try to improve product development productivity from twenty to thirty percent in a business that already achieves seven percent profit than in the Automotive Products business that is losing money."

Carl said, "I think we're getting the message. It all comes down to return on investment."

Al said, "Welcome to the real world — of capitalism."

DISCUSSION

How did wishful thinking become such a huge problem in product development and, as this chapter points out, in business strategy, too?

We worked in both manufacturing and product development. In

manufacturing, wishful thinking is almost unheard of. There is relentless testing and preparation to eliminate production variability.

We also see this difference in expectations between product development leadership and the engineering teams. We visited a company in Germany this past year and the vice president over product development assessed the knowledge sharing across projects as being at the sixty percent level. He told me about his operation's new best practice database, how it worked or was supposed to work, and concluded proudly that they had solved that problem. He clearly picked up from the blank stares of the engineering teams in the room that he was alone in his conviction. To his credit, the next few minutes of discussion was a real education for him — the death of wishful thinking at least for a little while. We prefer not to do assessments with just the company leaders. These assessments are often what they wish them to be, not what they actually are.

Wishful thinking is prevalent in business strategy as well. For IRT, a spreadsheet exercise has convinced Al Frank that cost reduction and acquisitions can increase profit from three to ten percent in one year. He believes it even after visiting his former company and seeing that the walls are crumbling.

Thanks to Toyota, nowhere is the difference in strategy more striking than the automotive industry. Starting in the 1970s and accelerating in the 1980s, a wave of Japanese automobile imports caused the Big Three automakers to slash costs and acquire companies. GM has been aggressively cutting costs including workers for nearly 30 years. During that period, GM bought Daewoo, Saab, half of Isuzu, and 20% of Subaru. How's it working? GM lost 50 billion dollars between 2005 and 2007.

After CEO Don Peterson significantly improved Ford by implementing Dr. Deming's teachings and introducing the Taurus in the late 1980s, his successors aggressively cut costs, and purchased Mazda, Volvo, Range Rover, and Aston Martin. Peterson bought Jaguar. By 2001, Ford was a wreck. The company's quality ratings were the lowest ever and it had experienced a horrific exploding tire problem. By 2007, the company was selling or mortgaging nearly everything in an attempt to remain solvent.

Chrysler went from near bankruptcy in 1979 to the most profitable auto company in the world in the 1990s, in terms of profit per vehicle.[1] The acquisition of American Motors in 1987 was a huge success and the

Grand Cherokee one of the first very profitable SUVs. Then it merged with Daimler in 1998. In 2007, Daimler unloaded 80% of Chrysler for essentially nothing to Cerberus Capital Management, which is cost cutting aggressively to try to find a size at which it can be solvent.

Meanwhile Toyota's rise has been nothing less than spectacular. Unlike the oil companies that all benefit from high prices of crude, Toyota has achieved its hyper growth and industry-leading profit at the expense of entrenched competitors. Toyota's strategy is the opposite of the Big Three. Toyota grows organically. But the difference is Toyota bases its success on knowledge.

Contrast the comments of Toyota CEO Katsuaki Watanabe with what you hear from other CEOs. In a recent HBR interview, Watanabe said, "I will not allow the same problem to reoccur." Replying to a question about designing low cost vehicles for developing countries and whether Toyota will have to trade off quality to meet aggressive cost goals, he states, "I told our engineers, let us not focus on developing low cost automobiles. Let us develop technologies and processes that will allow Toyota to manufacture all our vehicles at lower cost."[2]

Here is the CEO of the world's most successful manufacturing company, whose products are the envy of the competition, and he isn't talking about specific products. He is talking about knowledge.

His first comment speaks of solving problems once and for all. In other words, he doesn't want to pay to solve the same problem twice (or more). Not allowing problems to recur is hard enough to do in a company of three hundred. He expects that problems will not recur at Toyota with three hundred thousand employees! His second comment speaks to knowledge reuse and he expects engineering innovation to be reused across the company, even though Toyota builds over nine million vehicles a year ranging from the ten thousand dollars for a two-seater Yaris to the six thousand pound Sequoia to the hundred and twenty-five thousand dollar Lexus LS600.

Beginning in the next chapter we will explore the secret to achieving Toyota-like domination.

---

1 Liker, Jeffrey K. *The Toyota Way: 14 Management Principles from the World's Greatest Manufacturer,* New York, McGraw-Hill.

2 Stewart, Thomas A., Raman, Anand P. (2007), "Lessons From Toyota's Long Drive," *Harvard Business Review,* July-August, pp. 74-83.

Chapter 6
Discovering a New System Model

Model includes finding models for new alternatives for solving the root cause, and that modeling should be done at the simplest level of detail possible to allow for broad understanding and discussion.

Tuesday Morning: National Lean Conference, Tampa, FL

I was enjoying the ten-minute walk over to the convention center, a nice break from the typical drive in traffic into the plant. And it was great to have had the weekend off. That gave me time to do some thinking about the issues we faced. Of course, I was somewhat preoccupied with the events our cousins had planned. I didn't want to come off as the stereotypical, nerdy engineer. In fact, my wife had warned me to have fun. And I did. I felt refreshed.

I entered the cavernous building and looked around. Finding the registration area was going to be a challenge. Either I needed to follow signs, which I never could find, or just follow the hordes of people that all seemed to know where they are going. The long, tall escalator seemed like a good bet. The people on it going up were empty handed and the ones coming down were loaded with stuff. I got on and noticed some pretty nice looking backpacks on the way up.

Amazing — at each conference I attend, the dress code gets more and more lax. Lots of people were wearing shorts. In the early years, I recall a coat and tie was practically a requirement. But I must admit, my golf shirt and slacks were a lot more comfortable. I guessed there was no going back. It made me wonder what happened to companies that used to make men's hats. The only time I saw someone wearing one nowadays was when I was stuck behind some guy driving 15 miles an hour in a 35 mile zone. No doubt hat makers went to the same place as their predecessors that made buggy whips.

It was time for my first decision — get some coffee and a pastry or register.

I decided to register. I had not taken the time to plan my day and I needed the agenda schedule.

The first business after registering was to organize all the stuff. I knew now the reason for the backpack. Luckily they had a nice pocket size guide.

I got my coffee and a blueberry muffin, and looked for a place to plan my morning. One thing I hated about attending these things alone — nobody to collaborate with on which sessions to go to. I also felt somewhat conspicuous, as I clearly was a loner. Many groups were obviously made up of people from the same companies.

The opening session in the main ballroom was for everyone, so I headed straight there to read, and to find a decent seat before the rush began. The conference attendees were a mixed group. Most were interested in Lean from a production perspective, but there was also some emphasis on product development.

I found a good seat, and it occurred to me that it always took a few minutes to decipher the agenda at all conferences like this. I actually had several goals — certainly one was anything that would help our thinking in product development. But I also had some manufacturing technology areas to investigate.

Before long, I had decided on my morning schedule for the breakouts. It seemed as though everything was now Lean something or other on the agenda. I wondered why lunch wasn't listed as Lean Luncheon. Actually, looking around at my fellow conference attendees, that might have been appropriate.

The opening keynote address was typical — entertaining, motivational, but very little content. I headed out with the hordes looking for the right conference room. The first session was about visual planning systems, which certainly seemed appropriate and consistent with our Responsibility-Based Planning cornerstone. Each session was scheduled for one hour — forty-five minutes of presentation and a fifteen minute Q&A. I settled in at the back of the room. I'd attended enough of these to make sure I always left myself an easy exit plan.

The session turned out to be quite interesting. It was about Obeya room setups at Toyota for visually planning and controlling on conference room walls. We'd done a lot of large displays in manufacturing and in the past had set up what we called war rooms. There were some interesting tips on how to organize information. It was worthwhile, but it was hard to concentrate with all the big issues facing us back home.

I was the first to exit the room. Where was the coffee?

I headed to the main area scouring the place for that heavenly dark liquid. My cell phone buzzed. I looked at the number, assuming it would be my wife.

Oh Lord, it was Jack. I wondered if he's calling about the A3s I left for him. Surely he remembered I was coming here.

I pushed the button. "Hello, Jack."

"Hi, Jon. Sorry to bother you at the conference but I wanted to give you a heads up."

I felt better that he knew I was at the conference. "Sure, okay," I said.

"Sorry I was out of town last week and we didn't get a chance to talk. You need to know that Brenda has accelerated the decision making on her plan. She's arranged a meeting with Ray and the rest of the leadership team next Wednesday. To be honest, I don't have anything to use to hold her off. I know you don't have any silver bullets, Jon, but I wanted you to know."

Damn, what the hell was I doing attending this conference? "I don't have anything substantive, Jack, but we have been making some interesting progress. No big revelation though, at least, not yet. What's the plan? I can be back there tomorrow."

"No need for that," he said. "We can talk about it next week and plan our response. Let's meet on Tuesday. Maybe you'll learn something this week that will help. By the way, I liked the A3s you left, and I support those goals. You'll find my comments and a few questions in your e-mail."

I pushed the end button. Bummer, did I feel down. Here I was at this stupid conference and Jack was fighting for the future of the company. Had Al convinced Brenda to accelerate the decision based on our meetings? I didn't think so. He seemed more reasonable than that.

What should I do? I had a better understanding of the problem but no solution.

"Jon, is that you?"

The voice came from behind and I turned to see the most refreshing sight I could have seen at that moment. "Jan, how are you?" I extended my hand.

She brushed it off and gave me a hug — just what I needed at that moment.

"Wow!" I said. "Hugging you has gotten difficult." She was very pregnant. "You look great."

"Thanks." She laughed. "I signed up for this conference four months ago. Not sure if I am going to make it through this week. They need a lot more rest rooms."

"Is it a boy or girl, or do you know? "

"A boy, due in two months," she said.

"I bet you name him Doyle, right?" I could not hold back a smirk.

She laughed again and said, "That's funny. You know, one of my husband's nephews has a pet rat. We named him Doyle. I just love to say, 'Hello Doyle,' every time we visit. So, how is everything at IRT?"

"Let me get some coffee," I said. "Then I'll fill you in. But I have to warn you, it's not good."

"I need to go to the ladies room." She pointed. "Let's meet over there in a few minutes. I'm dying to know more."

I waited in the coffee line, wondering whether to head back home. My interest in the conference had evaporated. The problem was, I wasn't sure what I'd do when I got there. That we had no plan, other than our old one that wasn't working, gave me a case of nervous stomach. We were almost certain we knew why it wouldn't work, of course, but we had no idea what to do about it. Doggone it all. Brenda would have no trouble whatsoever shooting it down in flames.

I got myself a cup.

Also, my wife was still at her cousin's house and would be disappointed by an early departure. That made logistics an issue. Regardless, it would be good to sit down with Jan. It was great to see her again. She had certainly helped us understand the Toyota system. I wondered how much difference her leaving made to our effort— It would be impossible to ever know.

"Jon, over here!" Jan had commandeered a little corner seating area with a view of the river.

I took a seat across from her.

She said, "So what is happening? By the way, I am in no hurry, there is nothing on the agenda that interests me for the next hour — but we can talk later if you'd prefer."

"No, this is great," I said. "In fact, I'm thinking about heading back today to help Jack prepare for a meeting that could define his future . . . and mine as well."

Jan's brow furrowed. "That sounds serious. What happened?"

For the next 30 minutes or so, I described all that had happened including the arrival of Brenda, the lack of support from Charles and Nathan, and the rather lackluster improvements so far from implementing each of the cornerstones.

Jan listened intently and said very little.

"The bottom line is, there's no evidence we can point to that says we're going to be successful, and that means there's no way to counter the quick fixes Brenda is proposing. We don't have the support we need, and frankly, I can't think of what we might do differently."

I could see tears welling up in Jan's eyes.

"Sorry about my emotions," she said with a choked up laugh. "Part of it is my pregnancy, but you can't imagine how bad I feel now for leaving — although I am not sure what difference I could have made."

I wanted desperately to make her feel better. But before I could say anything, she perked up.

"Actually, I think it must be fate — my leaving. If I'd stayed, I wouldn't have known to do anything differently. But now I do know. Jon, you need to stay at least for the rest of today. I can help. We need to get to work."

"I appreciate it, Jan, but you're here with another company. I can't ask you to do that."

Uh-oh, those tears were coming back. She said. "Jon, it was really tough leaving IRT. But I had to because of my husband's family issues with his Dad. I really hated to disappoint you and Jack. The truth is, after my episodes with Doyle, I was thinking about quitting engineering — and I love engineering. You wrote that great letter of endorsement — and that's what got me my job. Did I ever tell you about Jack calling me into his office right before I left?"

I shook my head.

"I thought he was going to try to make me feel guilty. He didn't. He gave me a great pep talk about realizing my potential and wished great things for me. He understood completely. That's why I think our meeting today was meant to be." She leaned toward me. "Jon, there's only one session I want to attend today and we can work around that. All I ask of you is one thing. Take my boss — actually my boss's boss, our president, Ron Morrison — to dinner tonight. That was one of my goals today."

I laughed. "No problem," I said.

"Actually, he's the reason I know we can help," she said. "It's really not all that hard. Although we still have a long way to go, getting started is very straightforward." Jan paused and looked at her watch. Then she said, "I'm supposed to meet Ron in a few minutes at a session on Lean Six Sigma. We have really never done much with that and he wants us to understand it. Can we meet for lunch? Then we'll work the afternoon. I guess it would be wise for me to brief him on this."

"All right," I said. "This gives me time to call Jack and let him know you're gonna save us. I'll meet you at the entrance to the ballroom at lunchtime."

"Great," she said. "But don't you dare tell him I'm going to save you."

I got up as Jan stood to leave, then sat down and called Jack's number.

Donna answered. "Hi, Jon. Got a suntan yet? Brenda's in with him now — with the door closed. But you can talk to me until they finish. Oh, don't worry, they really never spend much time together — just long enough to get really mad — the both of them." She paused. "Things aren't going so well, are they?"

"You could say they've been better" I said. "By the way, Jan is here. We're going to work on this together for the rest of the day."

"Tell her hello. Is she still as pretty as ever?"

"Yes, but has gotten quite large." I waited a couple of moments to allow the image to sink in, then added, "In a family sort of way."

"Super! Tell her, 'congratulations.'" Then in a whisper, Donna said, "Jon, I shouldn't tell you this, but I'm pretty sure that Ray is retiring as CEO. I'm also quite sure Brenda is replacing him."

Oh no, I thought. There goes Jack's career and IRT as we know it.

"Does Jack know?" I asked.

"As much as I know," she responded. "Brenda just left. I will transfer you to Jack. Please, don't tell him I told you."

"Hi, Jon," Jack said. "What's up?"

He didn't seem in the mood for small talk.

"Donna said you were talking with Brenda," I said. "Anything different from your call earlier?"

"Well, not really," he said. "We're still meeting with Ray next Wednesday. But I do get the feeling Brenda is the one calling the shots. I'm afraid we may be on the cusp of a new era at IRT." He paused, then said, "Jon, you mentioned that you might come back early. Well, there's no need for that — unless you have a rabbit in your hat."

"Actually, I've decided to stay. It may be possible that I can find that rabbit here. I just ran into Jan, and she thinks she can help. She wants to try."

"Tell her 'hello' for me. I was very sorry to see her go."

"Let's plan on meeting Tuesday. I want to work with my team on Monday. In fact, since Al is involved, please see if you can get Brenda there, too. Might as well go down fighting."

"Okay, will do. But don't expect miracles."

I closed my cell phone. It was apparent that Jack had just about given up. But I wasn't quite ready for that. Not yet. I decided to go find a place Jan and I could work.

Jan and I had lunch. I caught her up on everyone at IRT and let her in on the impending promotion of Brenda. I even told her that Jack seemed resigned to what was going to be a big change of direction at IRT. We planned to work all afternoon and confirmed the plan to have dinner with the Sonic Solution president, Ron Morrison. We made our way to one of the cubicles the hotel had set up for small meetings.

"This will work just fine," Jan said. "It even has a flip chart."

"I got that from the hotel," I said. "And the best part is the ladies room is right over there."

"Good thinking, thank you," she said with a chuckle. "Okay, where do we start?"

"Well, I explained earlier how each business unit had taken one of the cornerstones to pilot and at best had some good continuous improvement, but nothing approaching our goals. Also, in our last team meeting, we decided to take the LAMDA approach and try to understand the root cause of our lack of improvement."

"And did you find it?" Jan asked.

"I think so," I said. "But I'm interested in your thoughts. I used the metrics you developed, both the sliding bar one, and the productivity one based on the twenty questions. We really hadn't changed much on either. The root cause we identified was that we're stuck in a paradigm of design-then-test which drives our loopbacks and other issues — rather than the Toyota paradigm of what we called 'test-then-design' that focuses on learning first, then designing."

"Interesting way to look at it," she said. "And I like the 'test-then-design' slogan. It's catchy. I think you're right. But we never actually approached it like that. Let me walk through our story and we can build from there, okay?"

I nodded and she took a breath.

"When I went to Sonic Solutions, I made a presentation to the leadership team on what this Toyota system is all about. I presented the four cornerstones pretty much the same as I'd done at IRT. Ron was quite interested. We did invite Allen Ward in for some LAMDA / A3 training. Our initial metrics were in the thirteen to sixteen point range — versus IRT at around twenty. We were pretty similar, and like Jack, Ron wanted to move ahead aggressively."

I nodded that I understood.

"But there are and were differences. Here's the first one. We are much smaller than IRT. We only have forty engineers total in two businesses. That makes things a lot easier because we can focus and get up to speed quicker. Also, Ron was adamant that we were not going to try to simply copy all of Toyota's practices. We were too small to do that. For example, there was no way to organize our engineers into functional groups. We had functional subsystems, but our engineers had to bridge across them. Ron encouraged us to understand more about why Toyota does what it does and to customize that logic for our culture and size. Ron had also heard what the president of Toyota North America stated regarding what a company needs to do to be as good as Toyota. Three things."

Jan stood and wrote on the flip chart:

- **Keep everything simple**
- **Make it visible**
- **Trust your people to do the right thing**

"Ron liked that a lot and he encouraged us to keep it in mind as we thought through how to implement. Oh, and something else. Two statements from Allen Ward also influenced his thinking."

She turned to the flip chart and wrote:

- **Product development at Toyota is primarily about developing functional knowledge about products. Great products will emerge from that knowledge.**
- **Great conflict makes great cars**

I said, "Doesn't Ron believe the four cornerstones are important?"

"Yes, he does. He absolutely believes in the cornerstones as a great way to understand the key Toyota capabilities, and he thinks they are very important for getting everyone on the same page. But believes they are a ***result*** of the implementation, not necessarily the ***way*** to implement. For example, he fully appreciates the need for the Entrepreneurial System Designer, but does not think it has to be specifically a Chief Engineer structured just the way Toyota does it. He'd probably say that IRT was trying to be too prescriptive."

I nodded. "And he might have a point."

"One thing for sure — he'd say you have to implement as a system — not in pieces."

"Okay, Jan, you definitely have my undivided attention. What did you do?"

She laughed. "I'm getting there. Remember, patience is a virtue. By the way, we retook the metrics a few weeks ago. Our results were over thirty percent now overall with a projection of about sixty within the next year. That's roughly a three to four times improvement over about a two-year time frame. More importantly, on our first project, the team estimates that we have already achieved the 60% level, and we've already achieved fifty percent faster time-to-market. In addition, we project growing another fifty percent faster in next cycle, meaning we will have cut product development cycle time in half in two cycles."

"That's impressive," I said. "The suspense is killing me. What's the secret?"

"First, Ron led the effort himself. He didn't delegate. He worked with us, his managers, and we came up with three simple principles that got us started." Jan stood and wrote:

- **Capture everything that is learned in K-Briefs**
- **Engineers must understand customer needs**
- **Remove knowledge gaps before design**

"By the way," she added. "I like your 'test-then-design' slogan for the last statement."

"What's a K-Brief?" I asked.

"Just our name for an A3, which is short for 'Knowledge Brief'. Ron won't let anyone make an important decision without one. He told the whole company 'knowledge doesn't exist unless it is captured on a K-Brief'. That changed everything. All of a sudden everyone was using LAMDA and documenting what they learned on K-Briefs. All disagreements had to be settled with facts that were documented knowledge — no more debating contests. Wishful thinking was replaced by fact-based decisions. It really was the dawn of a new day."

I said, "I heard they have a saying at Toyota that nobody is bigger than the knowledge notebook. Tell me about the engineers and customer needs."

"Ron would not accept specifications as the reason design decisions were made, so he paired up engineers and marketing people and sent them to customers to find out exactly what the customers wanted."

"Interesting," I said. "At Toyota, the Chief Engineers fill that role."

"We are not Toyota," Jan said, "and we haven't been training people for twenty years to be Chief Engineers. Ron requires that the customer needs be documented on what we call Customer Interest K-Briefs."

"How did you achieve 'test-then-design'?"

"Ron decided we were going to do it," Jan replied. "It was that simple. Ron was acting vice president of engineering at the time and he made the engineers prove their designs to him personally."

"He's president of the company," I said. "When did he have the time?"

"He scheduled Integrating Events when he was in town and the design engineers had to prove their recommended designs would meet the customer's needs and meet our manufacturability goals."

"I still can't fathom how Ron could do this himself."

"Remember we use K-Briefs for everything, so Ron could read the K-Briefs and understand what was going on very quickly. First, he scheduled an Integrating Event to find out what we knew how to do, and most importantly, what we didn't know. We quickly realized we had a lot of knowledge gaps. So engineers learned what customers needed. They then built and tested prototypes to create the proof or knowledge needed to convince Ron they had feasible designs. This process greatly increased insight into customer needs and the innovation required."

"Let me make sure I understand," I said. "The Integrating Events were primarily points in time where Ron verified that the knowledge justified the design decisions being made. I always thought of Integrating Events as the points where you reduce the sets being considered during set-based design."

"Actually, it is both," she said. "Selecting an alternative is an early design decision. Selecting a drawing tolerance is a much later design decision, but both must be based on known knowledge, or it is a guess. But remember, it is not 'does the knowledge exist' but 'show me the knowledge.' The standard K-Briefs made the knowledge visible and understandable for Ron, and everyone knew it."

"Have you released any new products using this approach?"

"Yes and we met our schedule, beat our cost goals, and achieved our best. quality ever." Jan laughed. "Ron made Engineering spend months proving to him they could design a high speed test machine that met customer needs and cost goals. Sales people were going crazy because no one was designing anything. Once all the design concepts were proven the machine was designed in a month and worked perfectly."

She paused to let that sink in. Then smiled

"I have to go to the ladies room. Why don't you get some coffee — and bring me a Coke, please?"

As she was leaving the room, I said, "Don't you dare go into labor until we get through today."

"Oh, all right, I promise. At least, I hope not."

When I returned from the conference lobby with coffee and Coke in hand, she was drawing on a new sheet of the flip chart.

She said, "I assume this is a typical high level view of processes at our companies. We both know how detailed these can get when all the gates and steps are documented, but I simplified it for ease and to make a few points" She pointed at the figure on the chart."

"Right," I said. "I can see us in that chart, although Doyle might insist on a lot more detail."

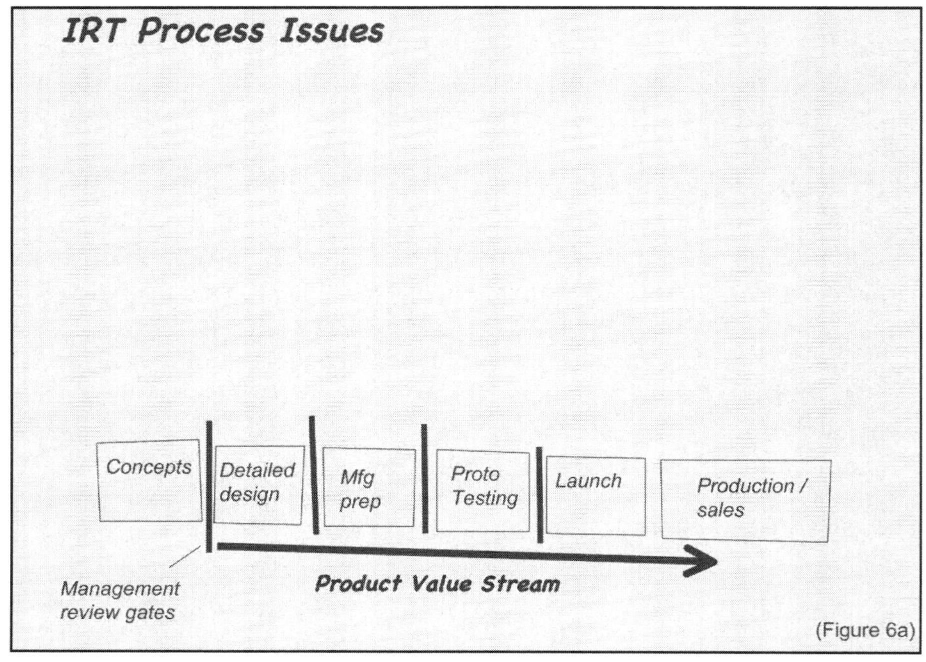

(Figure 6a)

She modified the chart slightly.

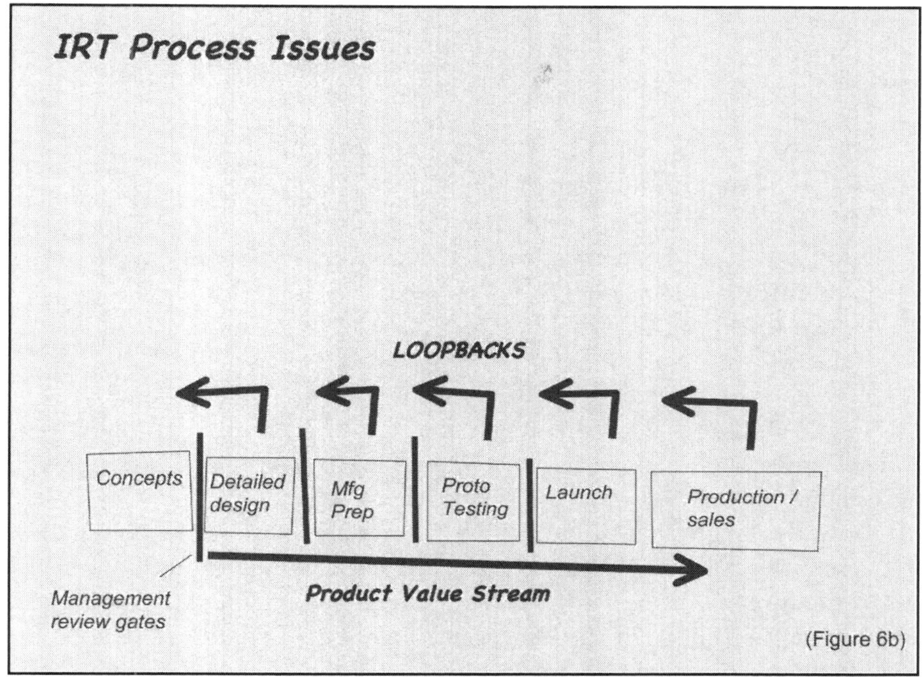

(Figure 6b)

"What happens, of course, is that loopbacks begin, and they cause all the issues in our metric charts — right?"

"Couldn't agree more," I said. "That's indeed what we call our root cause, the design-then-test-then-redesign-until-we-run-out-of-time paradigm."

"And the fundamental reason is you don't have the knowledge to make all the decisions that you have to make, right?" she said. "And these are both product and manufacturing process decisions — all made with limited knowledge of the limits and trade-offs having to do with customer interests and manufacturing capability. Not only that, often the specs, which we can't meet anyway, are allowed to be changed by marketing — or whomever. It's a process out of control.

"And that's one project," she continued. "In reality, there are application driven derivatives, there are similar products, there is next generation work, and all are in a state of knowledge flux. Then there's all the knowledge in the heads of the engineers of what didn't work — and from a learning perspective, that is really the most valuable knowledge. So how do companies try and solve this knowledge flow problem? They create knowledge databases that engineers are supposed to keep updated, or with some sort of search capabilities on product documentation. And the results are always poor. And there are reasons for that."

She flipped the chart and wrote:

- **If you can find relevant knowledge, you don't know if it applies to your situation.**
- **If you can make it apply, is it still up to date?**
- **Or if you find multiple bits of knowledge you can apply, how do you resolve conflicts?**
- **And knowing this much effort may be required to reuse your knowledge, does it even make sense to look?**

"Jon," she said. "I know I'm preaching to the choir, but I'm being a little dramatic to emphasize how simple the solution is. Now sit back and drink your coffee while I modify the chart."

"We did two things." She pointed to the chart. "First, we recognized that there's a Knowledge Value Stream that cuts across projects. We call it a value stream because all the knowledge needs to be defined and managed with the same rigor as the product definition in the Product Value Stream. This implies something very important — that the knowledge learned applies across projects. I will talk more about that in a few minutes."

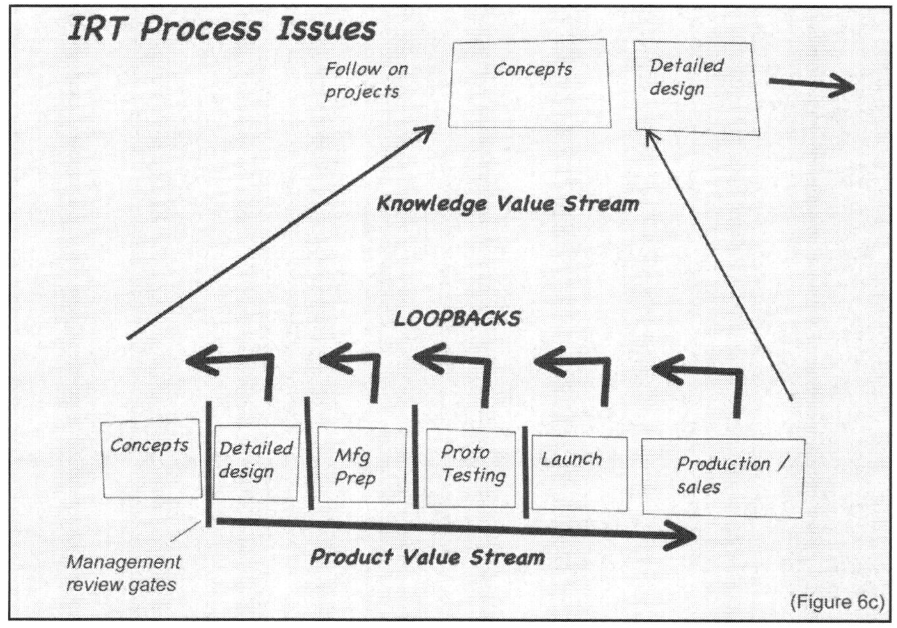

(Figure 6c)

I said, "I'm struggling a little with your emphasis on value stream and it being managed. Can you explain that a little more?"

"Yes — because it is critical," Jan said. "Remember that Toyota organizes and develops product capabilities from the bottom up. They are always innovating at the subsystem, or functional level, and then bringing this together — integrating it — at the system level. The subsystem innovation must be across projects. It has to because they use it — and it needs to build — from project to project. The Knowledge Value Stream is the ongoing development of product and process functional knowledge. The Knowledge Value Stream is fed from three sources from current projects — from the early set-based learning, from problems solved after design release including issues that arise in prototype testing as well as any production and warranty problems, and also from general production best practice knowledge. Raw research should also feed this value stream for effective application into future projects. This cannot be fuzzy or incomplete knowledge.

"Okay, I understand the logic, but I'm not sure I see how it all plays out in reality."

"Fair enough," Jan said. "But let's look at all the key Toyota tools and see how they apply in this simple model. First they use all the same CAE/CAD/CAM tools as everyone else. That is the language primarily used in the Product Value Stream to create detailed design and all the documentation required to build the product. But let's review the key tools for the Knowledge Value Stream."

She went to the flip chart, found a blank page, and wrote:

- **LAMDA — The learning process**

"You know this one as well as I do," she said. "It's Toyota's learning process for creating robust reusable knowledge. Even if you had a system for reusing knowledge, if the knowledge is not correct, the system will fall apart. But the 'D' in LAMDA requires that the knowledge be visible."

She turned back to the flip chart and added:

- **The K-Brief (A3) — visualizing the learning**

"Whereas LAMDA is the learning process, the K-Brief is the documentation of both the learning process and the results from the learning. Both are important. Allen used to say that the A3 was simply documenting the LAMDA story in a simple standard reusable way. It is the documentation of the Knowledge Value Stream. Durward Sobek, who followed Allen Ward into Toyota and who works with us today, stressed that the A3 was also the mentoring tool as well as the documentation tool, and that may be its most important role."

I said, "I understand the premise of the A3 and the power, but I worry about the manual use of A3 size paper as a primary way to communicate and control knowledge."

"I understand what you mean," she replied. "That's part of why we call them K-briefs, to allow A3 thinking not to be associated with only paper documentation. Note that if computer documentation is used, it needs to maintain the simplicity of a single page A3 and provide the ability for the reader to follow the LAMDA storyline. By the way, making good K-Briefs that will stand the test of flow across projects is very difficult. We have found that single page documentation for communication is much tougher than writing multi page reports for test documentation. The K-Briefs are a living part of the knowledge flow — not a historical reference."

Jan paused while that sank in. "All right," she said, "those are the tools that drive the Knowledge Value Stream. What's missing?"

I said, "The problem is, I don't see how it all fits together. We build products, not A3s."

She nodded. "True enough. The value streams must be integrated, right? But the knowledge must be the basis for the product, not the opposite. That's your test-then-design paradigm versus the design-then-test paradigm. The Knowledge Value Stream must feed the Product Value Stream." Jan turned back to the flip chart and said, "Now I am going to add the second and critical part. Drink some more coffee while I update the chart."

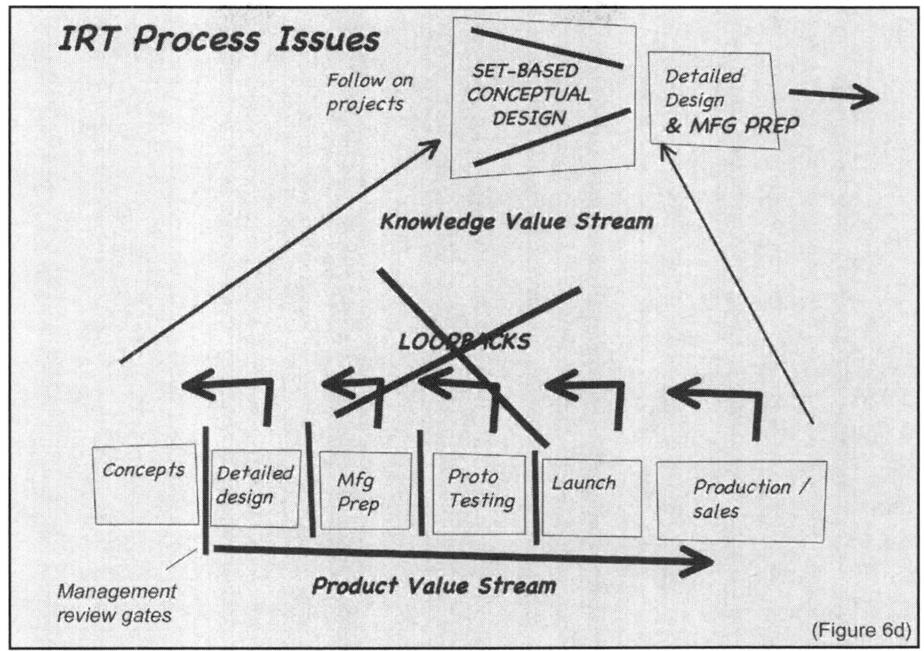

(Figure 6d)

She turned back to me and pointed at the chart. "Now, here is the real magic of Toyota and what we had to figure out how to do. We learned how to generalize the knowledge for early robust decision-making. We call this Set-Based Concurrent Engineering, which really gets to the heart of that Toyota cornerstone. It's using the existing knowledge both to understand the sets of possibilities and to optimize the design decisions through visual trade-offs. This also allowed us to systemically eliminate the loopbacks and to concurrently perform detailed design and manufacturing preparation — all because the knowledge was both right and formatted for reuse. By the way, I called it Set-Based Conceptual Design on this chart to emphasize the power of applying set-based principles very early in the design process."

"Jan, I hear your words, but I must admit, it sounds a little like 'a miracle happens here.' I don't see how this all fits together."

She said, "Do you remember, Jon, when Allen made the statement that the most important thing he learned about the Toyota Product Development System was one thing."

"Vaguely," I said. "But Allen told me a lot of things that still haven't fully sunk in."

"I understand that feeling," she said. "But this one made an impression on me. He said that Toyota's insistence on trade-off curves was the most important thing he learned. I didn't really understand at the time, but I do now. Toyota uses trade-off curves to generalize the knowledge in the Knowledge Value Stream for inexpensive product and process learning and decision making."

She went to the board and said, "This is the next key tool," as she wrote:

- **Trade-off curves — a tool for generalizing knowledge for set-based decision-making**

"We need to talk about this for a few minutes, because I don't think we ever understood the power of this while I was still at IRT. Remember when we were trying to understand Set-Based Concurrent Engineering? Donna used her cooking example of sets of recipes. She kept meticulous records — knowledge on the results. And she customized dinner parties based on putting together sets of solutions."

"I remember," I said. "It was a good way to understand the concept."

"But what if it was wrong?" Jan said. "Well, not wrong, exactly — Just incomplete. Donna said she focused on only one new thing and did a lot of testing beforehand to get it right. I believe that Donna was actually creating a new recipe based on trade-off curves in her head — a knowledge bank she'd built from years of experience. We assumed she was just adapting recipes she had documented, but I believe she was innovating based on trade-off curves she knew because of her experience. Knowledge breeds innovation. Also," she said, "do you remember the bicycle example?"

"Yes, I used it," I said. "Still do — for very effectively describing set-based development. Are you telling me that was wrong, too?"

"Sorry," Jan said, smiling. "Again, it wasn't really wrong, just incomplete. It describes the power of set-based design by the elimination of risks by designing bicycles using sets of interchangeable components: frames, wheels, and so forth, versus designing a totally new bicycle from scratch. What if you looked at a bicycle from a fundamentally different perspective, not from the standpoint of components, but from the point of view of the fundamental interactions of the physics that drive all decisions?"

I'm sure I must have looked dazed.

She returned to the board. "I need to draw a little more. Could you get me another Coke? I need also another trip to the ladies room."

By the time I returned from the main conference lobby, Jan had finished her chart.

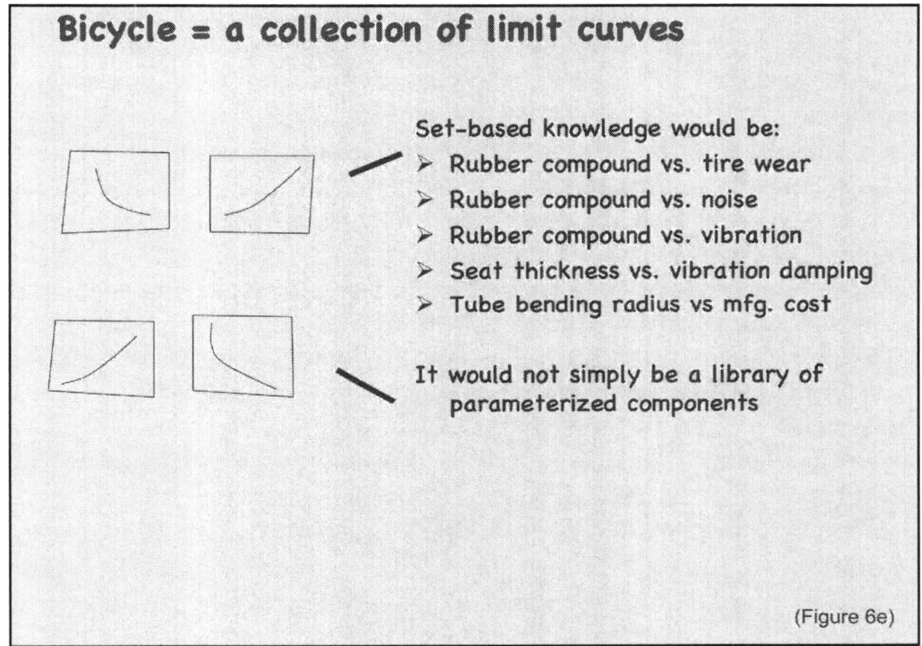

Bicycle = a collection of limit curves
Set-based knowledge would be:
Rubber compound vs. tire wear
Rubber compound vs. noise
Rubber compound vs. vibration
Seat thickness vs. vibration damping
Tube bending radius vs mfg. cost
It would not simply be a library of parameterized components

(Figure 6e)

She said, "Let's look at a bicycle based on physics. What if we'd known all this? Wouldn't we have taken set-based principles to an entirely different level?"

"Sure," I said. "But that is incredibly detailed, and most of it is interrelated."

"Now, some knowledge isn't really trade-off curves," Jan continued, "but rather more general design rules that need to be remembered. But those can be generalized the same way as trade-off curves — generalized such that they apply to the whole ranges of values that you design within. That ensures they are widely applicable to future design problems."

With a bit of a gasp, I said, "That is an explosion of knowledge."

"And any of it that you didn't know when you made a design decision would be a potential loop-back. Or at best a non-optimized decision. Right? Let me ask you a question. I know IRT has the best manufacturing in your business. In fact, most of your competitors don't even do manufacturing. How much of that knowledge are you leveraging to the benefit of your customers?"

Before I had time to respond, she said, "And how much frustration is created among your manufacturing people when your design engineers continually make the same mistakes? For example, using tolerances that are too tight? Think of the wealth of knowledge in your manufacturing that's absolutely wasted because you have no way to communicate it. That's unacceptable to Toyota. And it is to us, now. It should be to you as well."

"Jan," I said. "There's no way to argue against your logic. I now have visions of millions of A3s with generalized design rules and trade-off curves on my lap. How do I figure out how to use them effectively? I hope you also have that figured out."

"Well, yes and no," she said. "Enough to get us started because of our size, but maybe not enough for you. We need to stop now for today. I want Ron to help on the next discussion, and we can work some more in the morning. By the way, I want us both to go to a session early tomorrow called 'Simulation Driven Design.' Then we can discuss the last issue." She let out a sigh. "I also need to rest a little. This baby is working on my back. I told Ron 6:30 for dinner, is that okay?"

"Sure," I said. "How about that restaurant right across the river? I heard it was good."

"Fine," she replied. "We'll meet you there."

I spent the next hour walking around the river walkway reflecting on what Jan had said. Her company was building a system around the flow of knowledge — more specifically generalized knowledge, such as trade-off curves that defines visually the impact of design decisions on customer interests. They were copying the Toyota philosophy of development, where we were primarily trying to copy key Toyota practices, the four cornerstones, individually. She had made a good point: while the four cornerstones may be a great way to understand the Toyota system, they may not necessarily be the best way to implement the system.

Oh well, at least the walk did me some good physically, although I still didn't see how to apply what I had learned from Jan.

I made a reservation for six-thirty and arrived at the restaurant a few minutes early, surprised to find Jan and Ron already there.

Ron definitely projected himself as the leader of the company. He was quite well dressed. It occurred to me I should have shined my shoes. But before long his ready smile and easy-going demeanor, set me at ease.

We took a table outside with a good view of the river. Normally, I felt a little uncomfortable spending IRT money on entertainment, but not his time. Jan had already earned it. Both of them were giving their time to help IRT. I was going to be as gracious a host as I could possibly be. I picked up the wine list and surveyed the entire list, not just looking for reasonable prices.

We discussed our companies and roles during dinner. Ron was quite interesting. He had come to Sonic Solutions about five years earlier with a mandate to make it profitable. He'd done just that and had invested heavily in building a strong Lean Manufacturing environment and solid supplier relationships. He was both president and acting head of engineering. Marketing and Manufacturing vice presidents reported to him.

While waiting for dessert, Ron asked Jan to summarize for him what we'd discussed and what we'd like him to comment on. Jan recapped our discussion, including the different approaches.

Ron listened intently but did not offer many comments.

Then Jan summarized what Sonic Systems had accomplished:

- **We had identified the critical subsystems**
- **We had named the knowledge owners**
- **We had trained the engineers on LAMDA / K-Briefs**
- **We had trained the engineers on set-based rules and trade-off curves and how to organize them**
- **We had written concept papers for new projects with broad tar gets for implementation**

She then looked at me and said, "What do you think is missing for success?"

"I don't know," I said. "Seems as though you have all the pieces in place."

"Actually, there is one key missing part." She turned to Ron. "What is it, Ron?"

Ron laughed. "I don't know either. You've got me worried now that we're missing something."

"Change leadership is missing," Jan said. She shook her head. "Ron, I was trying to be your straight man. That's what Ron brought to the

party — Leadership. And it's critical. I believe that's what's missing at IRT — an absolute commitment to the change. Your leadership has been allowing you to try out pieces, rather than insisting on real change." She paused, and then said, "Ron, you remember that day when you decided to move ahead? Tell Jon what you had in mind and what you did — because it changed everything. None of the rest of us ever looked back because you never looked back."

"Well, it all made sense," Ron said. "We all knew that we continually made design decisions without the right knowledge to do so. We knew it resulted in the metrics you've seen. It affected how we scheduled. In reality, we had to schedule everything as quickly as possible in fear of the loop backs that always occurred. Our timing on decisions was out of synch. We would make some decisions well before they needed to be made in order to support decisions we suspected were most likely wrong. Marketing was frustrated we couldn't get anything out to meet their customer commitments and they would be changing specs to meet new commitments. In reality, this was the first approach that seemed logical to reverse the trend."

Ron paused when our desserts arrived. Then he continued. "Jan mentioned the training we had taken. None of it was hard to understand, but it did take a commitment to technical knowledge. We had to slow down and do things right. The problem was we were waste deep in alligators. How could we change to robust engineering when seemingly the only way to make a schedule was to jump to solutions we knew would be wrong?"

Ron paused again and took a bite of his cheesecake. He seemed to notice I was waiting for the punch line and smiled. "You're hoping for some great leadership maneuver, but there wasn't one I could find. I just said that, as far as I was concerned, knowledge didn't exist unless it was correctly documented on a K-Brief, and that I was going to hold Integrating Events on each project. Unless we had the knowledge, we wouldn't move forward."

Jan said, "One of the project leaders said we'd never get anything out on any schedule if he did that. What was your answer, Ron? With that answer, I knew, and every one else knew, you were serious."

"I just told him that all his projects were way over schedule, so how would we notice?" Ron said. "It has taken us about nine months to start seeing the change, but every project goes through an Integrating Event early on to assess what knowledge is needed to design and manufacture the product, and most importantly what knowledge is missing. That ensures that we have the knowledge — maybe not the optimized knowledge — but at least enough knowledge to get our products out the door. We have changed, and we recently modified our product development process to reflect the changes." He looked at Jan. "Did you talk to Jon about managed conflict?"

"No, I didn't," Jan said. "I wanted to discuss the overall leadership issue first. Jon, Allen Ward mentioned that 'great conflicts make great cars.' That only works if the knowledge is available to settle the conflict, and in most companies, it's not. There's a lot of conflict, but it is an endless debate. That was certainly true here between marketing and engineering as to what was possible. And marketing usually won, because the marketeers were generally better debaters."

Ron said, "This all changed when all knowledge had to be documented on K-Briefs and used for resolving conflicts. Everyone started to play fair. You can't argue against knowledge in the form of trade-off curves, for example. Knowledge changes everything. It's as simple as that. Capture the knowledge in terms of generalized rules and trade-off curves, and then use it for decision-making. LAMDA is proving a great and robust learning system."

"However," he added, "remember that we don't make money selling knowledge. We are not a research institution. We make money selling products that are enabled by the knowledge. The key for us is the effective ability to integrate the knowledge into the product decisions and do it on a set schedule. That is what the Integrating Events are all about — they pull everything."

Jan added, "Jon, I wanted you to talk to Ron because IRT needs to make that level of leadership commitment to success, or it won't work. You can't poke at this. You need to do it."

"Let me ask a couple of more questions." I asked, "How about the four cornerstones Allen taught us as the basis of the Toyota system? Do you see any conflict?"

"No, none whatsoever," Ron said. "Nor is it inconsistent with the thirteen principles in the Liker — Morgan book (Toyota's Product Development System, Productivity Press, 2006). But all that is focused on characteristics of a system that Toyota has been developing for decades and now supports a huge company, not how you'd necessarily implement it at a small company like Sonic. LAMDA learning and our subsystem owners ensure the Expert Workforce. Managing generalized set-based knowledge enables set-based concurrent engineering. Our managed conflict between the project leader and the knowledge owners ensures entrepreneurial system design, and there is no way to develop set-based knowledge without Responsibility-Based Planning. In reality, it just made more sense for us to focus more on the flow of knowledge and let the cornerstones develop from there. I understand you are focused more on implementing each of the cornerstones. I think that would be fine as long as you recognize knowledge is the mortar that holds it all together."

"And," I said, "the mortar is LAMDA as the learning process, the A3s or K-Briefs as the documentation, and the trade-off curves as a way for generalizing knowledge for reuse. Right?"

"Yes," Ron answered. "That is a reasonable way to look at it. But it all becomes the system."

"Another question." I said, looking at Ron, "It seems that you personally are the glue that is holding this together. You are personally managing the conflict between the project leaders and the functional knowledge owners. I don't see us being able to do that, or that you can keep doing it. Can you? Also, how are you managing all the knowledge on the K-Briefs?"

Jan said, "Jon, your questions raise the last issue I wanted to discuss. We can do that tomorrow or now."

"Actually, I would like to do it now," Ron said. "We know we are on the right path, but questions like yours are not fully resolved. I'd like to discuss them."

The timing was great as the waitress showed up. Ron and I each ordered a glass of port. Jan got some more iced tea.

Jan said, "Jon, we discussed earlier three of the Toyota tools: LAMDA, K-Briefs, and trade-off curves. Tonight, we've discussed the role and importance of leadership. There's another key Toyota tool that ties it all together. It's the Toyota Checklist — or Checksheets as we prefer to call them. These are the knowledge standards at Toyota. Toyota really doesn't control all of the individual A3s, but at the end of every car project, the functional managers all review the current knowledge and update the Checksheets. These become the knowledge standards for the next projects' Integrating Events, or reviews. Actually, Ron is currently acting as the knowledge standard bearer for us at the moment. We need to migrate to a real system."

'Let me make sure I understand," I said. "Because Ron will not allow projects to move into detailed design unless the knowledge exists on K-Briefs, then he is in fact acting as a living Checksheet, whereas Toyota has a well defined knowledge control system built around Checksheets."

"Yes," Jan answered, "and we are working on doing that."

Ron added, "Realistically, I only focus on the key knowledge issues, or trade-offs, but even that is a large step from where we were. We know that the Toyota Checksheets get into significant detail on manufacturing standards and rules. We have significant manufacturing knowledge that we want to build into these Checksheets. However, we know we have to build a system to do it. I don't see us using manual knowledge notebooks the way Toyota did."

"The good news is that it is conceptually simple," Jan said. "The Checksheets simply make visible how design decisions impact a wide range of customer interests. The Integrating Events define when design decisions are going to be made. The Checksheets simply link the two by making the knowledge available to the right people at the right time in the right form. We just have to generalize and catalog the knowledge to do so."

Jan added "Jon, remember earlier when we discussed the Knowledge Value Stream as being the flow of knowledge across projects. The Checksheets are the knowledge standards for the Knowledge Value Stream. LAMDA, K-Briefs, and trade-off curves are how and what you learned. The Checksheets are the approved learning — the learning that must move forward to all future projects."

"Okay, it's getting late," I said. I'd absorbed about all I could in one night, and I needed to rethink our strategy. "I really appreciate your time today. Let me summarize what I think are your key messages."

On my notebook, I wrote as I said out loud:

Required System Changes:

- **Expose and Capture the Knowledge through LAMDA / K-Briefs**
- **Generalize the knowledge for reuse in the form of trade-off curves or design rules**
- **Make the knowledge available for all decision making via Checksheets**
- **Use Integrating Events to pull the knowledge into the product design on a set schedule**
- **Fix what is broken and capture new knowledge through**

LAMDA / A3s and then standardize into the Checksheets
- **Determined leadership must ensure that none of the above is optional**

Ron stared at my list frowning and then said, "Jon, you are thinking too much as an engineer. Those are most of the tools, but it doesn't adequately reflect the people and leadership issues. May I?" Ron reached for my notepad, took out his pen, and wrote as he spoke.

Required leadership commitment:
- **Get the developers committed to the change. The four cornerstones presentations, books, and articles are great to do this.**
- **Free the developers to follow LAMDA and document the results properly by eliminating wasteful activities. They know where the wastes are.**
- **Look at the knowledge yourself and appreciate it.**
- **Review with the knowledge — no exceptions.**

He said, "Jon, if the developers are on board, and if top management is on board, then all others can join, or be thrown overboard. Sorry to be so blunt. The problem with so many of all our past improvement initiatives is this: Middle managers thought the initiatives were smart, engineers thought they were stupid, and top management listened to the middle managers. The engineers like this robust problem solving and the way must be cleared for them to do it. At Sonic, we really don't have such mid-level management. At IRT, I understand you do. But I think you have the engineers on your side. You and Jack have done all the right things in setting the goals for them, and getting them to understand the Toyota system and cornerstones. But you haven't freed them so they can do it right."

"One last question," I said. "Ron, are there any metrics that you are now collecting to show this is working?"

"Actually, I am not a great believer in a lot of metrics. So many seem to focus on process effectiveness. I prefer to look at customer acceptance of the product, timing of delivery, profit, and product reliability. Our first product through the process achieved all of those — it was the first time, actually, that I remember meeting our initial schedule commitments. However, there is one that we are beginning to use that is quite telling. That is the percent of our engineering resources used after design release. Traditionally, we know it is well above 50%, probably more like 70%. That is a measure of our loop-back problem. We feel it should only be in the 10% range. That is a lot of wasted engineering time by not learning first. Our project leader on the first product estimated that it was almost zero after design release. We think this will be a quite useful metric for evaluating our change process."

After an exchange of closing pleasantries, we broke for the evening. On the way back to the hotel, it seemed to me things were a lot clearer — even if my next steps weren't.

DISCUSSION

Toyota is a real company and has been both the inspiration of how good product development can be and the model for change. There have been no other models to follow — just theory and conjecture. Although IRT is a fictitious company, it illustrates a fairly representative composite of current product development practices. This chapter introduced a new company, Sonic Solutions, which, while fictitious, is patterned very closely after a real company, Teledyne Benthos, that is described in the case studies at the end of this book. The importance of this is that we are now developing new models for change inspired by Toyota's development paradigm but not strictly following that company's specific practices. We feel that is tremendously helpful as we start having new models to follow.

So, what new revelations have been discovered in this chapter and with this new company? The first and probably most important is that product development can be thought of as being made up of two distinctly different value streams. The traditional value stream is the process for developing the specific product. That is where almost all the improvement focus has been over the years. Define the process for designing the product and ensure the process is followed. The second value stream is the planned growth of the functional knowledge that makes up the product. This value stream should be the basis both for ongoing innovation and for ensuring the quality of the product. It provides the balance for product development decision-making. A Toyota Chief Engineer once made the statement that "Great conflicts make great cars." The conflict is the integration of the two value streams. But the knowledge flow should come first as it does at Toyota.

Let's look again at the Toyota tools from that perspective. Realistically, Toyota uses much of the same tools in the Product Value Stream as everyone else. They use basically the same CAE/CAD/CAM tools. They make product drawings. They make manufacturing process plans. However, they also follow the PDCA / LAMDA process for cross-project learning and knowledge development; they use A3s for documenting and spreading that learning. They use set-based rules and trade-off curves for generalizing the knowledge for reuse, and they use Knowledge Checksheets to standardize the knowledge and for reviewing with it. In other words, they have a completely different set of design tools for the Knowledge Value Stream. This value stream is about developing Set-Based Knowledge because its basic goal is to create ongoing sets of generalized solutions that can be optimized and integrated into products — but always on a cadence. That is why Toyota does not miss schedules. This Knowledge Value Stream will always keep the innovation flowing.

Chapter 7
Preparing an Alternative

Discussion includes understanding and evaluating the alternative solution models from many perspectives and looking for more alternatives if needed. The steps of LAMDA are easily blurred, but the process should play out as tremendous learning is happening.

Monday Morning: IRT

I did a lot of reflecting over the weekend. Jan and I had continued to discuss our companies and approaches through the rest of the conference. It had been quite energizing to work with her again. Her enthusiasm and optimism were refreshing. One thing that bothered me, though, was the size of Sonic Solutions versus IRT. The implementation principles should be the same, but I knew that the change issues always became magnified, probably exponentially, as the size of a company became larger. She did mention that a company in New Zealand, about twice the size as IRT, was making good progress. As a result of her connection with Allen Ward, she'd helped them get started, and she said she felt confident she could put me in contact with them.

The good news was what we had been doing was correct. The four cornerstones do reflect the Toyota system very well. This had been widely communicated and well received and accepted by the engineering community.

What we had not done was recognize that the four cornerstones and the underlying Toyota development philosophy are about the flow of knowledge. That's really the basis for the Toyota system — the continuous flow of knowledge across projects in such a way to ensure quality decision making at every project review, which were Toyota's Integrating Events. So we were implementing the pieces, but not the system. Sonic Solutions had recognized that the Knowledge Value Stream actually must lead the Product Value Stream. Their thinking was that implementation must begin with robust knowledge flow — both the capture and reuse. That can only happen if the knowledge is such that it flows readily from project to project. That indicated that the knowledge must be generalized, visualized, and organized for effective cross-project flow. That's the power of set-based knowledge. Then all the cornerstones would follow naturally.

One thing Al and Brenda had brought to the party was the importance of profit. That is really what IRT — or any company for that matter — is in business for. It's also important for the profits to be at a level that makes them financially appealing to investors. And even though investors typically don't focus on it, the profits must be sustainable. So, why does the flow of set-based knowledge across projects resolve this? And, more importantly, why would the lack of it cause inconsistent profitability?

I had arrived at the plant early on Monday. This was going to be an interesting week. The meeting wasn't scheduled to start until ten o'clock. I decided to go by the cafeteria and have a real breakfast. I also needed to review the slides I'd made up over the weekend based on my meetings with Jan. I was feeling anxious. My career, Jack's career, maybe more important, our legacies, were in jeopardy. Not only that, the future of IRT was on the line. I smiled to myself as I realized I was inadvertently humming the Rocky theme as I walked.

I got a tray, went through the line, and headed for a seat at the back of the cafeteria. As I sat down, the feeling came to me that there was hope. The important task was to figure out how to implement here what Jan's company had been able to do. In the first place, we were simply too big to have one person running every aspect of the program. Second, Al had to support moving forward on this and to agree to use his influence to hold Brenda off long enough for us to at least have a chance to develop a viable plan.

Al was a wild card. He seemed to be a soft-spoken guy, but outward appearances could be deceiving. I hoped he wasn't the one who was pushing Brenda to forget about Knowledge-Based Development and proceed with layoffs.

At a little before ten, I entered the conference room and plugged the projector into my laptop.

Carl and Greg came through the door at ten o'clock sharp.

"Anyone seen Al?" I asked. My anxiety level was climbing. "I moved the meeting from nine to ten because Al said he had a meeting with Brenda at nine."

Carl said, "What are we, chopped liver?"

Greg said, "I'm afraid we'll find out about that soon enough." He looked at me. "I read your e-mail, Jon, about Jan and her company. That was a badly-needed break."

I said, "We still have a lot of work to do to figure out how to make it work here. Even so, much of what they've done will work here, and they're willing to help us. So tell me, how was your visit to CTC?"

Carl said, "That company is a freaking disaster!"

"No kidding," I said. "Did Al feel the same way? Hold on, let me call Al's office."

I dialed his phone and was directed to voice mail. I left a message.

Carl said, "To tell the truth, I'm not sure what Al was thinking. But it looked like he was paying attention."

"Let's get started." I said. I put up the first slide. "Based on my meeting with Jan, I created a few slides to redirect our thinking a bit. This is just a recap. What happens here also happens at Jan's company, Sonic Solutions and no doubt at most companies. Most of the learning takes place late in the product development cycle, and we don't, or don't know how to, reuse what we learned on the next program."

Greg said, "That's us."

Al entered the room.

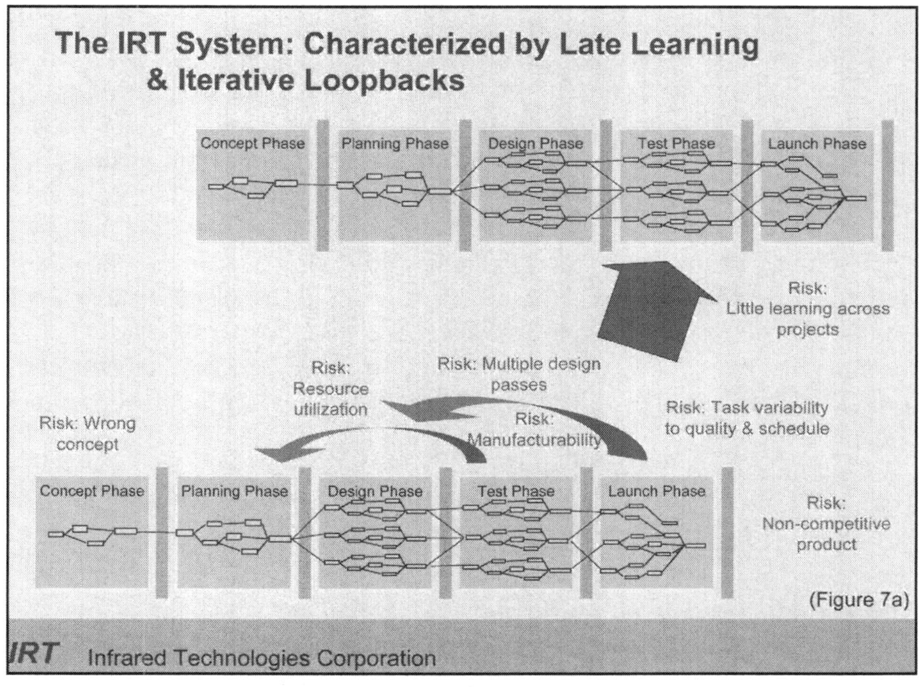

(Figure 7a)

"Sorry," he said. "My meeting ran over."

I said, "I'm sure it was interesting and important. Anything you want to share with us?"

"No," Al said. "I read your e-mail about the Sonic company and their program. It sounds as though you had a worthwhile trip."

"Yes, it was definitely productive. I'm presenting what I learned right now. The first slide is a recap. It shows how well intentioned programs go wrong and what is learned does little to benefit the next program. But, on the other hand, what happens if the knowledge from one product development always is transferred successfully to the next. How many of those risks would go away?"

Al said, "Jon, pardon this question, because it might sound rude, and I am not an engineer, so bear with me. It seems like all companies should do that routinely. I know we — and every company I have worked for — have spent considerable resources to solve that problem. Is it really that big a problem, and if so why?"

Greg said, "Actually, that's a good question, and to be honest, it is probably the biggest example of wishful thinking today by management. Jon, let's take a few minutes to discuss this. After all, it is at the root of the problem."

I nodded and sat down

Greg walked up to the flip chart and started writing.

Knowledge flow fails because it is not trusted to be accurate and robust

He turned to us and said, "Let's say, an engineer solved a problem two years ago like the one I have today. I don't know him or her and I don't know all the conditions. So I won't use the information. Also, since it is not controlled, how would I possibly know if the knowledge is current? It's information but it might just be hearsay — not verified, managed knowledge."

Greg added to the flip chart.

That's if I can even find it

He said, "If I'm under time pressure, and when aren't we all, there's no way I am going to spend my day looking for knowledge that I probably can't use even if I find it. I will reinvent it instead. It probably makes sense to me to do so even if the information does exist somewhere and is reliable, we all know what I'm doing is wasteful. It comes down to the fact that knowledge must be in my face when I need it or I'm not going to use it."

He started writing again.

If I find it, is it applicable?

"I'll be darned if I am going to spend a day studying a test report to understand all the conditions, when in most cases the knowledge will need considerable adjustment to apply to my situation. Probably should, but human nature kicks in and so I won't."

He turned back to the board.

Finally, is it easy to understand?

He turned to us and said, "If the knowledge is not visual and easy to understand, it's virtually useless. Realistically, all these factors I've written up here must be solved. Any one of them will have the effect of killing knowledge flow across projects. There may be others, but I assume you get the point."

Al looked from one of us to the next to let that sink in. Then he said, "This easily explains the poor productivity metrics we defined before. If knowledge doesn't flow freely across projects and generations of products, then it's like every product starts from scratch and a huge amount of knowledge has to be reinvented, right? What a waste."

I said, "It's actually worse because much of the reinvented knowledge turns out to be incorrect and this leads to loopbacks, reliability issues, and manufacturing problems. Ask anyone from Manufacturing. They are horribly frustrated about the same design problems occurring over and over. The problem is we don't know what we know."

Carl said, "Actually, if we only used what we know. We have a great resource of design and manufacturing knowledge, in infrared technology, but it largely resides unused and untapped in the minds of the knowledgeable. We have to solve this problem. A random cut of twenty percent of our people is a random cut of twenty percent of our knowledge base that we will never capture and build from."

Al leaned back, seemingly in thought.

Carl apparently sensing an opening in Al's defenses suddenly stood up. "Al," he said, "what did you see at CTC on Friday? Greg and I saw a company completely out of control with respect to engineering knowledge and a strategy that would ensure a complete free fall of that knowledge for years to come. You say that what Jon just presented made sense and yet you took us to visit a 'best practice' company that was as bad as we have ever seen. So what did you see?"

Al was looking at me, I think hoping I would divert Carl back to my presentation, but I wanted to hear his answer, so I just stared back.

Al said, "I certainly realize that we got two totally different perspectives from Engineering and Finance while at CTC. Frankly, it bothers me and I have been thinking about it all week. It is also not only about short versus long term, but raises the question, what is the basis for long-term profitability? Is it what markets we're in? Is it about timing? Is it about reducing expenses? Jon, your charts are implying that the knowledge and the ability to apply that knowledge is the underlying basis for sustained profitability, and that any strategy that undermines that is doomed."

"And Brenda's strategies do just that," Carl said emphatically.

"I understand," Al said. "Give me some time to think through this."

I decided to rescue Al, and I passed him Ron's business card. "Ron Morrison at Sonic Solutions offered to talk to Brenda on the subject. Give him a call. I am sure he would be glad to discuss it with you."

I said, "Good discussion. That's the reason that Jan and Sonic Solutions made knowledge flow its own value stream, separate and distinct from the typical Product Value Stream. This makes the flow of that knowledge visible, real and managed. Think of the four cornerstones. We've always applied them in context with just the product development of a single project. In reality, the cornerstones, the Expert Workforce, Set-Based Concurrent Engineering, Responsibility Based Planning, and the System Designer all really fit better in context of the integration of those value streams. Let's revisit Toyota from this perspective, and let me outline what I propose we copy."

I put up a slide.

I gestured to it. "Toyota relentlessly solves problems and captures knowledge using the LAMDA learning process and documenting the learning and results on A3s. This makes the knowledge robust, understandable, and visual — and also trustworthy since the A3s are owned by the functional organizations that create them."

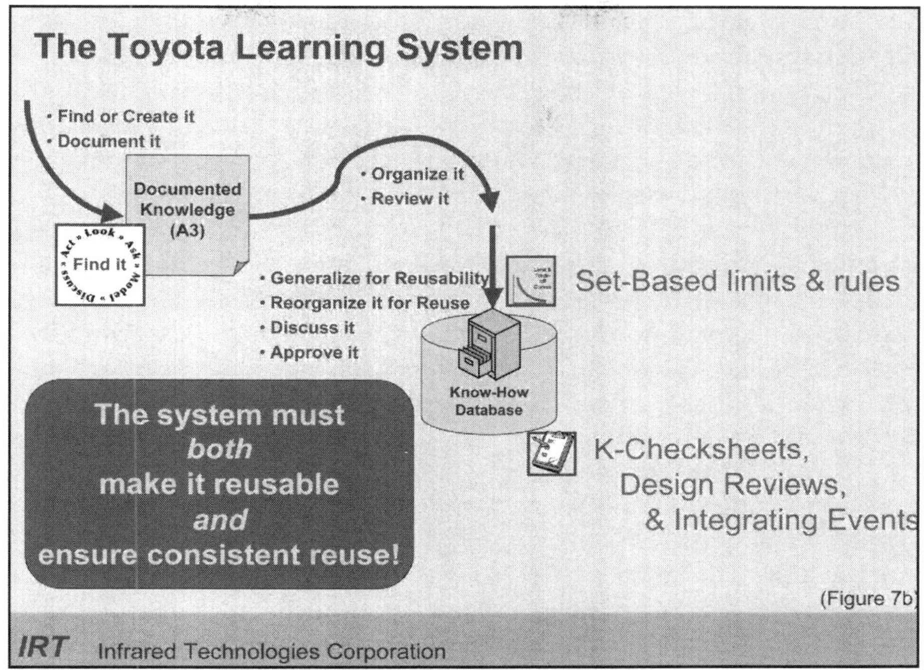

Carl added, "Greg, that handles two of the issues on your list. But, Jon, why have you emphasized set-based limits on this chart?"

I said, "Let me explain. When we find a solution to a specific problem we have what Toyota, or Sonic Solutions, calls point-based knowledge or single-event knowledge because it's a solution to a specific problem. This applies to product design as well as manufacturing. Point-based or single-event knowledge is only reusable in the exact same or very similar situations, which unfortunately almost never occur. Set-Based Knowledge is how you generalize the knowledge for reuse."

Carl said, "Hold on, I'm a little confused. We've always thought of set-based design as sets of design possibilities. You appear to be using a broader definition."

"I am. What did Al Ward say was that the most important element in the whole Toyota Product Development System?" I wondered if Carl or Greg would remember. Fortunately, Jan had reminded me.

Greg and Carl stared at each other.

I said, "I'll give you a hint. Remember the Harvard Business Review article where Katsuaki Watanabe, Toyota's CEO, said he told his engineers not to focus on developing low-cost automobiles, but instead to focus on developing technologies and processes that would allow Toyota to manufacture all their vehicles at lower cost?"

"Trade-off curves," Carl correctly answered. "I just never thought of them being synonymous with Set-Based Knowledge, but it does make sense. A trade-off curve, in its simplest form, can show the impact of a set of design decisions on a customer interest."

"Right," I said. "Toyota's success is built upon what Sonic calls Set-Based Knowledge. It is made up of trade-off curves and other rules generalized across sets of decisions that establish the customer, technical, and economic relationships between design decisions. This is what enables Set-Based Concurrent Engineering. When the chart says 'generalize for reusability,' it means to turn your point-based knowledge into Set-Based Knowledge."

Carl and Greg were nodding in agreement. Al wore a blank stare.

I asked, "Al, does this make sense to you?"

"I read about trade-off curves and feasible regions in the material you gave me, and it said these curves are used extensively. I think I know how they are used in engineering to show the feasible and infeasible regions between design decisions. But how are they developed?"

"Our best engineers develop them naturally," Greg said. "Actually, I think all of our experienced design and manufacturing engineers have their heads full of trade-off curves based on their experience. It is this embedded knowledge that make our best engineers so intuitive. They might not actually know the exact curves, but they know where the knees in the curves are so they can stay on the safe side. The problem is the curves are in their heads. The curves need to be documented on A3s so everyone can understand them and actually build on them to create new knowledge."

Carl said, "And every time someone retires, or is laid off," he looked toward Al, "those curves walk out of the company — unless they're captured as visible, reusable knowledge. I've created several over the past year. For many, I was able to develop formulas using my graduate school test books. Formulas are my first choice because they're faster and cheaper. I also built a few simulations, which I verified with experiments. A couple of times, I had to design fairly expensive experiments with enough prototypes to create a curve. The best part is that other engineers in Civil Avionics are using my curves for their designs. So they've stopped having to ask so many questions. The A3s become a natural mentoring tool"

I said, "And this discussion leads into what is possibly the most critical thing Toyota does to make all this work. They standardize the knowledge into knowledge checklists — or Checksheets — and review all their design decisions against these standards. They update them after every project based on all the new knowledge. The functional managers are responsible for the updates and for ensuring the standards are adhered to. The Checksheets align the Set-Based Knowledge limits for design decisions at the defined project review points, which are their Integrating Events. The functional managers and chief engineers use these for resolving design conflicts. It's pretty simple really."

Al said, "Okay, I think I'm getting it. LAMDA is the learning process for creating robust knowledge. The A3 makes the results visual and understandable. The knowledge is generalized for reuse into set-based rules and trade-off curves, and the Knowledge Checksheet is the resulting standard that is continually owned, maintained, and used for validating the design standards. Right?"

Carl said, "Nice summary. Maybe you do have some engineering blood running in your veins. Notice, also, that all of Greg's knowledge flow issues are resolved."

Al's puzzled look returned. "I'm confused about trade-off curves and Set-Based Knowledge. Can you help me understand the difference?"

I said, "Here's a slide that shows how it works. Carl, can you explain?"

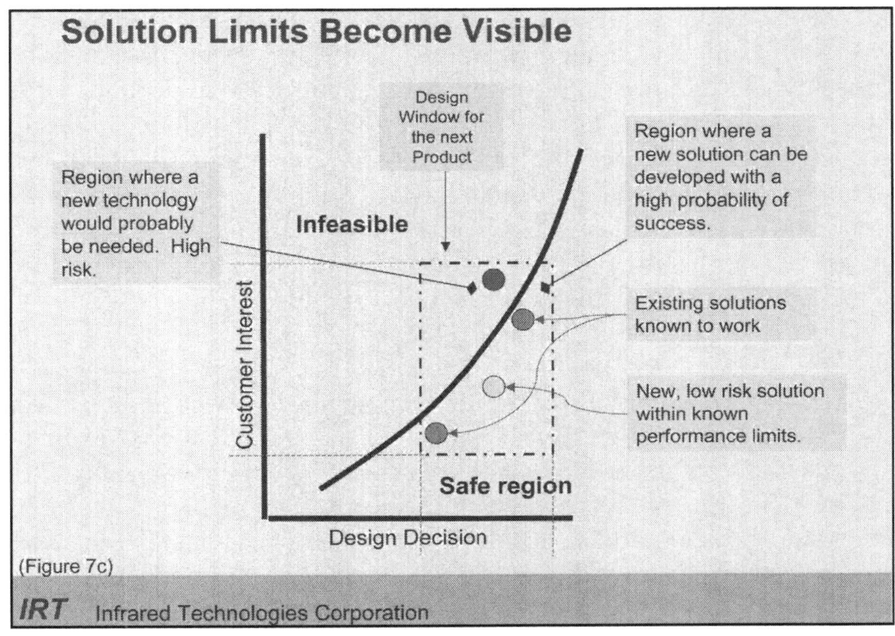

(Figure 7c)

Carl stood and walked to the screen. "In this example, the feasible region is below and to the right of the curve. The dotted rectangle shows the design window. The circles indicate known feasible designs. The design alternatives can be visually and rapidly evaluated with regard to both risk and reward."

Greg said, "Most of the product development performance improvements in Civil Avionics are due to these curves."

Carl said, "The best part is that while everyone uses my curves, I can do research to figure out how to move the curves."

Al asked, "How are they used in Marketing and Manufacturing?"

"In Manufacturing," Carl said, "trade-off curves show the tolerance limits of different manufacturing processes. Product design engineers need to know these limits before they make their design decisions. In reality, set-based design is the optimization of customer interests to a number of known limits from multiple perspectives. These become the trade-off decisions — I hope you appreciate that these trade-off decisions can involve some rather intricate relations between related decisions."

Al said, "It sounds like a huge undertaking."

"But remember," I said, "we already have most of the knowledge, we just haven't made it visible as set-based knowledge generalized for reuse. The pay back should be huge because once we have that knowledge flowing, everything else ought to fall into place. Sonic's president said they schedule Integrating Events early to define what knowledge is needed in order to design a product, and to identify what knowledge is missing. He said he will not allow a design decision to be made without the necessary knowledge. In fact, if you think about it, any design decision that is made could impact a customer in some way. If, in fact, anyone in the company knows that impact, and it is not communicated, then that's a huge waste of knowledge. To learn first and then design is a huge paradigm shift, because we have been trained to freeze the specification and finish the design as soon as possible."

Carl said, "So that's how they achieve 'test-then-design.'"

"Yes," I said, "and the rate of innovation has significantly increased. We're too big to rely on one person to manage the knowledge across four businesses, but Ron does that at Sonic. He also insists all conflict be resolved with knowledge. No debating contests. No opinions and wishful thinking. Knowledge talks and everything else walks. And Ron insists engineers must understand customer needs. An engineer can't say he made a design decision because he received a specification from Marketing."

"Sounds great to me," Carl said. "No more Marketing BS."

Greg said, "What about problems encountered along the way?"

"Great question," I said. "They capture all solutions in Problem A3s, create new rules or trade-off curves, and update the knowledge in their Checksheets. The functional managers and the chief engineers integrate the Knowledge Value Stream with the Product Value Stream."

"Jon, that description is interesting," Greg said. "I remember the quote from the Toyota chief engineer, that 'great conflicts make great cars.' This makes the logic of that crystal clear."

I said, "That is a great lead-in to my next slide." I put up the chart. "I'm going to suggest a new term, 'Lean Knowledge Management,' to describe what Toyota has effectively done — they have established a knowledge management system that actually works, long-term — and that seems to be the foundation that drives everything in the Toyota Product Development System. It's also the basis for what Jan's company is doing, although with some different approaches. The common ground is that it is a continuous, closed-loop cycle of learning, generalizing, organizing, applying to design decisions, and improving. There's a clear distinction of roles for owning and designing with knowledge, with healthy conflict allowing the knowledge to drive decision-making."

Greg said, "I like that phrase — Lean Knowledge Management. Lean is about removing waste. We know most knowledge is wasted. Good management is the key."

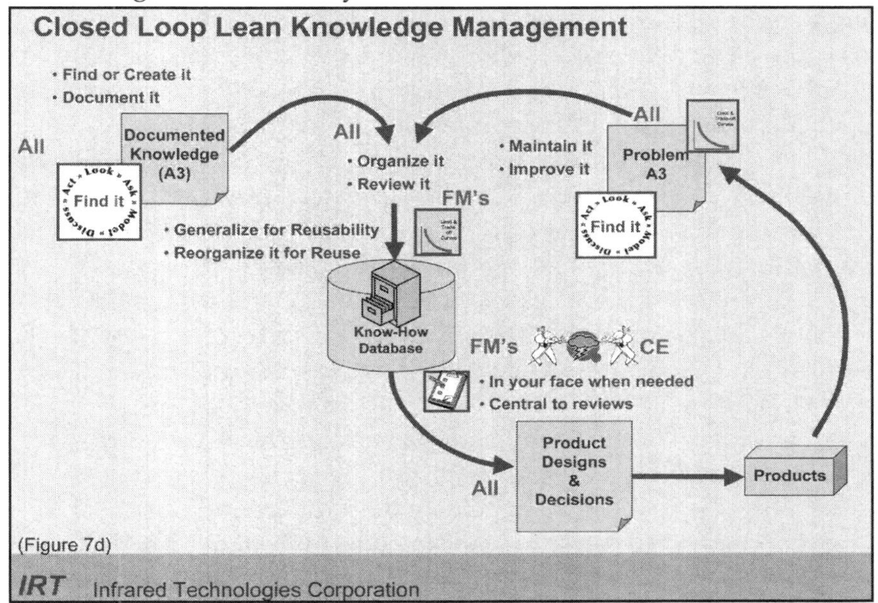

(Figure 7d)

"I understand Toyota," Carl said. "But how does Sonic Solutions find their knowledge? And how do the engineers know which trade-off curves are needed for particular design decisions? And how do they know how the different curves interact?"

I said, "They develop causal diagrams that map trade-off relationships as they need them so engineers can see the interactions between curves. The causal diagrams plus relevant A3s contain all the knowledge to be reviewed before a design decision is made. They haven't implemented the Knowledge Checksheets — they hope we can help them think that through. Ron uses the A3s or K-Briefs, as they call them — short for Knowledge Briefs — for capturing the knowledge. He personally polices knowledge standards. Actually, this is pretty consistent with Toyota. Much of the knowledge glue is in the heads of the functional managers and chief engineers."

I thought for a moment, and then added, "Actually, Ron believes there are not that many curves that drive their key product level integrating decisions, so they focus on those. He's aware of the huge amount of best practice knowledge — or rules of the road — particularly from Manufacturing. They have not yet integrated this level of decision-making into the review process, but they plan to.

Carl said, "This last chart and knowledge standards or Checksheets resolves a personal issue I have had for awhile. I have always assumed the knowledge embedded in all of our A3s is where our knowledge would continue to live, and I have had to take it on faith that somehow we would be able to find that knowledge when we needed it. In actuality, the A3s and LAMDA are the learning process. The knowledge is organized into the Checksheets of design standards.

"That's right," I said. "The functional managers are responsible for doing that — in trade-off curves where possible, but they can be simple rules for manufacturing. The knowledge is learned on one project, coalesced and made the visible standards for the next. This is the so-called Toyota Engineering Checklist, or Know-How Database, or knowledge notebooks. Jan commented that she had heard a top level Toyota executive say that their knowledge notebook was the fundamental key to Toyota's success."

Greg added, "That's why Integrating Events are so important as they naturally pull the Checksheets into the review process."

Al said, "I know you guys believe that dollars and cents is the only thing that matters to me so let me speak to that for a minute. It would seem that having Integrating Events, that don't slip, based on accurate trade-offs between design decisions, is a huge competitive advantage on the revenue side. Jon, didn't Brian say 'give me good timely products on a predictable schedule with high quality,' and he could sell them? This would say that any actions detracting from that capability would be wrong." Al leaned back and seemed take a moment to think.

The others just stared at the slide still on the screen.

Greg broke the silence. "Did Sonic Solutions focus on the cornerstones at all?"

I said, "I asked about that. Ron and Jan said that once knowledge is captured in Set-Based format and organized for reuse, implementing the cornerstones is relatively straightforward. The Set-Based Knowledge represents the work of the Expert Engineering Workforce. Sonic schedules Integrating Events early to identify what knowledge is missing for a new product. The engineers have to find or create the missing knowledge, which is Responsibility-Based Planning. Once they acquire the knowledge, they proceed through the Integrating Events doing Set-Based Concurrent Engineering. Optimal design decisions result from the tension between Ron and the project managers, which is Sonic's version of the Chief Engineer."

Carl asked, "What is the timing of these Integrating Events? And how did Jan's company integrate them into their process?"

"Good question, Carl," I said. "I really quizzed Jan on that since they have a phase gate system similar to ours." I put up the next slide. "The main thing they did is replace the fuzzy front end with what they call the Set-Based Concurrent Engineering Phase. They installed two key Integrating Events. One at the very start — to answer whether they have enough functional knowledge to make a good system. In other words, they had at least one viable solution set for all their functional subsystems. Ron has refused to let project managers go past this point without verifiable knowledge on K-Briefs — or A3s if you prefer that terminology. Then they have another key Integrating Event, called the Set-Based Transition Integrating Event, when they converge on each of the functional subsystems. After that point, they use the gates they already had in place, because there should not be any further knowledge failures or loopbacks. The phase gates should work fine in that environment for detailed product and process design."

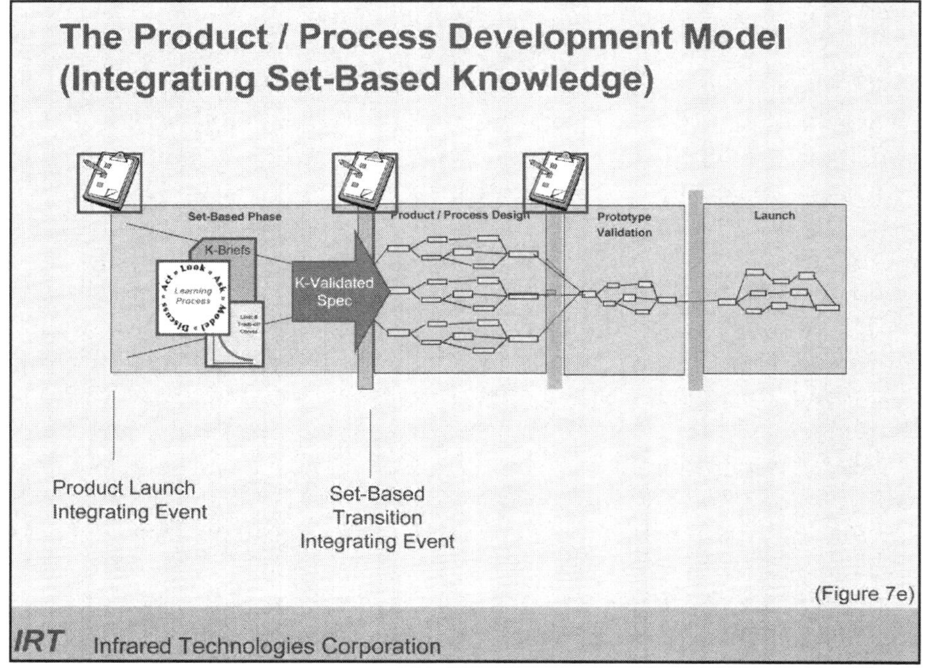

(Figure 7e)

"Interesting," Carl said. "That actually is pretty simple. How do they select the timing on the Set-Based Transition Integrating Event?"

"Again, pretty simple," I said. "They back up from the launch date based on the length of time for detailed CAD design and CAM process design, including the tooling cycle for each major subsystem. Once the unscheduled loopbacks are eliminated, project scheduling is simple. That's why Toyota doesn't miss schedules and can maintain a cadence of products. Jan and Ron are confident they will be there within a couple of product cycles."

Carl asked, "That second Integrating Event would have to consider a huge number of design decisions, wouldn't it?"

"Ah, I forgot to mention that," I replied. "That is actually multiple Integrating Events, one for each subsystem. The timing of each is determined by the timing to get each subsystem through tooling into production. Remember, the goal is to make all decisions as late as possible, but no later. Manufacturing capabilities will largely dictate the timing of the Set-Based Transition points."

"So Manufacturing is driving the timing of innovation?" Greg asked. "That thought bothers me a little."

"That's not the way to look at it," I responded. "Innovation is being driven through the continuous development of the Set-Based Knowledge. The Integrating Events just drive the level of integration into any specific product. As Al would say, you make money by delivering products, not promising products."

"So, Set-Based development really ends at these transition points?" Greg said. "Is that right?"

"Not necessarily," I said. "I believe that inexpensive Set-Based development ends there at the end of the conceptual or Set-Based Phase of the project. Once you move into the time zone required to manufacture the product, either you are risking schedule and sales, or you are going to have double or more expenses for detailed design and process development. Toyota does do this. If the Chief Engineer needs more knowledge, he can and will authorize additional expenses for more than one detailed design. What Toyota doesn't do, nor should we, is to move ahead hoping for a manufacturing miracle to make up the schedule. The key point is that moving across the Set-Based Transition Point is a major change in expenditure rate."

Carl said, "Jon, my head is spinning. Your meeting with Jan has taken me to a different level of understanding of the overall system. In a way, once you pass the Set-Based Transition Points for each subsystem, you are really starting into a manufacturing-like process with real concurrent development of the product design, CAD, with the manufacturing process (CAM)."

"Yes," I said, "and as long as you have knowledge, you can start all of the other actions to bring the product to market — sales material, training manuals, and so on — all on a well defined schedule. In my opinion, the typical task-based scheduling and workflow systems will work just fine after this point. If you are not still designing through loopbacks, the traditional scheduling systems are a good match.

Greg said, "Jon, this discussion and your Product / Process model are tying some things together for me. See if you agree with my thinking. The Knowledge Checksheets linked with the Integrating Events effectively make the right knowledge visible at the right time. The Integrating Events define when we need to make decisions to maintain the schedule, and the Checksheets are the collective knowledge of how those decisions will impact the customer interests. Right?"

After my nod, he continued. "And if the knowledge in the Checksheets is set-based curves or ranges, then the Integrating Events will allow set-based decision making because it makes the trade-offs visible at the right time. Right?"

Carl said, "Ahhh, yes, the Checksheets are set-based knowledge — curves and such. That helps distinguish them from the checklists that we've been using, sorta, for years. That's been bothering me a bit up to now. I can't see how we'd use our current checklists early in the design process. They mostly list things that need to be done, but things that we would never have done that early. So, we'd just check them off saying okay we'll remember to do that. That would be a fairly pointless exercise early in the process."

"Yes, good point," I said. "That's why Jan said they call them 'Checksheets' rather than 'checklists'. Our old checklists are lists of the good design practices that we want to make sure that we do during detailed design. They have been valuable but, realistically, have not been consistently used or maintained. These Knowledge Checksheets are different. They are not just lists of best practice detailed design rules, but rather, they list the approved knowledge about how our early design decisions will impact the customers of our products."

I followed up. "Once you realize that there are set-based curves captured in the Checksheets, it becomes clear how they enable true concurrent engineering. And that solves a long standing issue of mine from my manufacturing days. Currently, we have no way to elevate manufacturing technology issues — such as the limits on our ability to manufacture new detector arrays — no way for them to be considered at the right time when the project managers are making their technology decisions. We in Manufacturing know the impact certain decisions will have on us. If we want to make sure the design engineers factor that impact into their decision-making, we simply need to make sure that impact is in the Knowledge Checksheet that will be used at the Integrating Event where that decision will be made. With that, Manufacturing — and our suppliers, too — have a very clear way to communicate to the design engineers. And not just on the current project, but all future projects."

"Wow, that's powerful," Greg said. "Everybody in the company will know exactly how to communicate to the design engineers: get the knowledge into the right Checksheet such that the engineers can see the impact that their decisions will have. Leading up to those Integrating Events, you know those design engineers are going to look at those Checksheets. They are not going to walk into a design review without having made sure their designs conform to the Checksheets."

I said, "And everybody also knows how to get involved in the design process — at the Integrating Events, ensuring their Checksheets are adhered to. In a way, it makes the design process itself clearly visible to all."

Al, who had been taking all this in, said, "Prior to this discussion, I wasn't trying too hard to understand Checksheets. assuming it was just some engineering-specific tool, but I think I get it now. A Checksheet is simply a list of the set-based curves and design rules that constrain the decisions you will be making in an Integrating Event. It simply displays what you know when you need to know it. Right?"

"And how you want to see it," I replied. "It makes it easier for the engineer to design with the knowledge than without it. No need to search some huge database of knowledge . . . it's already organized based on how and when you make decisions."

Al nodded and said, "Getting back to Sonic Solutions, how long did it take them to see benefits?"

"Ron said they were seeing the progress in nine months. He also said his first products are shipped twenty-five percent faster than they would have with their old system. He predicts the cycle time will be much faster next time because they now have a broad base of knowledge captured in K-Briefs for reuse. He expects cycle time to be cut in half in two product development cycles."

"But Sonic Solutions is a technology company," Al said. "Won't they need all new technology for their new products?"

I said, "They are innovating much faster than they ever did before because they know the limits of the product and manufacturing technologies, and they know which curves need to move to achieve the next level of customer satisfaction. That's where the technology development is — at the functional subsystems. Now they can plan functional innovations orchestrated to achieve a rhythm of innovative products and derivatives and no longer have to depend on a lucky home run."

I paused and took a breath. "Okay," I said. "Now let me show you another slide. I call it the Learning-First Product Development Model. It's not just the Toyota model. It also represents Sonic Solutions and it should be our model. This slide shows how the knowledge flows across product lines. It's the reuse that increases productivity. Sonic has doubled their productivity already, and Ron believes they will double again as their Set-Based Knowledge grows. We would build a Knowledge Value Stream that is used across all four businesses. We can do this and double our productivity in two years."

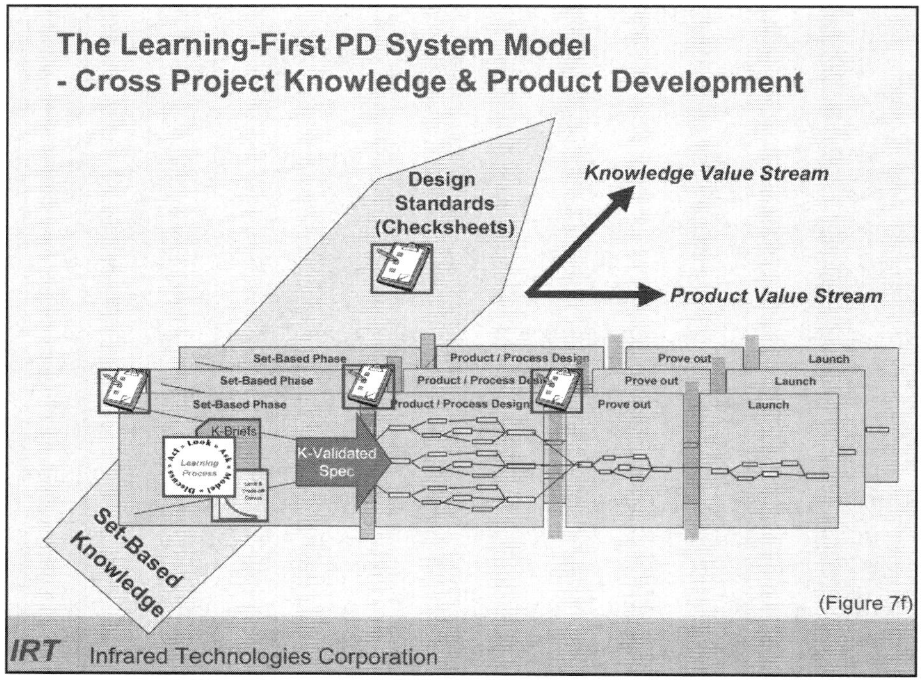

Carl said, "That's an interesting summary slide, Jon. It emphases the concurrency of knowledge and process development, and that it takes both to make the system. I wish I had that slide in an argument I had with your buddy Doyle a few weeks back. He was arguing that Set-Based Design was actually not Lean because the alternatives that did not go forward on a project were inherently waste. That actually would be the case if the knowledge didn't flow seamlessly across the business. In fact, that needs to be the heart of product development. If people know what doesn't work they won't waste time with it."

Greg said, "I also like the simplicity of that chart. It provides a simple answer to another question that's been raised in the past. One project in my area had front loaded engineering recently, based on the common perception that it would avoid some of the late design variability that messes up our schedules. The problem is they didn't really know what to focus on up front to remove the back-end variability, so their costs and schedules actually became worse. Early set-based learning not only reduces variability naturally by developing backups, it also generates knowledge that provides flexibility if decisions need to move later. The consistent flow across projects of the set-based knowledge delivers free early learning from prior projects."

Al glanced at his watch. "Jon, I really have to run to another meeting Brenda wants me to attend. You've given me a lot to think about."

I said, "Any thoughts or further questions?"

"No," Al said. He gathered his things, then paused. "Greg, Carl, may I speak with Jon alone?"

"Sure," Greg said. "Come on Carl."

Carl said, "Make sure you scan the room for bugs."

Al closed the door behind them, turned and sat across from me.

"Jon, you've made tremendous progress in the last week in figuring out how to implement this. But IRT is out of time. Brenda and Ray and the Board of Directors want to take immediate action to improve profit. Brenda's proposing a 20% across-the-board workforce reduction this quarter. Profit will increase to seven percent next quarter as a result, and investors will finally have confidence that this company will do what is necessary to earn a decent profit."

I said, "Is it a done deal?"

"It's very close. I'm told Jack is the only executive fighting it, and he really can't stop it — although he might be able to delay it for a little while."

Al stood.

"Do me a favor, Al, and think about what you heard today," I said, as he moved toward the door. "I'll see you tomorrow when we meet with Jack and Brenda."

"Oh, I will," Al said. "We haven't gotten a chance to discuss in depth how our meeting went with our former company. From our traditional financial view, it was positive, but as Carl and Greg pointed out earlier, it's doubtful that's the case from a long-term strategy point of view. I need to do some thinking. Trust me on this, neither Brenda nor I have anything but the best intentions about the future of IRT. We are both here for the long-term."

Al opened the door. "Do me a favor. Send me your slides," he said as he left.

DISCUSSION

We introduced the view of Set-Based Knowledge flow in the last chapter as a separate value stream. We built on that in this chapter. The real magic of Toyota is that they have effectively integrated the flow of innovative knowledge into a planned cadence of product releases. That is what needs to be copied. Set-based development must have a life of its own that flows across products. This means the knowledge must be generalized for set-based decision making. This is our concern with so many of the piecemeal efforts to implement Toyota practices we have seen, whether they are based on each of the four cornerstones in the first book or on selected principles of the thirteen discussed in the Morgan / Liker book, as well as whether they are driven from the top down or through internal guerrilla warfare activities. If they are all focused only on specific projects as pilots, we believe it is unlikely that a complete system will develop that achieves the huge potential productivity gains that might otherwise be possible. If, however, the pilot Lean activities are all executed in context with an overall system model, then the business results can prove to be dominating. We believe that the Learning-First Product Development model described in this chapter provides a good framework to work with. The basic premise of this model is quite simple: the Knowledge Value Stream and the Product Value Stream integrate early in the Set-Based Phase of the project. That is the true meaning of Set-Based Concurrent Engineering. At a bare minimum, a top down commitment to such a model is important to assure the system view of the transformation is always maintained.

Chapter 8
The Battle for the Future of the Company
(Evaluating the Alternatives)

Discussion continues with a different level of stakeholders. When do you know enough? That is always the issue.

Tuesday: Meeting with Jack and Brenda

I woke early and couldn't get back to sleep. Today was the day I'd either get a reprieve from Brenda, or not. Was IRT out of time? It could well be Brenda didn't want to hear about KBD. All signs pointed that way. After all, she'd moved up the meeting with Ray to Wednesday. I wondered what Al would say, but I was not sure whether anything that he said would make any difference. He seemed to understand what I told him, but he'd stopped well short of saying he'd support KBD rather than Brenda's cost reduction plan.

I was also concerned about Jack. I'd sent him an e-mail yesterday afternoon with my recommendation but had not heard back from him, which was not like Jack. He'd said he wanted to review conclusions and recommendations. At the very least, I wanted an acknowledgement that he had received my plan. I had to wonder whether he was about to be fired or forced to resign. What a way to end a forty-year career. If things went the wrong way, there would be a stampede for the door.

Since I was awake anyway, I decided to drive to work early. For nearly thirty years, I'd left the house at six. The drive was a whole lot more pleasant with less traffic.

I arrived at 6:30 and got myself a cup of coffee and a muffin. The meeting was to start at eight because Jack liked early meetings. I still didn't have a response from Jack. I flipped through my slides again. I was tired of looking at them. I put my feet up on my desk and thought about whether I should have retired a year ago and worked on my golf game. I'd know soon. It was 7:10, so I thought I'd swing by Jack's office on the way to the conference room — still no Jack.

I entered the conference room and staked out the front left chair, which was right across from where Jack always sat. I hooked up my laptop and turned on the projector.

Good. Everything worked. I placed six copies of the A3 entitled, 'IRT is not meeting goals for market leadership or profit ≥ 7%' in the middle of the table for reference. I didn't expect many questions since Jack and Brenda had already seen them.

Brenda Caine entered the conference room at 7:40. "Good morning," I said, totally surprised. She looked as if she was dressed for a business party. She was wearing a navy blue suit without a wrinkle. Every strand of hair was in place.

"Jon, I was hoping to catch you," she said. "Did you visit CTC last week with Al?"

"No, I couldn't make it but two of my engineers, Greg and—"

She interrupted. "Too bad, I was hoping you could have seen what they've accomplished." She put her small computer bag and purse on the conference table across from me, where Jack always sat, and walked to the white board and wrote:

	3 Years Ago	**Today**
Profit	**2%**	**10%**
Market share	**16%**	**20%**
Stock price	**$12**	**$30**

"Three years ago, CTC was in as bad shape as IRT is today," she said. "My strategy, the same strategy I'm proposing for IRT, increased profit from two to ten percent. It increased market share in the core business from 16% to 20%. And yesterday the stock closed at over 30 dollars a share."

She handed me a press announcement and said, "Yesterday, CTC announced they're buying another medical company and continuing their cost reduction. As you see, the stock went up nearly five dollars. CTC stock is recommended for retirement plans. Mutual fund managers are buying CTC stock for their portfolios. Investors recognize that CTC is a well managed company."

"I was briefed by Al and my guys about CTC—"

"Jon," she interrupted again, "I know you've worked really hard on your Toyota project and you've started to make some progress. But IRT doesn't have time to pursue a company wide transformation that requires years to produce a meaningful return on investment."

Greg and Carl appeared at the door.

Brenda said, "I'll be back at eight o'clock." She left.

Greg said, "What was that all about?"

I was still reading the press release.

"Jon?" Greg said.

"Greg, Carl, good morning," I said.

Carl said, "What were you talking with Brenda Caine about?"

"This," I replied and handed him the press release. "I'm afraid this meeting is going to be a waste of time."

Carl read out loud. "CTC plans to cut a third of the workforce at the company it is acquiring." He handed the release to Greg. "Insanity."

Greg read it over as the executives filed into the room and picked up coffee and muffins, which Donna had provided and had placed in the back of the conference room. Nathan Jorgenson, who headed Military Products, wore a new suit and sat at the end of the table. Charles Osgood, the head of Automotive Products, sat next to Nathan. Doyle sat behind Nathan in a chair against the wall. Neither of them looked at me. Greg and Carl took seats nearby, behind me. Christine Dumas, the head of Security Systems, and Wayne Tillotson, who was over Civil Avionics, took the two seats on my left. Also, Brian Hawkins from Marketing and Sales took an inconspicuous spot at the back of the room.

I was surprised to see Jack's direct reports at the meeting. I thought just my team would be here, plus Brenda, Jack, and Al. I wondered whether Jack or Brenda had invited them. Having this all canceled was one thing, but in the presence of Nathan, Charles, and especially Doyle was another. The prospect made me uneasy. I turned to Greg and asked him to make more copies of the A3.

I glanced at my watch. It was eight o'clock. Jack came in and walked to the chair opposite me. He placed his laptop and folder on the table and pushed Brenda's laptop and purse to the middle of the table just as she was entering room. She glared at Jack from behind him.

"Mr. Holder," she said in a controlled tone, "are you looking for my lipstick?"

Jack shot her a wry smile. "I doubt there's anything in there I want."

Brenda sat next to Jack and pulled her purse and laptop in front of her.

"It's eight o'clock," Jack said. "Let's get started."

I looked at Brenda. "Has anyone seen Al?" I asked.

"No, I haven't," Brenda replied.

"Let's get started," Jack said again, looking at his screen.

"Jack," I said softly, "did you get the slides I sent you yesterday?"

"No," he replied looking at his e-mail. "When did you send them?"

"About 2:00."

Jack stared at his e-mail. "Never got them. Let's get started."

I put up my agenda slide just as Al walked in. "Sorry," Al said as he sat down next to Brenda. His eyes were bloodshot and bags puffed out beneath them. He looked like he was even more tired than I was.

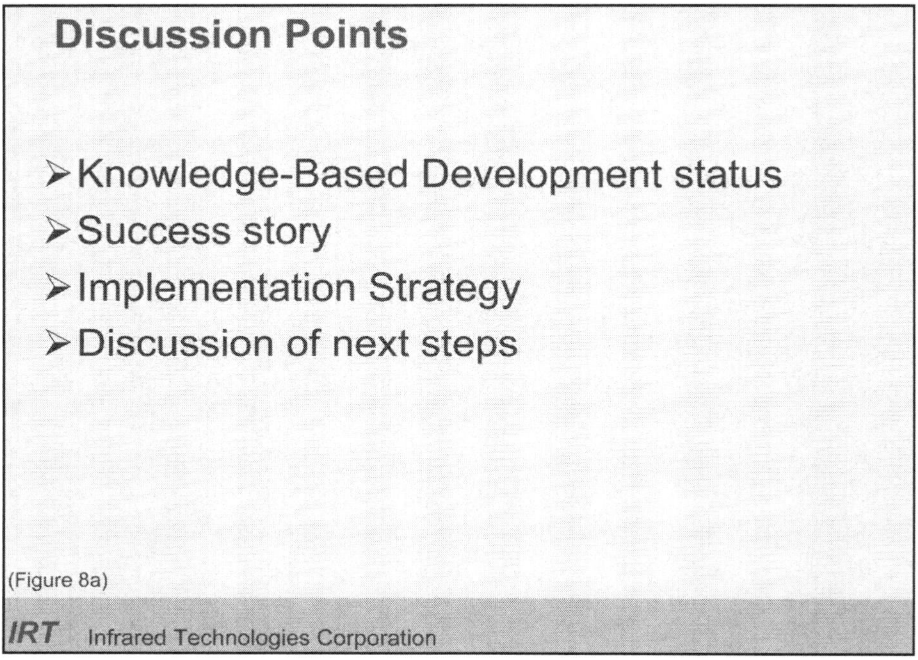

Discussion Points

- Knowledge-Based Development status
- Success story
- Implementation Strategy
- Discussion of next steps

(Figure 8a)

IRT Infrared Technologies Corporation

"Here's the agenda for today. The goal is to understand where we are and what we need to change for implementing our KBD system. I will be recommending that we change the name to Learning-First Product Development (LFPD)," I said. "Any questions? Anything to add?"

"Let's get to the punch line," Jack huffed. "Is this going to work or not?

I looked around the room and saw a lot of unfriendly faces. Doyle whispered something to Nathan and they both chuckled. I imagine most of them thought this meeting would mark the end of Knowledge-Based Development and the end of me — at IRT at least.

I said, "Yes, Jack. Given a chance, this will work. In the last year, IRT improved its product development performance from nineteen to twenty-three percent, a twenty-one percent increase. That's probably the largest increase ever, but it's far less than I had hoped."

"We improved in Civil Avionics from nineteen to twenty-five percent, which is a thirty-two percent increase," Wayne said. "And I believe this year's new products will be a significant improvement."

"Security Systems improved from twenty to twenty-five, a twenty-five percent increase," Christine added.

Nathan and Charles were silent.

"What progress have the other two businesses made?" Jack asked.

I showed this slide.

Product Development Performance Assessment

	Initial Score	After 1 Year	% Increase
Civil Avionics	19	25	32%
Security Systems	20	25	25%
Automotive Products	19	22	16%
Military Products	18	20	11%
IRT Average	19	23	21%

(Figure 8b)

IRT Infrared Technologies Corporation

"That's about what I expected," Jack said.

"Let's not forget," Nathan said, "Military Products still delivers the most profit of any business."

"Go ahead, Jon," Jack said, brushing off Nathan's comment.

"Last week, at a Lean conference, I ran into Jan Morris who used to work at IRT," I said. "She was our resident expert on Toyota product development, so her loss was felt. For the past year, she's worked for a small company in Massachusetts that has doubled their product development performance in one year and has already reduced product development cycle time by twenty-five percent. They're the triangles on this chart. We are the diamonds. Toyota is the circles. According to the president, he and his team fully expect this thinking to allow them to dominate their markets within the next few years. Here's his business card." I took two of his cards and passed one to Jack and the other to Brenda. "He said he'd be glad to discuss it personally."

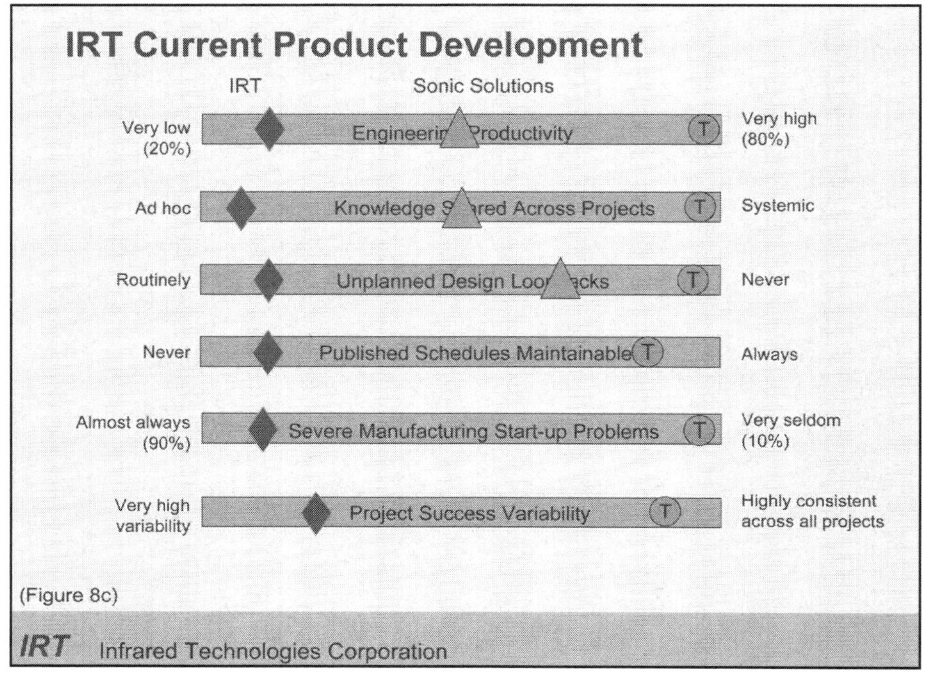

(Figure 8c)

"What were we missing on our implementation?" Christine asked.

"We assigned one of the four cornerstones to each of the businesses to pilot with the plan to integrate them all together later," I said. "We should have kept it as a system and built the knowledge foundation first. The other oversight was thinking this can be driven from front line engineering groups. It has to be led from the top. I had dinner with Ron and Jan last week, and he is leading the change actively. What they have accomplished is very impressive."

Greg returned with additional copies of the A3 and gave them out.

"Jack and Brenda have seen these," I said. "This is the problem we've been solving using LAMDA. This one describes the problem and the root cause analysis. Any questions on the problem description?"

Everyone studied it for a minute.

Problem: IRT is not meeting goals for market leadership or profit ≥ 7%

Problem Description

- IRT market share and profit have both declined over the last 5 years.

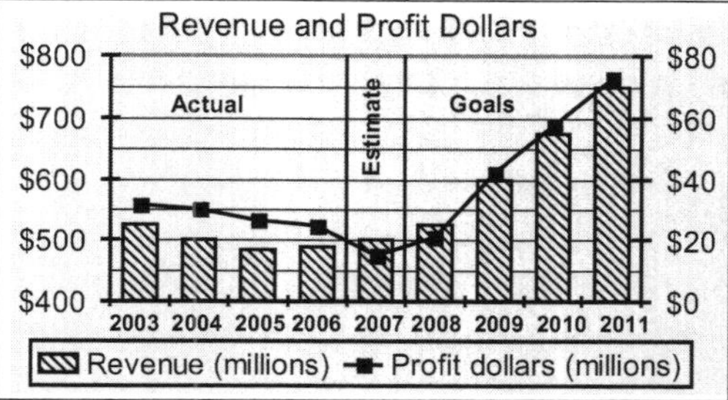

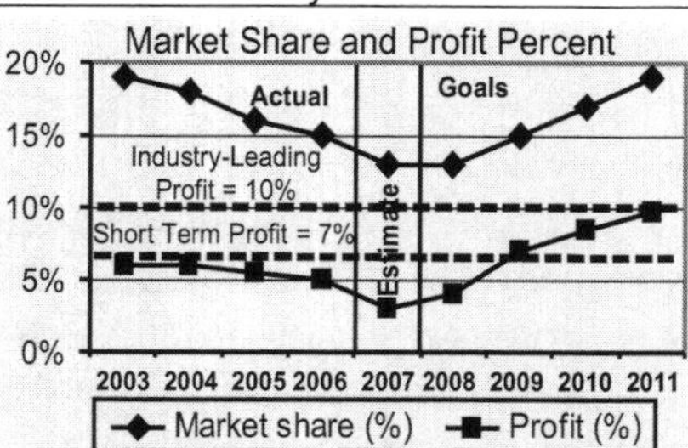

Assumptions:

- Gross Margin = 30%
- Fixed costs = $140M thru '09 (people incl. benefits - $100M, buildings, etc. - $40M)
- 5% annual increase starting at end of 2009, only if profit goals are met

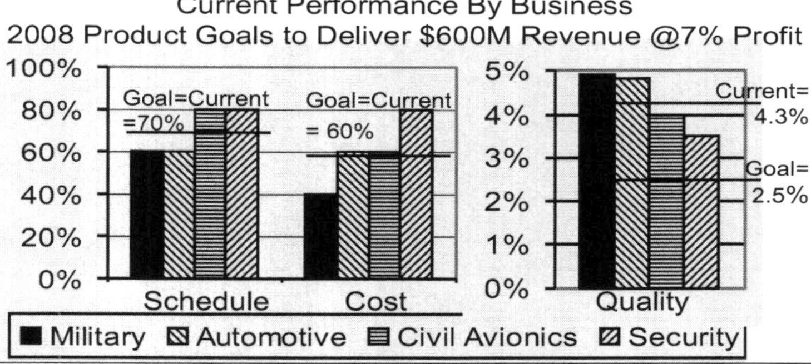

2008 Product Development Goals to deliver $600M revenue @7% profit in 2009:

- Schedule:
  - 70% of products deliver quantity by committed date.
  - No slips within 4 months of 1st customer shipment (4 in 2007: Military-2, Auto-2).
- Cost – 60% of products meet cost-of-sales target.
- Quality – total annual failure rate ≤ 2.5%

(table 8a)

"It clearly shows how poorly this company has been performing and how far we have to improve," Jack said.

"I see you included my goals," Brian added.

I said, "Could you explain those for us?"

"At Jon's request," Brian announced, "I have done an analysis that shows we can achieve seven percent profit and overall market leadership if we raise our revenue by a hundred million dollars. My sales force says if we do the following then we can achieve that increase in revenue by year after next — meet 70% of our schedules; no late surprises that change our customer commitments; meet our cost plans; lower our quality failure rate from 4.3 to 2.5 %."

Brenda said, "I have two issues with this. First, we don't want to wait until 2009 to reach an acceptable level of profit. We want at least seven percent profit starting in the first quarter of next year. Second, I can't imagine how we could ever achieve the profit goals without significant cost reduction."

"Any other comments or questions?" I said.

"Just a comment," Christine said. "We've been using this approach in Security Systems for a couple of months now and it really improves productivity, particularly management productivity. There are more facts on this one piece of paper than we would typically see in an entire slide set."

"We're starting to use it too," Wayne said, "for the same reasons."

"Any questions or comments on the root cause analysis?" I asked.

"Your conclusion is a leap of faith," Nathan said.

"You're criticizing the essence of what we do," Charles added. "If we don't design and test, we can't innovate. The selection of a design pulls the needed innovation."

"What you are advocating here," Doyle said, shaking his head, "is process destruction, and the result will be complete chaos."

"Selecting the design as soon as possible tells the organization what they will be working on, which removes confusion," Nathan chimed. "It also tells my people what I am committed to doing."

I'd been worried about how I could bring people along who hadn't been in all the discussions we've had over the last two weeks.

"If you follow the root cause analysis," I replied, "which was prepared using real data, you will see that our problems are caused by the fact that we commit to product design decisions before we know they will work. That is the nature of our design-and-then-test product development process."

There was moment of silence while everyone studied the root cause analysis.

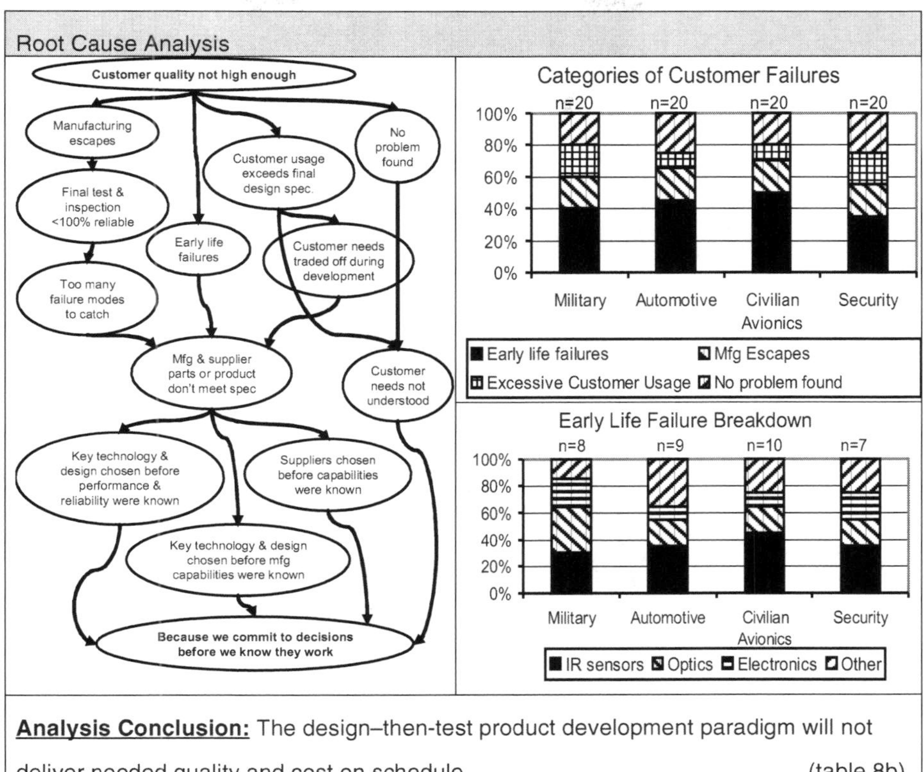

"I agree with it," Wayne said.

"Me too," Christine added.

"Jack, what do you think?" Brenda asked.

"I think they hit the nail right on the head," he answered. A vision of Jack hitting Nathan, Charles, and Doyle on the head flashed through my mind.

"Interesting," Brenda said. "Tell me how you solve this problem."

"Jan introduced this concept to me," I said, showing the next slide. "This is the development model, Learning-First Product Development, that Sonic Solutions uses as their system vision. The revelation is that there are really two value streams in product development: Product and Knowledge. We, and nearly every other company in the world, focus on the Product Value Stream. Toyota focuses on both. Knowledge flows across projects and is integrated into the design decisions for specific products. These two value streams are developed concurrently with clear ownership of each. At Toyota, the functional managers own the

Set-Based Knowledge that flows across the projects, and the Chief Engineers own the Product Value Stream decisions.

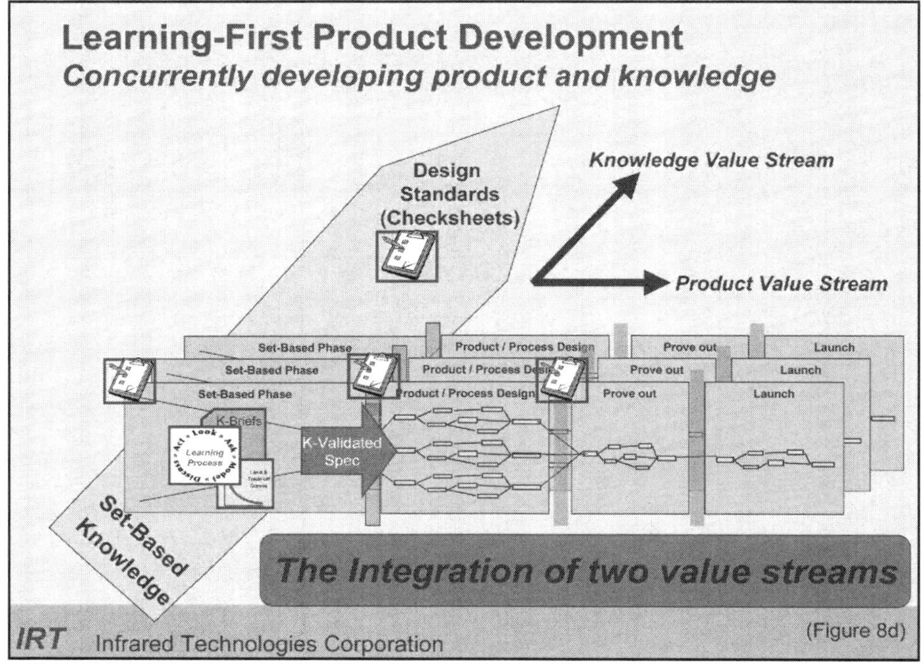

(Figure 8d)

Christine said, "Why is the knowledge in the diagonal arrow called Set-Based Knowledge and what is the significance of the K-Validated Spec?"

I said, "Christine, do you remember last week when we talked and you expressed concern that your set-based efforts seemed to be too focused on geometric sets and you felt you were missing something. The thing we were both missing is that set-based design does not have to be based only on physical properties, but also on performance parameters as documented in trade-off curves. Trade-off curves and generalized rules are used to define sets of possible design solutions in the set-based phase, which is the earliest and cheapest phase of Learning-First Product Development. This is why you start with wide targets and narrow those targets through the set-based phase until the spec is validated with known knowledge. Does that make sense?"

"Absolutely," she said. "And that is why Toyota is always looking for where the solution doesn't work; they want to know the ranges."

"Yes," I replied. "More on that in a few minutes."

Without waiting, I immediately advanced to the next slide. "The language is different in each value stream. Product knowledge is unique to a project. The Knowledge Value Stream must be directly usable across projects. Similarly, Toyota focuses equally on both, and their integration

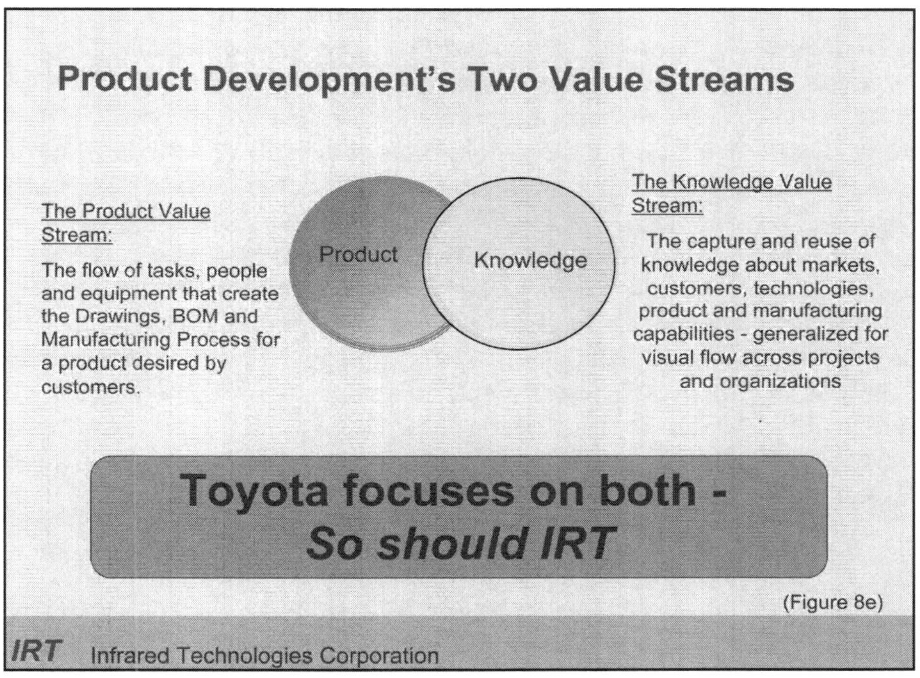

Product Development's Two Value Streams
The Product Value Stream:
The flow of tasks, people and equipment that create the Drawings, BOM and Manufacturing Process for a product desired by customers.
Product
Knowledge
The Knowledge Value Stream:
The capture and reuse of knowledge about markets, customers, technologies, product and manufacturing capabilities - generalized for visual flow across projects and organizations
Toyota focuses on both -
So should IRT
IRT Infrared Technologies Corporation

(Figure 8e)

early in what they call the Kentou, or study phase. Realistically, we have focused primarily on the Product Value Stream, with really no awareness that the other even exists."

"I'm curious," Brenda said, "how did we miss knowing all this?"

"Why we didn't know what to do is a long story," I said. "But the bottom line is that it was my responsibility. We didn't know all we needed to know about implementation. As I mentioned before, we didn't approach it as a system. We now know how to do this, and the Massachusetts company is willing to help us."

Nathan piped up. "This is exactly what I suspected Jon would say. We spent a whole year basically getting nowhere and now he's telling us it is much harder than he thought, so we need to redirect our money and more time and cause more disruption. Let's end this thing and get back to work."

"Nathan, I know you oppose this," Jack said. "Hell, everyone knows you oppose it. But a lot of people have invested a lot of time, and I want to hear what they've learned. Did it sink in when Jon mentioned earlier that a little company in Massachusetts has successfully implemented this?"

Nathan said nothing.

"I didn't think so," Jack grumbled. "Go ahead, Jon."

Charles said, "Jack, I'm with Nathan on this. We have to be honest with ourselves. No one in this company knows how to do this."

Jack turned an icy stare toward Charles, and I continued. "Charles just raised perhaps the most pertinent question. How do we do it? Based upon what I've learned this is what I recommend. There are three steps to address the root cause and achieve the objectives we just discussed. I will explain each one."

"Jon," Jack said, "I just found the e-mail you sent me in my junk mail."

Pointing at the first statement on the Implementation Plan slide with my laser pointer, I said, "It all starts with the Expert Workforce that can create and document Robust Visible Knowledge. This is LAMDA and A3s. We have proven that our people can solve problems more effectively with LAMDA and A3s and we can teach it. But these techniques have not yet become standard operating procedure, which in some cases is causing extra work."

Learning-First Product Development Implementation Plan

1. ***Robust Visible Knowledge Development***
   - Train everyone on LAMDA / A3's
   - Use for all problem-solving and decision-making
   - Management leads by example
2. ***Knowledge-Based Product Development***
   - Test-then-design
   - Identify Chief Engineers (project owners)
   - Define and schedule Integrating Events
   - Establish the Knowledge Value Stream. Knowledge Owner, and Checksheets
   - Capture what is learned in Set-Based Knowledge
   - Lead creation of new knowledge and establish cadence of innovation
3. ***Set-Based Concurrent Engineering***
   - Sets of possible design solutions are defined using trade-off curves generated from the Knowledge Value Stream
   - Chief Engineer leads elimination of weaker solutions until optimal product and process design is found

IRT Infrared Technologies Corporation

(Figure 8f)

"A key success factor," I continued, "is that everybody uses it and management leads by example. Ron, the president of Sonic Solutions, asserted that knowledge does not exist unless it's captured on a Knowledge Brief — that's his term for an A3. That alone changed the way decisions are made at Sonic. No more wishful thinking. No more debating — just sound decision-making based upon facts."

Charles jumped in. "I have not seen that level of acceptance in my organization."

"Nonsense, Charles," Christine said. "I've seen some of the A3s from your people. They believe in it and can do it, but they also know you don't care."

Thank you Christine, I thought. "The second step is Knowledge-Based Product Development. It ensures test-then-design, which is the underlying principle behind what we call Learning-First Product Development. This means that design decisions will not be made without documented knowledge that proves there is at least one feasible solution for both the customer and manufacturing. At Sonic, Ron did police this personally. He required that engineers show him their Knowledge Briefs, and he decided if there was enough knowledge to make the decision. Ron has recently hired a Chief Engineer to fill this role."

"Sonic must be a really small company," Nathan said, "and Ron must not have much to do."

"You're partially right," I replied. "Sonic is smaller than we are but Sonic has nearly eliminated all their loopbacks."

"I'm sure they eliminated their innovation too," Charles quipped.

"Actually, the opposite is true," I said. "And this is an important point. If we know what our limitations are up front, then we have more time and more options available to remove the limitations. If we know what knowledge is missing up front, we have more time to find or create the knowledge we need. We know we can create simulation models and build and test prototypes in days, weeks at the most. We have done so on many occasions for our Six Sigma projects and research prototypes. The reason is because we ignore most of the details required for the full product design. Sonic built a prototype that proved they could cut the size and cost of their machine in half on their first project."

"You're saying that we should be doing a lot more testing up front," Wayne said. "That makes sense."

"Given our financial situation," Nathan argued, "we don't have money to do extra testing up front."

"We seem to have money at the end of the process to fix everything that doesn't work," I replied.

"Nathan," Jack said, "do you have any idea how much money it costs when your products are late to market and riddled with defects?"

I said, "The point is, it is far cheaper to obtain the knowledge needed before you design the product with cheap and fast prototypes and a few customer visits than it is to find out what doesn't work after the design is complete."

"I have to say something here," Brian announced. "Our quality problems and late schedule slips are killing us. I was on the phone last night pleading with one of our largest customers not to cancel their order. Fortunately he's giving us another week. Hell, Nathan, it's your product."

"It's not as hard as it sounds," I added. "At Sonic, Ron plays somewhat of a Chief Engineer role. He schedules Integrating Events at the beginning of a project to determine what knowledge is needed, what technologies and manufacturing processes limit the achievement of customer needs, and what knowledge is missing. Then the engineers innovate, but it is targeted innovation because they understand the relationship between what their product and manufacturing technologies are capable of doing and what is important to customers. Engineers also team up with Marketing and visit customers to obtain that side of the missing knowledge."

Everyone was quiet so I continued. "The Knowledge Value Stream is also established in this step, and that is the most significant new concept I learned last week. Every time we solve a problem or make any design decision, we fundamentally have a single point solution. Our solution only applies to the problem at hand. This is a fundamental reason why knowledge does not flow across projects. The people who might be able to use the underlying knowledge don't know it exists or whether it applies to their problem or product. The knowledge must be generalized for as wide a range of applicability as possible. That's what trade-off curves are all about. Trade-off curves make visible a continuous set of possibilities. If your problem or product appears anywhere on that chart, then that trade-off curve is knowledge that applies to you. We know how to do this. This provides the basis for their ability to do Set-Based Concurrent Engineering — they know the ranges and limits of their design decisions."

"The last step," I said, "is *real* Set-Based Concurrent Engineering. The reason I say 'real' is because we've experimented with this in Security Systems. Basically, we've identified more alternative designs and kept them alive longer. Real Set-Based Concurrent Engineering requires the Knowledge Value Stream. Toyota starts with thousands of alternatives in the form of set-based rules and trade-off curves and narrows them down through analysis and testing until the optimal product and process design is found."

I concluded with: "None of these steps is hard if we put our mind to it. Ron, at Sonic, made the statement that it was quite straight forward — just capture the knowledge and use it relentlessly. We can double product development performance in a year and keep increasing from there."

"Jon, I followed that pretty well," Brenda said. "Can you give me a simple example of the difference between a point solution and this generalized Set-Based Knowledge? It seems that much of your logic is based on that premise."

I had actually thought about that as a possible question. I now hoped my answer would work, and not appear overly simplified.

"Let me put it this way," I said. "My wife likes a nice green lawn. I know if I make the decision to put an inch of water on the lawn a night, I will have a green lawn. That will make my wife happy, until we get the next water bill. Then I will find out she wants two things — a green lawn and a low water bill. At that point, my problem is that I only have point-based knowledge. I know one inch of water will keep my lawn green. I don't know how much less water I can use and still keep a green lawn. I also don't know how those same decisions affect my water bill. But I could easily set up some experiments that would allow me to understand the minimum amount of water that will keep my lawn green during different weather conditions, generalize that knowledge into sets of decisions and ramifications. From that, I can optimize across many solution sets." I paused, and then added, "I hope that gives a simple idea of how trade-off curves can become the generalized Set-Based Knowledge that flows across projects. At Toyota, as it should be here, any problem is not solved until the limits of that solution are known and documented."

Brenda nodded and said, "I assume it could also get quite complicated with many interactions of decisions and ramifications to customer interests." Then, with the first smile I had ever seen on her face, she said, "I appreciate your keeping it simple for us finance people."

My eye was drawn to Doyle, who looked as though he felt compelled to show that he was relevant. He said, "Yes, the principles are solid as long as they are kept simple. But our products are much more complicated."

Carl immediately spoke up. "Interestingly, Doyle, our engineering history is full of great trade-off curve applications. Maybe you remember back to your engineering days. Non-dimensional multi-parameters were defined that allowed a wide range of set-based decisions, such as the relationships of Nusselt Number, Reynolds Number, and Prandtl Number — all for defining heat transfer and fluid flow parametric relationships."

Doyle just shrugged, as if he actually understood, but didn't agree.

I continued. "This next slide shows in more detail how these three steps deliver our goals."

Learning-First Product Development Implementation Plan

	Step	IRT Benefits
1.	***Robust Visible Knowledge Development*** ➢ Train everyone on LAMDA / A3's ➢ Use for all problem solving and decision-making ➢ Management leads by example	➢Already provided 32% and 25% benefit in Civilian Avionics & Security Systems respectively. ➢Broader adoption and leadership will continue to increase productivity
2.	***Knowledge-Based Product Development*** ➢ Test-then-design ➢ Identify Chief Engineers (Project Owners) ➢ Define and schedule Integrating Events ➢ Establish the Knowledge Value Stream: Knowledge Owners and Checksheets ➢ Capture what is learned in Set-Based Knowledge ➢ Lead creation of new knowledge and establish cadence of innovation	➢$600M revenue, 7% profit in 2009 ➢1.5-2X increase in product development productivity, breakthrough innovation. ➢Company market leadership, leadership in 3 of 4 businesses ➢Knowledge is reusable across all businesses ➢Industry-leading innovation
3.	***Set-Based Concurrent Engineering*** ➢ Sets of possible design solutions are defined using trade-off curves generated from Knowledge Value Stream ➢ Chief Engineer leads elimination of weaker solutions until optimal product and process design is found	➢$750M revenue, 10% profit in 2011 ➢Leadership in all businesses ➢3-4X increase in product development productivity

IRT Infrared Technologies Corporation (Figure 8g)

I paused to allow everyone to digest the slide.

"What makes you so sure," Brenda said, "that steps one and two will deliver six hundred million in revenue and seven percent profit year after next?"

"The experience of Sonic Solutions," I replied. "Their first product was on-schedule, below cost, and had their best quality ever, which is exactly what Brian is asking for."

"Sample of one?" Brenda said.

"Yes, but one more than I had a week ago," I replied. "Plus Jan mentioned a company she's worked with in New Zealand that's twice our size that's had success using the Toyota development system. She offered to put us in touch with them."

"Explain Checksheets," Wayne said.

"I've talked about test-then-design and the Knowledge Value Stream. Every time an engineer needs to make a design decision, he or she reaches into the Knowledge Value Stream of Set-Based Knowledge, and pulls out the knowledge he or she needs in what we call Checksheets. The same knowledge serves all businesses but the Checksheets are tailored for each product and each design decision."

"I don't want to sound negative," Charles said, "but this looks awfully complicated. Last year Jon was peddling the four cornerstones. Now he's added Knowledge Value Stream, Knowledge Owners, and Checksheets. What will he have next year when we're sitting here discussing what went wrong?"

"The difference between last year and this year is that Sonic Solutions has already successfully implemented most of this," I replied.

"Charles," Jack said, shaking his head, "Jon has taken a complex and potentially extremely profitable methodology, which only a few companies in the world know how to do, and concisely explained it in three steps, and you're complaining. You could at least make it appear that you are trying to make it work."

"Where are we in terms of implementation?" Christine asked. "How long would it take?"

I put up a slide. "As you can see, step one, Visible Knowledge training and implementation are complete in Security Systems. Training is complete and implementation is in-progress in Civilian Avionics. We need to accomplish steps one and two to meet 2009 goals, and by doing so we'll be well on our way to achieving the 2011 goals."

Learning-First Product Development Implementation Plan

	Step	Status / schedule / actions
1.	***Robust Visible Knowledge Development*** ➢ Train everyone on LAMDA / A3's ➢ Use for all problem solving and decision-making ➢ Management leads by example	➢Training and implementation complete in Security Systems ➢Training complete and implementation in-progress in Civilian Avionics
2.	***Knowledge-Based Product Development*** ➢ Test-then-design ➢ Identify Chief Engineers (Project Owners) ➢ Define and schedule Integrating Events ➢ Establish the Knowledge Value Stream: Knowledge Owners and Checksheets ➢ Capture what is learned in Set-Based Knowledge ➢ Lead creation of new knowledge and establish cadence of innovation	➢Integrating Events need to be defined and scheduled ➢Establish new roles / responsibilities ➢Identify knowledge owners and train in all businesses ➢Train in Checksheet development and defining sets of possibilities ➢Implement knowledge management system
3.	***Set-Based Concurrent Engineering*** ➢ Sets of possible design solutions are defined using trade-off curves generated from the Knowledge Value Stream ➢ Chief Engineer leads elimination of weaker solutions until optimal product and process design is found	➢Train in defining / seeing / utilizing trade-off relationships for Set-Based Design

IRT Infrared Technologies Corporation (Figure 8h)

"Jack," I said, "you asked me if we could do this and my answer is yes. If we implement immediately I believe we can achieve these goals."

I held up the A3.

"How far has Sonic progressed with this," Wayne asked.

"Sonic has implemented steps one and two," I answered. "They expect to be doing full Set-Based Concurrent Engineering on their next products."

Brenda said, "I am actually quite impressed, Jon, with your logic. I believe that we should pursue this Learning-First model as you call it as a pilot." She turned and addressed the room. "But this does not relieve the need for cost reduction, and we are under the gun to improve profit immediately. We don't have years to make these improvements, as I perceive your approach will take. This company is like an aging fighter who is too slow and too fat. We need to get down to fighting weight and get our quickness back. And we need to do it now. I've talked to the four business managers and we're ready to pull the trigger. The first order of business is a cost reduction, and a twenty percent workforce reduction is a key part. Nathan and Charles have already developed their specific plans. Jack, we've all agreed to execute the cost reduction plan."

Blindsided that Nathan and Charles had been independently working with Brenda, Jack stared at them for what to them must have seemed like an hour, and then said, "Is that really what you all want? You want to start firing the people? You think that's going to fix this company?"

You could have heard the proverbial pin drop.

"Jack," Charles said at last, "it's going to happen. Our costs are too high. We've been in denial for years. We need to cut costs before it's too late."

Nathan chimed in, "We have to reduce our expenses, and that is all tied to the people count."

Doyle nodded his head in agreement as Charles and Nathan spoke. Carl tapped me on the shoulder, but my stomach muscles were too tight to turn around.

Christine said, "I agree with Jon. We can do this. I'm not ready to throw in the towel yet, and start cutting people."

"I agree with Christine," Wayne said. "I don't want to stop my Lean development program. Maybe we can do both. Jack we're in a tough spot."

"Jack," Charles said, "you can't argue with the results CTC has achieved. They increased profit from two to ten percent while also increasing market share. And the stock went through the darn roof. IRT stock is essentially worthless."

Nathan added, "This company can't attract and retain top talent with worthless stock options."

Doyle was nodding in agreement so vigorously he looked like a bobble-headed doll.

"We have to face reality," Brenda said. "We live in an age of global competition and liberated economies. The result is extreme competition. We're doing things that other companies do faster, cheaper, and better. We have to reduce costs."

Jack shook his head. His face was flush. "Jon, what else do you have?" he said.

As I'd feared, the meeting seemed to be heading toward a foregone conclusion. Brenda had appeared to be listening, but her mind had been made up coming in. I felt I had little left to fight with.

"Brenda," I said, searching for words to turn this around. I had to say something. Brenda glanced at her watch. I decided to just say it. "I'd like a little more time to work out the details of how we're going to implement this before we decide for sure that we're going to cut the workforce. I learned a lot last week and I don't understand why we are in such a hurry. I thought we were waiting until all the new products were shipping."

Brenda smiled condescendingly. "You and your team have made a lot of progress, but we're simply out of time. We have a lot of cost reduction to accomplish by the end of the year, and we've waited and waited for the new products to ship. Jon, twenty years ago the global economy was Japan, Western Europe, and the United States. Everything else was called rest-of-world. Today, low-cost industries exist all over Asia, South America, and Eastern Europe. Our manufacturing operations and supplier base just plain cost too much."

I said, "Learning-First Product Development will address cost through technology advancements that benefit all products. Besides we can't afford to take the risk that quality deteriorates."

Brenda said, "Our quality is no better than what we can get from any number of much cheaper suppliers. Look, I've traveled all over the world. I've seen hundreds of manufacturing companies. Believe me when I tell you, we are not competitive. It's time we took advantage of globalization, rather than being a victim of it. It's simple economics."

Jack shook his head. His face was still flush. "Jon, do you have anything else?"

I looked at Al. Al looked down at his PC.

"That's it," I said.

"Thanks," Jack mumbled as he stood and walked out of the room. Brian followed him.

Brenda gathered her things and left. Al followed her.

Christine put her hand on my shoulder and said, "Great job, Jon. I definitely want to implement this in my business."

"Me, too," said Wayne. They left.

Nathan, Charles, and Doyle were all smiles in the back of the room.

"We can finally get back to work," Nathan said.

"This learning-first stuff will be dead in a week," Charles added.

Doyle said to Nathan and Charles, "I want to chat with you guys about some process enhancements." Before leaving the room, Doyle turned to me with his little arrogant smile and said, "See ya', Jon."

Everyone had left but Carl, Greg, and me. Carl held is head in his hands. Greg tapped his head lightly against the wall. I slowly packed up my stuff.

After a few moments I said, "How about I buy you guys an early lunch, or maybe we should call it brunch?"

"I'd call it an early last supper," Carl grumbled.

I drove the three of us to a little restaurant that serves breakfast and lunch only.

After we had ordered, Carl said, "At least I got some good news last night. My little brother got a sales job at a Toyota dealership in Denver. He and his wife are house hunting as we speak."

"Maybe he'll let you live with him," Greg joked.

"I'll live in a tent before I live with him," Carl replied.

"Jon, what are you going to do?" Greg asked.

"Retire," I said, "and play golf. I'm hoping for a mild winter. In fact, I may call Troy this afternoon. The days of him beating me are soon to be over."

"How about you guys?" I asked Greg and Carl.

"I'm updating my resume this afternoon," Carl said, "and calling people starting tomorrow. I'm a believer in the early bird and there aren't that many good jobs in this area."

"How about you, Greg?" I asked.

"I don't know," Greg said. "Part of me wants to stay but I know it's going to be different. I hate to say it, but I think I'm holding on to the past."

I raised my glass. "Here's to 31 years at good ole IRT." We toasted.

The waiter served our food

"This may have gone the wrong way," I said, "but we figured out how to implement Toyota-like Product Development, and it would have worked. I believe that and really appreciate all your help."

Greg said, "You know what I can't figure out is Al. Yesterday I thought he was coming around, but today he didn't say a word."

"He knows who his boss is and what she believes," Carl said. "So it really doesn't matter what he thinks, or what the truth is." Carl shook his head. "And he accused us of wishful thinking."

My phone rang. It was Donna. "Hello Donna," I said wondering what more could go wrong today.

"Jon," she said, "Brenda wants you in the Executive Board Room in fifteen minutes."

"What about," I said chewing my omelet.

"She just said to be there," Donna said.

"I thought you always included a topic," I reminded her.

"Where are you?" she asked.

"I'm having brunch with Carl and Greg."

"Take the fork out of your mouth and get back here," she commanded and hung up.

We grabbed to-go boxes and drove back. I hurried to Mahogany Row and headed for the Executive Board Room. Donna waved me over to her desk and said, "The meeting won't start for a few minutes because I just got a hold of Jack. He was up in the mountains."

I nodded. "He was probably hunting wild game with his bare hands."

"Look at this," Donna said and motioned me around to behind her desk so I could see her PC monitor.

It was a live protest of some sort.

"What is it?" I asked.

"The company that Consumer Technologies is buying staged a walkout after they learned of the plan to cut the workforce. They are having a rally against the merger and they want their CEO to be fired for agreeing to take ten million dollars to sell the company. Apparently, most of their Research Lab walked out."

"Who's the guy in the lab coat?" I asked.

"He's their chief scientist — some famous research Ph.D. He organized the whole thing."

"Is that what's-his-name?" I asked, "The movie star?"

"Yes, they invited a few actors. CTC's stock has dropped over ten bucks and is now under twenty dollars a share."

"Whoa," I said. "That's got to be embarrassing."

Just then, Al walked out of Brenda's office and over to Donna's desk.

"What's going on?" I said.

"Brenda wants to talk to us," Al said.

Al and I entered Brenda's office. She was on her cell phone in front of the window. "Gene," she said, "cut your losses and put it behind you. It will all be forgotten in a month." She waved us in. The bright sunlight exposed wrinkles I had not seen this morning. Maybe this had been rough on her, too.

Al whispered to Jon, "Gene is the CEO of CTC."

Brenda hung up and shook her head.

"How's Gene doing?" Al asked.

"He's a wreck," Brenda answered.

"I'm glad I'm not at CTC," Al said.

"He simply didn't do his homework," Brenda said. "He tries to buy a company in Hollywood, California, with the most narcissistic workforce in the country. They even had bleeding heart actors speaking at their rally.

She took a deep breath. "Jon," she said, "apparently you've made quite an impression on Al. He's been lobbying on your behalf for over an hour. He wants to delay the cost reduction until we have time to more thoroughly work out a plan for Learning-First Product Development. As soon as Jack arrives, I want to put that question to Jack and Brian."

Donna opened the door. "Jack's here," she said. "He and Brian are in the Board Room."

Brenda, Al, and I walked in the Board Room. Al sat in the front, across from Jack. Brenda sat next to him, across from Brian. I sat next to Brian.

"I'd like to continue the discussion we had this morning," Brenda said. "Al, I'd like you to share what you showed me."

"Sure," Al said, plugging his laptop into the projector.

"Since we're basing our recommendation on CTC, let me show you what has happened there."

Al put up a slide.

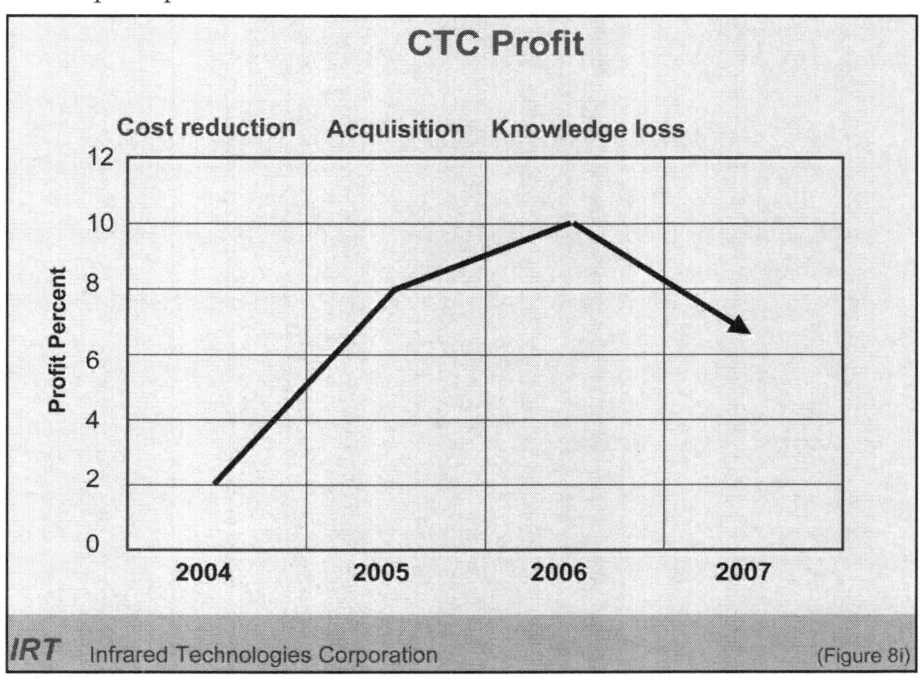

(Figure 8i)

"In 2004 CTC executed a broad cost reduction plan. Twenty percent of the workforce was cut and a building was sold. Profit improved from two to eight percent in 2005 because costs were reduced while revenue remained constant. Last year profit reached ten percent because CTC acquired a medical company with fifteen percent profit. This year profit is projected to be less than seven percent because so much knowledge left the company with the people who were cut."

Brenda cut in. "Seven percent profit is a lot better than two percent but the trend is clearly disturbing."

"I have to tell you," Brian bellowed in his loud voice, "a strategy that relies on mergers for growth scares the hell out of me because most mergers fail. My last company bought a business that was supposed to have a red-hot sales force. Most of them quit within a year."

Al said, "You're not alone. CTC's plan to restore their profit was to buy another medical company and cut their workforce. It looks like that merger is not going through. Now let me shift gears to IRT. We know IRT's product development productivity is fairly low."

"It stinks," Jack grunted.

Al said, "You're right, it stinks. Our product development productivity is so bad that we can't design a product without expensive and time-consuming unplanned redesigns. We can forget about innovation because everyone is consumed fighting fires just to get the products out."

Al glanced around. All eyes were riveted on him. "We have two options. The first is we can continue to be really bad at product development and cut the workforce and outsource manufacturing — which will probably make us even worse at product development — and we can roll the dice on acquisitions."

"Last week CTC provided two scores on our product development assessment," I added. "One for today and one for three years ago, and their product development performance has declined since the workforce reduction."

Al took a deep breath and put up his next slide.

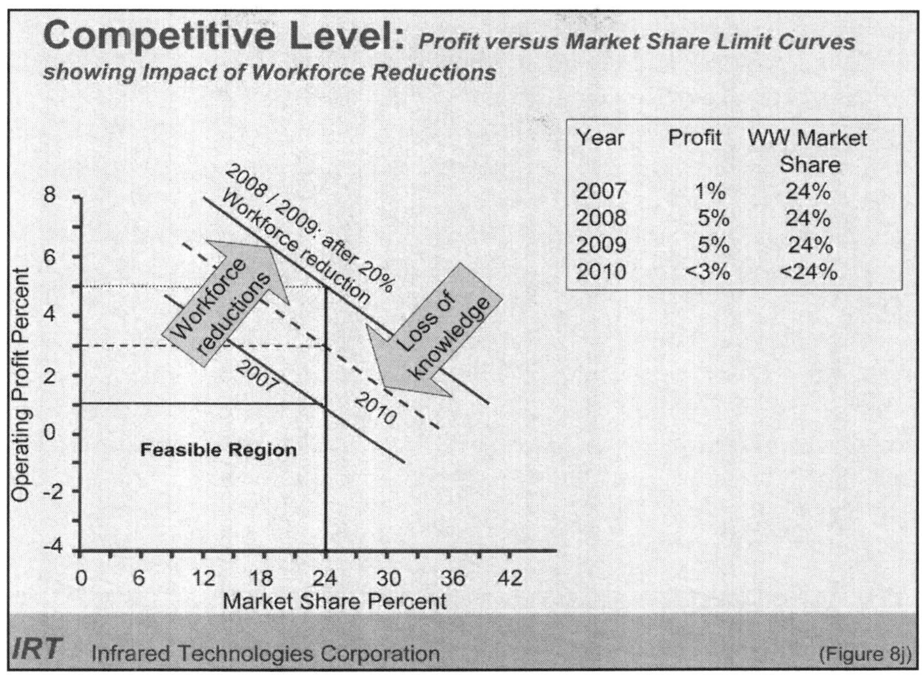

Year	Profit	WW Market Share
2007	1%	24%
2008	5%	24%
2009	5%	24%
2010	<3%	<24%

(Figure 8j)

"I prepared this model of what will happen in the Security Systems division if we execute a twenty percent workforce reduction. Jon taught me that trade-off curves are a big part of the Toyota system. This is an economic trade-off curve between profit and market share. In the short term, profit can be traded off for market share by lowering prices and visa versa along the trade-off curve. It won't really be linear, but that's an adequate approximation for the ranges of values we'd actually consider. But the key point is that profit and market share cannot intersect at a point higher than the trade-off curve. Any questions?"

"What is 'competitive level'?" Brian asked.

"'Competitive level' is what I am calling the curve," Al replied. "If the curve moves up and to the right the 'competitive level' increases."

Brian nodded that he understood.

Al continued. "A 20% workforce reduction will increase the competitive level in the short-term because cost decreases while revenue is constant, resulting in higher profit, higher market share or both. But the loss of knowledge will reduce our ability to compete in the long term."

"So," Brian said, "you're saying that a 20% workforce reduction will increase profit in Security Systems from one to five percent with the same market share, but that the loss of knowledge will push profit back down in two or three years?"

"Yes," Al replied. "That is my prediction."

"What do we do in two or three years?" Brian asked.

Al said, "To keep your profit up, we'd take action that would further reduce costs, such as outsourcing manufacturing or another workforce reduction."

"And a couple years later," Brian said. "What do we do then?"

"More workforce reductions and more lost knowledge," Al replied. "The loss of knowledge will always eventually result in loss of market share and profit. Thinking otherwise is wishful thinking."

I said, "Toyota wins by knowing more, learning faster, and applying it better. Toyota's competitors have been working the lower cost and acquisition model for years, to no avail. Any strategy that results in the loss of knowledge is doomed — unless the competition is losing knowledge faster. It is inevitable."

Al put up a new slide.

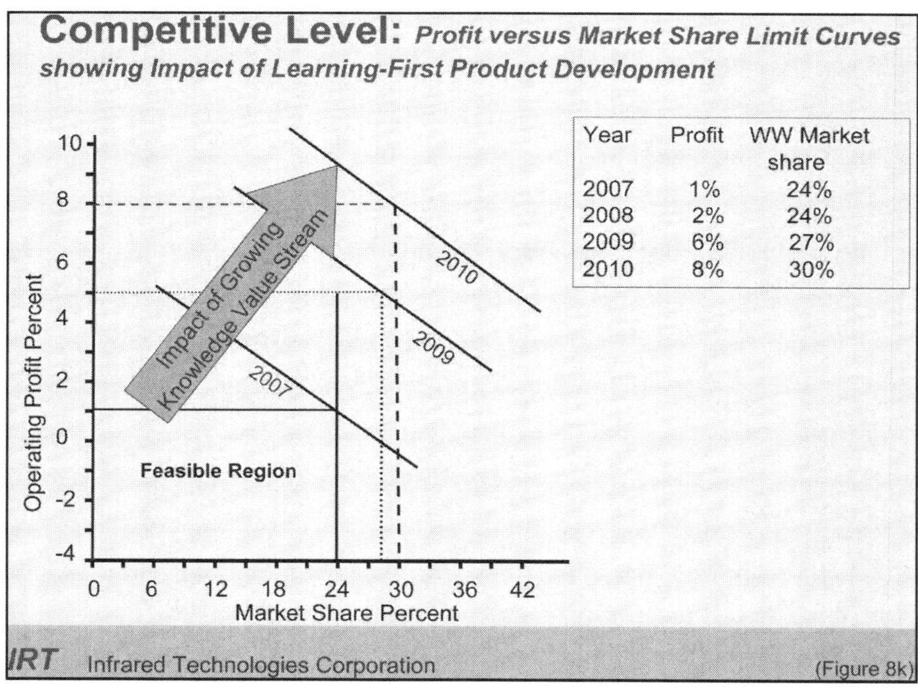

"Here's the other option," Al said. "Learning-First Product Development won't move the trade-off curve as fast as a workforce reduction due to the time required to train and implement. But I'm confident that Sonic Solutions results can be duplicated, which means Security Systems will do better the year after next under this scenario and continue to increase from there."

Brenda added, "Al thinks we will do better than this graph shows but I'd like to over-achieve, so I had him scale back 2010."

Al continued. "Brenda wanted a real example, so we came up with one in 15 minutes. The Y-axis is net profit on this chart because that was easier to find. For IRT we've been talking operating profit."

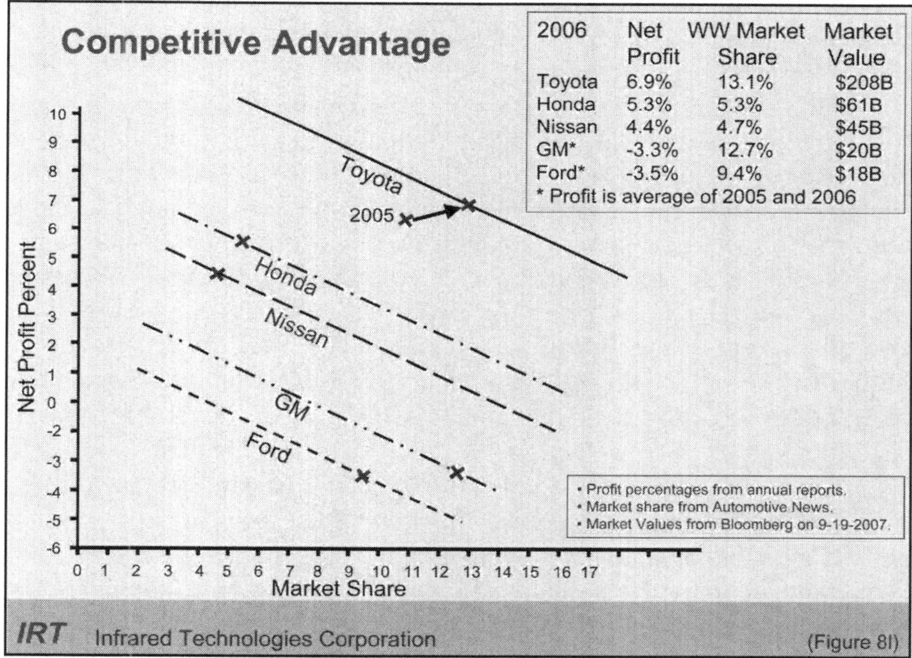

(Figure 8l)

"Look how far Toyota moved in one year," Brenda said as she stood, walked to the screen, and pointed at the 2005 point and 2006 line for Toyota.

Al said, "Bear in mind that Toyota has added roughly seventy billion in additional revenue in five years to bring the total to about a hundred and eighty billion."

"How did GM and Ford do in 2005?" Brian asked.

"We looked into that," Al explained, "but the problem is GM took a large restructuring charge in 2005 so net profit was negative 5.3%. In 2006 net profit improved to negative one percent. Ford did the opposite. It took a large restructuring charge in 2006 and net profit was negative 7.8%, down from positive 0.8% in 2005. The swings did not represent significant differences in business performance, so we decided to average them. In my opinion, GM and Ford aren't stable enough to draw any year to year conclusions."

"What about the other Japanese auto-makers?" Brian asked. "Are their product development systems like Toyota's?"

I said, "According to Dr. Allen Ward, Honda uses a similar product development system to Toyota, but they are more secretive. He knew that because he had talked to Honda's suppliers. He said Nissan and other Japanese auto companies do not."

"Where are Daimler and Chrysler?" Jack asked.

"In 2006, DaimlerChrysler's market share was 6.7%and net profit was two percent," Al replied, "so DaimlerChrysler's competitive line would be between GM and Nissan. I left them out because Daimler unloaded Chrysler and Daimler's stock has significantly increased since then, so their market share does not reflect the combined company anymore."

"Now let's get to the hard part," Brenda said, "Toyota's operating profit is ten percent and their net profit is seven percent and that's as good as it gets in the automotive industry. Its market value is a little higher than its revenue. But there are lots of companies that earn much higher percent profit and have market values that are several times their revenue."

Brenda looked around the room to make sure she had everyone's undivided attention, and then continued. "The question is how do we get IRT's profit consistently above seven percent and reach double digits in some years with strong growth, so we achieve a market value that is several times revenue?"

Wow, I thought to myself. *Ten percent profit and a two hundred and eight billion dollar market value doesn't cut it for Brenda.*

Al said, "The point is we have to figure out what to do with the Automotive Business. We don't want to spend three of four years improving profit from negative five to positive one. We think we can achieve the needed profit and growth in the other three businesses."

"I'll tell you what we should do," I said. "Let's create trade-off curves that showcase our technology and show them to Toyota and Honda and see if they'll buy our products."

Jack looked at Brian. "We should be able to do that."

"It's worth a try," Brian said. "We know our problem is we have the wrong customers."

I said, "Allen Ward said that Denso does that all the time to prove their products are superior to the competition, and Jan said Sonic showed their trade-off curves to their customers and their customers love them."

"We looked at the Toyota and Denso numbers over the last five years," Brenda said. "Toyota's profit ranges from seven to ten percent and Denso ranges from six to eight percent. If Toyota and Denso are the best, can we really expect to consistently achieve seven percent or better?"

"What's worse," Al added, "is that the auto industry suffers the most when energy prices increase. Material prices increase and the cost of gasoline increases. Do we want to bet that energy prices are going down? That sounds like wishful thinking."

"What's holding Toyota back?" Brian asked.

"They haven't figured out the next generation power source," I answered. "If they were selling plug-in hybrids with a 60 mile range that run on E-85 ethanol for a reasonable price, their market value would go through the roof."

"Right," Al said. "Or fuel cells or something that sets them apart from the industry. A lot of companies sell hybrids now."

"I wouldn't bet against them," I added.

"The point is," Al continued, "if you don't have the needed technology or know-how, then you have to acquire it. That needs to be the focus of our acquisitions, and also in what we contract out to suppliers. It is all about the intelligent growth and use of knowledge. That is the Toyota strategy and it should be ours. Broad people-cutting and risky acquisitions make no sense to me anymore."

Without waiting for reactions, Al rolled on. "Here's a slide that integrates the two strategies. Learning-First Product Development will build a vault of knowledge that is used by all four businesses. We still offload design and manufacturing activities that suppliers can do faster, better, and cheaper than we can, but instead of a workforce reduction, we move resources up the value chain to develop product and manufacturing capabilities that customers value."

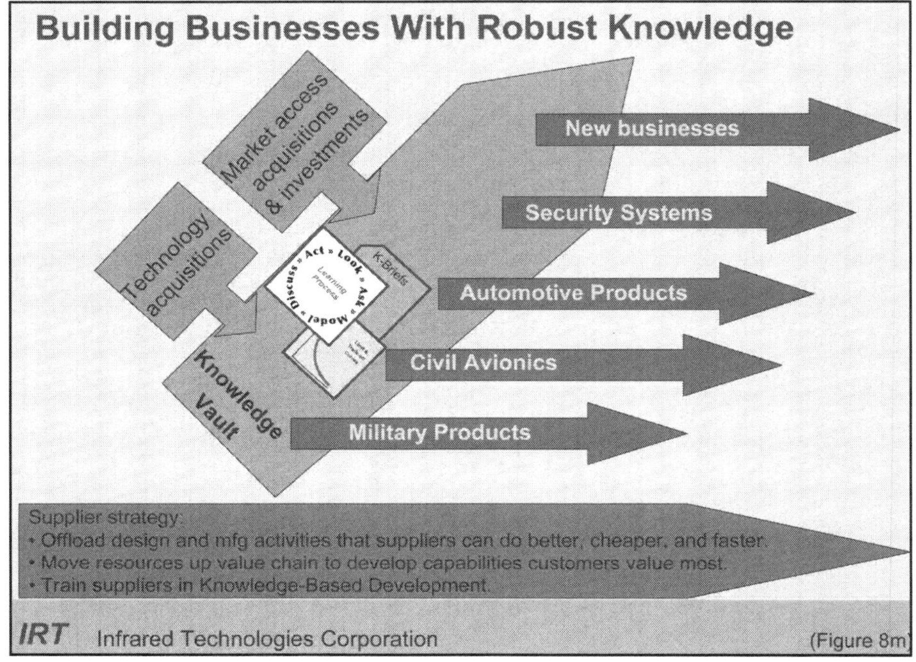

(Figure 8m)

"If this works," Brenda added, "productivity will be high enough that reinvesting in the businesses will earn a better return on investment than workforce cost reductions."

"Well put," Al said. "In two or three years our product development productivity should be two or three times what it is today so investments in the businesses will earn an acceptable return on investment. After we become proficient, we train our suppliers. But it's critical that we acquire important technology that is either locked up in patents or that we don't have the expertise to develop. We also need to acquire companies or make investments to expand our market access."

"Or we hire people with the expertise we need," Jack said, "and let them create the knowledge. Maybe I'm old fashioned but I think acquisitions should be a last resort."

"Good point," Al said. "I'll add that to the slide."

"Now," Brenda said, "what we're talking about is a major change in strategy, and I want to know how you feel about embracing this. Jack, I think I know how you feel."

"I want to tell you anyway," Jack said. "A year ago I read that one of Toyota's key philosophies is 'trust your people.' I strongly believe in that. I trusted Jon to pull this thing off, and he figured it out, although he had me a little nervous for a while. You know I want to put all my energy behind it."

"Brian," Brenda said.

"For me, it's pretty simple," Brian said. "Cutting people is wrong. Fixing our problems is right."

"Al or Jon," Brenda said. "Do you want to add anything?"

Neither of us did.

"This is what I propose we do," Brenda said. "We delay the decision on the workforce reduction a week. Jack, you and I will talk to Ron Morrison at Sonic as soon as possible. Jon, you mentioned earlier today that Jan would be willing to put us in touch with the leaders of a company in New Zealand that's twice our size that's implemented this strategy. I also want to talk to them this week. Jon, please set that up. I'd like to talk to their CEO and the executive team, and to invite everyone here to participate. And we still need a solution for Automotive Products. Jack, can you come up with a proposal by the end of the week?"

"Sure," Jack replied.

"Good," Brenda said. "I want to know by the end of the week whether we know enough to take this thing on. Anything else?"

"I'm curious," I said. "What caused you to change you mind about this?"

"After the meeting this morning," she said, "Al reinforced that knowledge is an asset, which if properly developed and deployed, can provide an always-increasing competitive advantage. There are few investments with that potential. I just don't know if we can do it in a reasonable time frame."

DISCUSSION

In the first book, the important role Product Development needed to play in leading this change was emphasized. In this book, and particularly in this chapter, we emphasize that this change is in reality a complete business system change and needs to be thought of that way. Product Development is not an island. It profoundly affects all other core business processes. As we have observed, the companies that have gone the farthest in the lean product development journey are the ones that have approached it from a broader perspective than product development alone.

In particular, the strategic planning, marketing, and manufacturing processes all have to be understood in the context of the complete business system. Indeed, the involvement of these areas needs to be more than just understanding and adapting to the changes. They need to be fully vested stakeholders in defining and implementing the new system. That is what this chapter was all about, as the financial perspective of change was integrated with the engineering.

Realistically, IRT still has not completed the discussion part of the change. The marketing and manufacturing sides of the company still need to be much more involved in both defining and executing the new system. They are huge sources of knowledge about the customer needs and manufacturing capabilities and as such need to play key roles in the successful implementation of the full learning-first model.

Chapter 9
Deciding on a Recommendation
(Can we do it?)

Discussion can compare alternatives but also needs to prepare the plan for implementing the alternatives. All planning needs to precede actually doing (i.e., PDCA).

Thursday Morning: IRT

I arrived at the plant at about 7:30 a.m. Yesterday, I'd spent the entire day setting up a conference call with the G&K Appliance Company in New Zealand. They were about twice the size of IRT, so I was hopeful they could provide some insight into how to implement this on a larger scale. Brenda had really pushed to have the meeting take place as soon as possible. I was concerned that her expectations for the meeting would not be realized. Except for what Jan had told me, I new almost nothing about them. I also felt somewhat guilty about getting Jan involved, but she didn't seem to mind. Perhaps it soothed her conscience about leaving IRT.

When I'd left for home yesterday evening, Donna and her counterpart in New Zealand were working out the timing details. The company was very gracious in agreeing to this conference call on such short notice.

I entered Mahogany Row. Donna was on the phone. I walked to her desk, and she handed me the phone.

"Jan wants to talk to you," she said. "I still can't believe you let her go."

I suppressed the urge to grunt and took the phone. "Hi, Jan," I said. "Haven't talked to you since yesterday. I really appreciate your time. Is everything set?"

"Yes, I think so," she replied. "We are meeting at two p.m. today your time, four p.m. my time, and eight tomorrow morning New Zealand time. Mac Fraser, who is your counterpart, will be on the line. He has guided the transformation. There's a possibility one or two others will be on the line as well, maybe the CEO."

"Really?!" I exclaimed. "That would be great."

"The CEO is iffy, according to Mac, on this short notice. But he is in town and will be on the line if possible. His name is Don Baldwin. Mac has led their program. Don is the inspiration. I hope this all works out, Jon. I really don't know where they are in their transformation since I left. You'd better prepare yourself. They might tell you not to try."

"Thanks, Jan." I said. "I was already worried about it without you reminding me."

"By the way, Jon," Jan said, "you know if Doyle is on the line — I am hanging up, right?"

"You're safe," I said. "It will be just Jack, Brian Hawkins from Marketing, Brenda, Al Frank who works for Brenda, and me."

I handed the phone back to Donna and said, "So what's the plan?"

"Do you realize that it is now about midnight tomorrow in New Zealand?" she said. "Wouldn't it have been a lot easier to find a company in the U.S.? You'll be in the Board Room at 2 p.m. Everyone knows where to call in." She glanced around as if to make sure no one was watching. "Jack and Brenda spent most of yesterday talking. I actually saw them smile some. So, tell me, is Jack just giving up or is Brenda leaving the dark side to come into the light?"

It occurred to me that my answer might go a long way toward Brenda becoming accepted by the rank and file of the company. "I think" I said slowly, "Brenda is listening with an open mind."

"Good!" she said.

I headed back to my office to think through some questions I might want to ask. There really wasn't much else I could do. I felt responsible for the outcome, but totally out of control of the situation.

I spent the morning debriefing Greg and Carl, who were feeling a bit left out of the process. We also thought through various scenarios, both for the meeting, and more important, for how we could gracefully redirect our implementation. Al joined us a couple of times. Carl now seemed to accept Al. It certainly was nice not to have to play the role of referee.

What bothered me most about this transformation was momentum and staying power. This had been the problem with our current change approach. We were piloting Toyota principles, but not piloting the actual transformation of the business. Jan's company overcame that because the president forced the issue by inserting himself into the role of knowledge police. The New Zealand company was larger. It would be interesting to see how they approached this. Brenda and Jack were going to push hard for progressive and impressive business results. The promise of a big bang result was not in the cards. But there would have to be visible pay back from the start — measurable benefits — and a clear path to domination of our markets.

I arrived at the Board Room about a quarter to two. I really liked this conference room — chairs upholstered in leather. It was a totally different environment than the typical stark conference room at IRT. Twelve people could be seated comfortably around the thickest mahogany table I'd ever seen. Donna was already there to ensure all the conference room voice connections were working. She'd already signed in as the conference leader.

"So, is it all working?" I said.

"I hope so," she said. "I've never done this across different days before. It still seems odd we will we talking with people that are already well into tomorrow."

Jack, Brenda and Al walked in together. Jack and Brenda took the two seats across from each other at the front of the room. Interestingly, Brenda took the seat that Ray normally took when he was in attendance. Al sat next to me, about half way back. Brian Hawkins, the marketing VP, came in and sat next to Brenda. I was pleased he was there. I now knew that I should have included him from the start. Marketing involvement is key, as is Manufacturing, when you think of this all as a system.

In order to not set expectations that were too ambitious, I began, "Jack, Brenda, you know that this meeting might not give you the assurances of success that you are looking for, right?"

Jack said, "We know. But it's another point of knowledge. We talked to Ron Morrison at Sonic yesterday. Besides, it will give me a chance to say hello to Jan."

"How did your call go with Ron?"

"The three things I really like," Jack said, "are the notion that knowledge does not exist unless it is captured in a Knowledge Brief, test-then-design, and that engineers must understand customer needs. We can implement those tomorrow and have significant impact on next year's products."

"Sonic has made great progress," Brenda added. "They have just about cut their product development cycle time in half, significantly reduced cost, and quality is the best ever. However, we learned there are two major differences between Sonic and IRT. Obviously Sonic is much smaller, but also their products are high price and low volume. Our products are higher volume and lower price. I think that's an important difference, but I don't know what it means yet."

I was hoping Ron would put Brenda over the top but it didn't sound like she was convinced yet.

As if on cue, a new caller joined and Jan announced herself.

"This is Jan Morris."

Jack said, "Hello Jan, this is Jack. Welcome back. Also, congratulations."

"Thanks," Jan replied. "It's good to be back, at least for today. I'm glad this isn't a video conference. I am approaching blimp size."

Jack introduced Jan to Brenda, Al, and Brian. And after a few minutes of small talk, another caller beeped in and a strong Scottish accent came through the speaker. "Good mornin', this is Mac Fraser calling from G&K Appliances in New Zealand."

"Hi, Mac. This is Jan Morris." She thanked him for helping and introduced all of the IRT people. I was impressed that she remembered the names.

Mac introduced Gary Gwynn, the VP over Manufacturing, Thom Anderson, the Center Head over several product lines, and Don Baldwin, the CEO of the company. Brenda seemed particularly pleased that Don was on the line.

I thought it was interesting that they seemed to have adopted some of the naming of the Toyota organization. I had not heard the use of Center Head outside the context of Toyota.

We spent a few minutes in small talk. There did seem to be a camaraderie based on common goals of lean product development. The New Zealanders seemed quite gracious and willing to help — even offered to host us to visit their plant. We all volunteered to go. Even Brenda commented that it would be true to the LAMDA principles. The small talk also got us used to all the different dialects of the participants.

Just as I was trying to decide how to start the business discussions, Jack took over. I relaxed somewhat. This was the way it should be.

"Let me tell you why we are calling," Jack said. "As a company, we are profitable but not to the level that our shareholders expect. We have bought into the Toyota principles, as taught to us by Allen Ward and Jan. We believe these principles will allow us to double our productivity in two years and quadruple it in four. That will give us the leverage to dominate our market." He took a breath and continued. "We're a year into our change. We've achieved about twenty-one percent improvement, but that's not good enough. We're wondering, are our expectations real? Is our approach right? We would like to hear from you about your experiences."

Brian, our Marketing VP, jumped in. "This is Brian Hawkins. I'd also like to get your feel on the impact that's occurred on your ability to innovate as a result of this system. I'm concerned that there's too much emphasis on knowledge gaps, and that will hamper innovation."

Gary Gwynn then spoke up from New Zealand. "This is Gary — over our production operations. You blokes haven't mentioned Manufacturing. That's where a huge amount of wasted knowledge is. Are you working that as a part of your change? We are now, but got started a little late — in my opinion."

Jack said, "Actually we haven't yet, but we fully appreciate the problem. Yes, we would like to hear your experiences there as well."

Don, the CEO, then said, "Those are bloody good questions. I will take some of them and let Mac discuss the implementation details. Our goal is similar to yours. We want to dominate the high-end appliance market as soon as possible, and want to show steady growth toward achieving that status. We have quality issues from the past that still impact us, and our metrics were similar to yours based on discussions with Jan yesterday. Our company has always been known for innovation. In the past, we would aggressively insert innovation goals into our funded projects, but we just couldn't get the products out of design. They seem to wallow forever until we'd have to back off on innovation in order to ship the product, or finally cancel the project. Cost overruns, loopbacks, resource shortages, and really overworked engineers, were the norm. We were in an endless swirl of debate."

Don paused for a second, then continued. "I believe the goals you stated are absolutely achievable, but you won't achieve them without absolute commitment from the top. Is your CEO on board with this change?"

"Absolutely," Brenda said. "Jack and I together have full authority to make this happen."

Don said, "Well, let me make you feel a bit incompetent. There is no logical reason for this to be as hard as it is. The engineers buy into this like no other initiative we have had. It makes perfect sense, and there is nothing bloody hard about any of it. What makes it difficult is that it is a complete new system that impacts everybody and it is a new paradigm that we don't know how to manage. That is why the leaders have to be involved — the management rules are different and nobody can be left out. Gary is right. We left Manufacturing out too long, also Marketing, and it is still hurting us — although we have largely corrected that, thanks to Jan." He paused. "I will now turn it over to Mac to discuss details. Recognize, he is an ornery old Scotsman, who says what he wants, and doesn't care who is in the room — including me."

"Oh, man," Mac responded with a laugh and Scottish accent. "I knew Don was going to introduce me that way, but I guess there is some truth to it. I will apologize before we start if I offend anybody. So what specifically would you like me to cover?"

I'd thought about the question beforehand and immediately answered. "Mac, I think we will all appreciate your candor. I would like you to walk us through the following:

- How did you get started?
- How did you progress through the change, and why that approach?
- What would you have done differently?
- Any specific recommendations for us?"

I looked around the table. "Any other requests from our side?"

Brenda said, "Yes, those are good. I'd also like any ideas about recognizing when there are problems and how to address them."

Mac said, "Good, I think I can cover all those. I would also like an open discussion from your perspectives. By no means do we have all the answers, but we are far enough along to know this is right and we will work out the issues. Back-sliding is not an option. Actually, that is my first advice.

"Now, to your questions. We got started when one of our engineers began reading the books on the Toyota system and passed them along to me. I passed them along to Don, who passed them to his direct reports. We all saw the differences and the potential. Since I was the one that passed the book to Don, he assigned me to make it happen.

"The first thing we did was to invite Allen Ward, a few months before his tragic accident, to visit us," he said. "But because it was such a long trip, we invited him for several days. Looking back, that might have been the smartest thing we accidentally did. Allen spent most of the time talking to the engineers in small groups in both of our major plants. By the end of the week, our engineering community was well exposed to the Toyota cornerstones. The engineers started the journey, and I believe were taking ownership of the change. Don has made it clear ever since that this would be a participative change."

Brenda said, "Pardon me for interrupting, Mac. That's an interesting point. Let me ask Jon a question — do our developers and engineers really understand and feel involved in this change, or do they view it as just another of the change initiatives invented and directed from the top?"

My reaction was that the engineers certainly would identify with this change more than a twenty percent layoff cost initiative, but once I thought for a second, I realized the answer was not that simple.

"A little bit of both," I said, honestly. "But realistically, our engineering community has bought into the principles, but not in a sudden dramatic way by immersing themselves quickly into them along with a no-holds barred management attitude. Rather, our piloting approach made it possible for the detractors to manipulate the change to some degree. As a result, we never jump started our momentum."

Mac said, "We do have our detractors, too. I call them slaggards. That's part of my job — to convert them. But I agree with the word momentum. Maintaining the momentum was my job, and Don always made it very clear as to our direction."

I said, "We definitely also have our slaggards as you call them. I must admit, sometimes I think they are winning. How do you motivate them?"

Mac said in a firm voice, "It depends on the problem. If they don't understand, I explain and encourage. If they are fighting our direction, I kick their bloody asses. It is not hard to tell their motivation."

His answer was so simple and correct, I felt silly for asking it. It occurred to me that Jan was probably trying to figure how to get Doyle to New Zealand.

Mac said, "We then quickly moved into lots of training in the Toyota problem solving methodology. We followed Allen's approach with the LAMDA methodology and the A3 as the documentation of the learning. We also learned to understand and develop trade-off curves of our capabilities to meet a wide range of customer interests. Surprisingly, we found that our problem-solving capability had gone downhill for years. We had lost the art of really digging to the root cause and permanently solving problems. We had overburdened our engineers to the point of routinely jumping to solutions. In his teachings, Allen focused on the waste of wishful thinking that was clearly embedded in our problem solving techniques.

"Now we ran into a bump in the road, and with Allen gone, we really had to fight through it by ourselves. Still are, actually," he said. "We were solving long standing problems, and we were generating lots of great A3s. We were also generating trade-off curves with many documented successes. We knew we were on the right path, but . . . but it was too hit-and-miss. Many engineers were still working as before — seemingly as though they didn't have time to do it right. We were having hundreds of A3s with good knowledge. But our ability to manage and share them with the people that needed to know was being overwhelmed."

Brenda said, "Mac, you are worrying me."

I wondered whether she was serious or just giving Mac a breather. I must admit that I'd thought the same things might happen, if and when we really got rolling.

With a genuine laugh, Mac said, "Actually, it's going to get worse, but remember, even with these problems, our engineering capability was clearly increasing. We now were developing knowledge for accurate decision-making. Here is an interesting result that we think is very positive. Prior to this switch, our engineers only did about twenty percent of the work before handing off to experts. We are now approaching ninety percent in areas where the knowledge is documented and reused.

"However," he said, "what we began to recognize was that our organizational structure was built for task-based administrative control — not for knowledge-based decision-making. We needed to reorganize to support this new thinking. We decided to follow the Toyota model quite closely. We defined our functional systems and organized the engineers into these functions. The functional owners would own and organize the knowledge. Chief engineers would be at the same organizational level but would be responsible for making the system level decisions. Center heads were named over the major business units. We actually reshuffled the deck as to who had what positions. The change from an administrative based system to a knowledge based system forces a lot of rethinking of roles and responsibilities — and leadership compatibilities."

Jack said, "Are you telling me that you actually did a mass reevaluation of your leaders to put them in new roles based on their capabilities to either manage knowledge and the people, or to design and integrate the products? Are you saying that their prior positions were not a primary consideration for similar roles? That's a huge commitment."

"That's Jack talking, right?" Don said. "In a nutshell, the fundamental change we are making is from a task-based system environment to one driven by good engineering decisions. The engineers will gladly make that switch. Not to have the project and knowledge ownership aligned accordingly will never work. So, yes, it is a huge management commitment, but it is one that we felt had to be made. We had reached somewhat of a comfortable plateau of robust problem solving. Then, we made this organizational commitment that made it clear we were not going back. We reorganized to ensure the principles would be maintained.

"That was bold," Jack said. "Did they all know what was expected in their new roles and how to interact?"

"No, they didn't at all," Mac answered with his strong Scottish accent, which seemed to vary based on his level of excitement. "That was the scary part of it all and the beautiful part. We threw the whole lot into the pond and said — 'swim.' But there was no doubt from then on as to our commitment."

Jan said, "That point for us was when Ron announced that knowledge did not exist unless it was on a K-Brief, and that no product would move into detailed design until he personally approved that the knowledge supported it. Everyone knew the rules were permanently changed."

Don Baldwin added, "Realistically, all of these changes are still sorting themselves out. It is a huge philosophical change when you move from thinking of product development as a series of prescribed tasks to one of learning, and the flow of the resulting knowledge into products. I don't see any continuous improvement approaches ever getting there. You have to change the environment, and then let continuous improvements take over from there. I don't perceive that you have made such a visible commitment — am I correct?"

"Yes, you are," Jack said in a way that clearly indicated he understood, agreed, and took responsibility.

Jan spoke up. "This is Jan. I'd like to comment to steer things away from what I fear might be the wrong place to focus. I completely agree with Don about the need for absolute leadership commitment and that the project and functional leadership must be aligned to knowledge-based decisions, not defined by tasks or compliance metrics. However, that does not mean that you have to organize exactly like Toyota. We are too small to organize that way — our engineers have to bridge across functions. But you have to have the healthy conflict between those who have the knowledge of your capabilities and those who have the knowledge of how to optimize that knowledge into great products for customers. Your organization must support that conflict. But it does not have to mimic the Toyota organization exactly."

"Good point, Jan," Mac said. "I absolutely agree with that. Another thing that an organization change of some sort does is show real top-level commitment. It helps maintain momentum. Do not allow an organization to stay in place that will not or cannot change from processes based on tasks to processes based on knowledge. Be realistic. Expecting the engineers to be rigorous designers and problem solvers and a management team focused on administrative tasks for progress will not be sustainable."

Jack and Brenda were taking copious notes. That was positive.

Don continued, "Yes, this organization change was positive, as it maintained momentum and began getting the right people aligned to the right jobs. But it brought us another problem, or an opportunity, to cast it in a positive light. We realized that this was not just a product development system, it was a business system affecting all areas of our organization. All of my reports began complaining. Marketing was complaining that engineering was not responding to their demands. Manufacturing complained that nothing was really changing from their perspective. The organization change in product development had stirred up a hornet's nest."

Mac jumped in. "Indeed it did, but it forced us to address this as a complete system. Looking back, we now realized our marketing and engineering relationship was completely broken. As a company, we survive on our innovation and keeping ahead of the customer on what he will want in the future, primarily in the realm of styling and features. What we didn't have was the ability to see all the knowledge gaps for reliability and quality. This allowed too many of our projects to be designed too early based on great ideas and wishful thinking. The new knowledge coming from our LAMDA thinking and trade-off curves was able to temper that, but the marketing processes were not aligned to that thinking. We had to change that."

I noticed Brenda give Jack a look that seemed to say, *What in the world are we getting ourselves into?* Jack actually appeared a little angry. I'd seen that look before. It generally meant he was blaming himself for not seeing all this before now, and reacting. I have to admit that I felt much the same. We'd taken the easy road, whereas these companies were attacking the problem from a system perspective.

Gary, the Manufacturing VP, added his perspective. "In Manufacturing Operations, we applauded the new emphasis on knowledge-based decisions but we still were seeing and complaining about the same design problems — nothing seemed to be changing. We were loaded with knowledge in Manufacturing — from simple rules to complex process relationships — that was not getting into the development process. Again, we realized this was a system problem that we had to address."

Mac said, "But remember, while we were recognizing these problems existed, we were still getting great benefits from our robust problem solving and the generation of limit curves. But we had to complete our system. So we called Jan to see if she could help."

Brenda said, "And how did you know to call Jan?"

Mac said, "When he was here, Allen Ward had referenced her and her company as making great early progress. He had given us her contact information. So we called her. Jan, why don't you take it from here?"

"Sure," she said. "When Mac called, we'd already come to the realization that this was a complete business system. Luckily our company was small enough, and our president had the vision, so he became the 'knowledge clearing house' for the system. This switched us from great problem solvers to a learning based development environment, recognizing that knowledge comes from everywhere — customers, marketing, sales, manufacturing, service departments — everywhere. In some form, almost everyone might be considered a customer of decisions made in the design phase. The goal for development was to systematize the learning and the resulting knowledge. That is really the essence of the Toyota message."

Jan took a breath and continued. "So when Mac called, I actually was quite excited because, as a larger company, they had to build all those system knowledge bridges in a larger scale than we'd had to. I was delighted to help."

Don said, "One thing I had promised was that this would be a participative change, not pure directive from the top. I suggested Mac invite Jan to New Zealand to lead an internal meeting of some kind to sort all this out. I thought an outsider could do a better job, particularly one with a background of knowledge and success. So we did invite her, and she accepted."

Jan laughed and said, "This was not a hard decision. I had vacation time and have always wanted to go to New Zealand. The fact that they offered to arrange sightseeing for me and my husband was icing on the cake. We had a great time.

"Anyway," she continued, "I suggested a two day meeting with leaders of all the organizations impacted — from marketing, to even key suppliers if they wanted. I thought three to five people from each organization would be good. My plan was pretty simple — get all the key Toyota principles on the table, understood, and then customize, in a participative way, all the new roles and responsibilities of each organization. Only the high level changes would be defined. Each organization would be responsible for adapting its own policies and procedures to support these changes. So we did that about six months ago."

Mac said, "Yes, and it worked out quite well. Don kicked off the meeting. We went through the principles, and then Jan had us work though all the key elements that needed to change. For each, we defined the system changes, then each organization thought through their new roles and responsibilities."

"What were the organizations in the meeting?" Jack asked.

Mac said, "Let's see. First off, we wanted the system to be consistent across our main plants and business, so we made sure we had leaders from all areas that would work together within their functions. The functions were:

- Design Engineering
- Project leaders, or chief engineers, from a Toyota perspective
- Knowledge owners, or subsystem functional leads
- Support engineering
- Manufacturing
- Procurement, also representing suppliers
- Marketing
- Human Resources
- Center heads, who are the business segment leaders"

"That's quite a crowd" I said. "How did you manage that, Jan?"

"I'll admit it worried me," Jan said. "But as it turned out, it really wasn't that bad. There were no Doyles in the room. Everyone wanted it to work. Oops, I'm sorry, that slipped out. That has become a common phrase up here."

A smile appeared on Jack's face. "Yes, we understand."

Jan said, "It was really important to have everyone there. The system change depends on everyone interacting and learning from each other, and it worked quite well. At the end, everyone reported back to Don concerning the changes required and the actions they would need to take."

I said, "Jan, what were the key principles you had them work through?"

"I knew you were going to ask that, Jon," Jan said. "I have them listed."

"Just a second Jan, let me write them on the board." I went to the large electronic white board on the side wall. "Okay, I'm ready."

Jan said, "I will read each and comment. The first is:

Review and define functional subsystems and knowledge owners

She paused, and then said, "This is critically important as it sets up the responsibilities for developing, owning, and reviewing with knowledge. This does not necessarily define the organizational structure. At G&K, it does, but not with us. The knowledge owner must own the knowledge that drives the design decisions for their particular functional subsystem, including manufacturing knowledge, right Gary?"

"You're right, Jan," Gary said. "That was tough for me to do, but this is an important point. My manufacturing knowledge in terms of know-how must be communicated and owned by the knowledge owner, even if the knowledge owner is in Product Engineering. My people work with him or her to communicate that knowledge, but the knowledge owner must feel responsible for ensuring the knowledge is included in the design decisions. Likewise, my people own manufacturing processes. The design engineers are responsible for giving me the knowledge I need to make good manufacturing process decisions. It's about knowledge accountability."

Don added, "In our company, at least half of our competitive advantage comes from Manufacturing, and although we brought Manufacturing in late, it is now a key part of our program. Great products emerge from the intersection of customer needs and technical opportunities. Manufacturing is ripe with technical opportunities."

Brenda perked up, "Can you explain your manufacturing involvement in more detail?"

"Sure," Gary answered. "In manufacturing, innovation is continuous so we prepare Checksheets of our latest capabilities for a particular type of product and hand them to Design Engineering before the product is designed. An example is what tolerances we can hold on refrigerator doors for various types of door designs, and believe me when I say the quality of refrigerator doors is very important to selling a premium refrigerator."

"Great example," Mac said. "In the past, Marketing would ask for the perfect door with perfect gaps when the doors are closed and perfect finish, etc. We in Product Design Engineering would prepare a design specification for the perfect door with very tight tolerances."

"Gary continued, "The only problem was we couldn't build the perfect door, so we had poor yields and lots of rework."

Mac added, "So the product would be late to market, cost too much, and have quality problems. Now Manufacturing gives us Checksheets that tell us what is possible, which tells us two things — what can we do today and where we need to target innovation for tomorrow."

"We have already seen an increase in the rate of manufacturing innovation," Gary said, "and new products are finally taking advantage of what we can do as opposed to setting tolerances that we can't meet. And we're rolling it out to our suppliers as we speak."

Brenda was still taking copious notes and nodding with agreement.

"Thanks Gary," Jan replied. "Well said. The next key element is:

Define the Set-Based Integrating Events for selected system types

She continued. "As we know, Toyota integrates the known knowledge into design decisions during a series of Integrating Events. This allows schedules to be made while at the same time set-based options are developed and refined. In reality, these are not that hard to define by each product type. We developed the first pass for all of the major product types during the workshop."

"Here's the next one, Jon" Jan said.

Reconcile the Integrating Events with the current process

She explained, "G&K had a relatively new phase gate system that was similar to the one used here and at IRT. As we know, the concepts of phase gates and Knowledge Integrating Events aren't even close to the same. However, it is proving to be more of a timing issue. Once the Integrating Event that transitions the project from the set-based phase to the detailed design phase is reached, then the traditional phase gates actually work quite well, because there should be few if any disruptions caused by knowledge loopbacks. The gates allow all the detailed design and manufacturing activities to be scheduled nicely. But early phase gates that conflict with set-based knowledge development need to be challenged and reconciled. Again, this worked quite well."

Jan said, "Here is the last one, Jon:

Understand and define Knowledge Checksheets and when to use

"Knowledge Checksheets are the knowledge standards at Toyota. These are updated at the end of every car project. It's the responsibility of the knowledge owners to understand, define, keep current, and review with these Checksheets. At Toyota, they are quite detailed, and they will end up so at G&K and Sonic. Remember, these are not only derived from problem resolutions, but also from all the known functional knowledge within the company. I expect manufacturing — as it is at Toyota — to be the source of most of the Checksheet items. When and how they will be used need to be discussed and agreed upon, at least in principle."

Then she added, "These were the objectives for the two days — to understand how this works and then for each group in attendance to define its new roles, responsibilities, the actions that would make it happen. It seemed to go very well. Mac, Don, Thom, Gary, do you want to add anything?"

Mac said, "Yes, it did go very well. We are working our way through the details, but there is nothing going to stop us — the pieces are all in place. We are not as far along in integrating Checksheets as a formal part of the review processes as we would like because there's still a lot of learning and knowledge building going on."

A new voice then entered the discussion, "This is Thom, the Center Head from a plant with both engineering and manufacturing on the South Island. I am up here for a series of meetings and decided to listen in today. I would like to comment on a couple of points from Jan's visit. For me and my team there, the role of Integrating Events became key as these were the new milestones that had to pull everything together. The

Integrating Events define the timing for product narrowing decisions and knowledge enabling decisions. We don't sell knowledge, we sell products that are created through knowledge. The Integrating Events are the anchors to ensure the proper integration and timing of knowledge insertion into products. At Toyota and how it should be here is that the timing of these Integrating Events can't float. This is what ensures that your company keeps a cadence of quality and innovative products flowing to your customers."

Brian leaned over to Brenda and in a loud whisper, so that all of us in the room could hear and said, "And that is how we make your profit goals — give me a continuous flow of good products and I will sell them."

Brenda just nodded.

Brian then said openly in his booming voice, "Have you seen, or are you worried about innovation being hurt by this effort, particularly the need for assurance that you have the knowledge before innovating? It would seem that the pendulum needs to be balanced between moving ahead with great new ideas against never taking technical risks."

"Good question," Don said. "Realistically, we were unbalanced before toward unbridled innovation that got stymied in years of wishful thinking. Understanding the technical risks against great innovative ideas early has allowed us to focus our early research on the technical risks and to optimize our go or no-go decisions. We can decide to be as aggressive as we want, but at least do so with a real understanding of the knowledge gaps. Late loopbacks on innovation failures are devastating to our ability to plan sales and marketing. Another real plus for innovation is that the set-based knowledge produces multiple small innovations that are waiting in the wings, and this allows us to keep products going longer by introducing rapid refreshes on a planned cadence."

Brenda responded, "You are saying, to some degree, that innovation before had somewhat a life of its own, but now is more integrated and planned with both products and technology development. Have you seen the rate of innovation introduced into products change? Has the time to market changed?

Don replied, "We are absolutely seeing — even in our infancy with regard to the overall transformation — decreased time to market, and more important, we are now able to have a real rhythm, or cadence of products that sales and marketing can depend on. This also answers your question on the rate of innovation. A rhythm of product releases also allows a rhythm of planned innovation. It's the cycle of relentless innovation that wins in our market. Long gaps in innovation let our competitors in. We want them chasing us, forever. If we stay ahead of them in knowledge, chase us is all they will ever be able to do."

"I know we are running out of time, so last question," Brenda said. "Don, are you absolutely convinced that you can make this happen in the time frame you have planned."

"Brenda," Don answered, "I am absolutely convinced that this is the only way for G&K to dominate our market. If we know more than our competition, if we learn faster than our competition, and if we know how to build that knowledge into products faster than our competition, then we will eventually dominate, and we will be unable to be caught. We have made the first step."

After a short pause, Don said, "Once you come to the conclusion, as I have, that the effective growth and use of product knowledge is the bridge to business domination, then that thought needs to play in all strategic planning. For instance, we are revisiting all our supplier and subcontracting relationships to leverage and never lose knowledge. It absolutely makes no sense, ever, to trade off long term knowledge growth for near term cost expediency."

Brenda looked perplexed, but it was time to wrap up the meeting, since we'd promised to take no more than an hour of their time.

I said, "We really appreciate your time and would like to continue an ongoing dialog."

Mac said, "Yes indeed, we would like that, too. We have a long way to go to dominate our market, but we will get there. Your experiences will help."

"We're running over," Don said, "and I have to run to another meeting. You are welcome to visit us anytime."

After some small talk we hung up.

"Jon," Brenda said. "Thanks for setting that up. If we decide to move forward, we will take them up on their invitation and visit them."

Man, I thought, what does it take to convince this woman?

"Jack," Brenda said, "Do you have a proposal for the Automotive Business?"

"Yes, actually I do." Jack said as he handed out 8 1/2 x 11 copies to everyone. "I had help from Al on this."

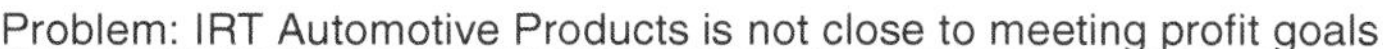
Problem: IRT Automotive Products is not close to meeting profit goals

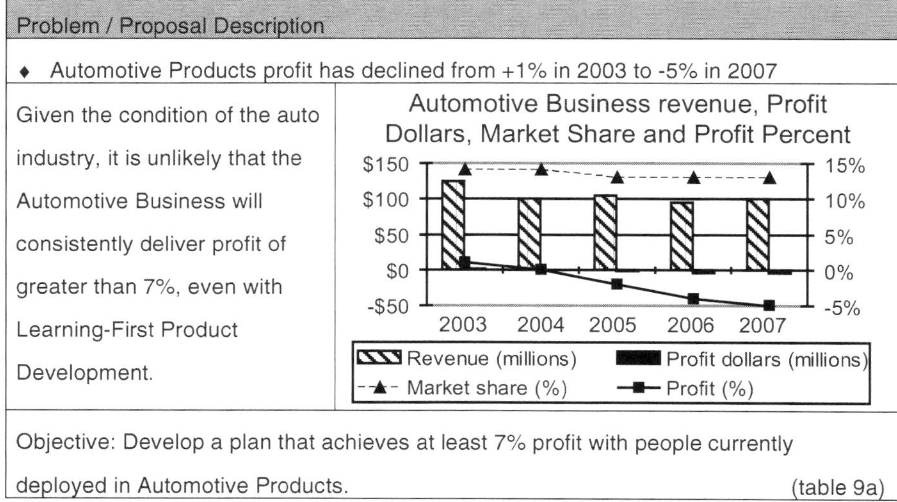
Problem / Proposal Description

- Automotive Products profit has declined from +1% in 2003 to -5% in 2007

Given the condition of the auto industry, it is unlikely that the Automotive Business will consistently deliver profit of greater than 7%, even with Learning-First Product Development.

Objective: Develop a plan that achieves at least 7% profit with people currently deployed in Automotive Products. (table 9a)

"First look at the problem statement," Jack said. "It shows that profit used to be positive and it has declined steadily to -5%. Revenue and market share have also declined."

"I have a detail point," Brenda said. "Add the word consistently achieves 7% profit to the objective. I want everyone to know that we always want to be over 7% and not bouncing over and under."

"Anything else?" Jack asked. No one spoke.

"Okay then, on to the Root Cause Analysis," Jack said. "As you can

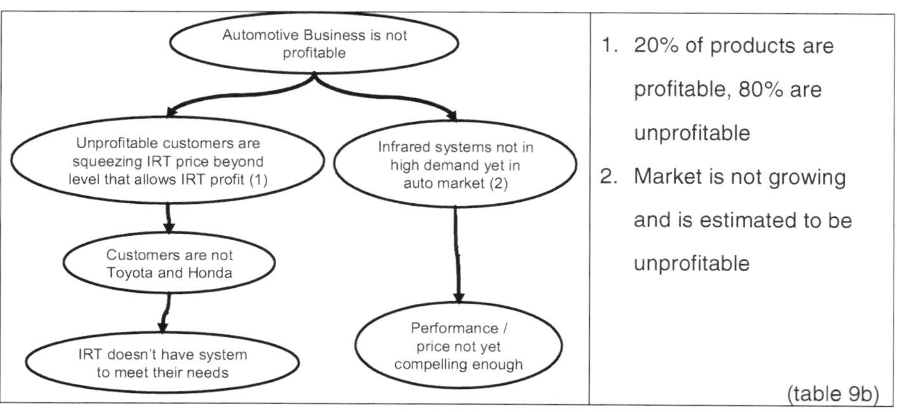

1. 20% of products are profitable, 80% are unprofitable
2. Market is not growing and is estimated to be unprofitable

(table 9b)

see, we have two problems. First, most of our customers are losing money, and they are squeezing us on price beyond the level that allows us to be profitable. Second, the market for infrared vision systems really hasn't materialized yet. Any questions?"

"If we stopped selling unprofitable products," Brenda said, "what would our profit be?"

"Three percent," Al answered. "The average profit of the 20% of sales that is profitable is about 3%."

"Don't forget," Brian said, "we have customer commitments that we have to honor."

"Are we ready for alternatives?" Jack asked. Brenda nodded so Jack proceeded. "Al and I came up with these. I suggested we view the peo-

Alternatives and Recommendations				
Alternatives		Pros	Cons	Recommended
1	Stay the course	Least disruptive	Unlikely to produce needed profit	No
2	Sell Automotive business	Proceeds from sales	Value of knowledge lost is greater than value of business	No
3	Close Automotive business and cut people	♦ Quick and easy ♦ Save costs	Knowledge lost from people leaving is unrecoverable	No
4	Show trade-off curves to customers	♦ Will improve productivity ♦ Everyone needs to be trained anyway	None	Yes
5	Retain profitable customers, phase out unprofitable customers	♦ Toe-hold in Auto market ♦ 3% now, 7% profit possible w/ Learning-First Product Development	Auto business will shrink to about $20M in revenue	Yes
6	Transfer people to other businesses over time	♦ Help other businesses grow faster ♦ Keep knowledge at IRT	Integration issues	Yes
7	Establish small new business creation group	Define new business opportunities and develop technologies that all businesses can use	Cost w/o immediate ROI	Yes

Table 9c

ple in Automotive as assets that we want to position to gain a good return on investment. In summary, I don't want to do the first three."

"Why not numbers two or three?" Brenda asked. "Why shouldn't we just get out of the Automotive industry altogether, rather than hold onto a small business with barely acceptable profit?"

"I would like to keep a small Automotive Business alive," Brian said. "The luxury car market is still doing quite well, and someday the technology is going to meet the needs of the customers and this business could take off. There is also prestige associated with selling IR vision systems to the luxury car market."

"Al," Brenda said. "What do you think?"

Al said, "Jack and I talked about a phased move of resources from Automotive to the other businesses. We would phase out of the lowest profit market segments and customers first and then we can see what is left and whether it makes sense relative to the other opportunities."

Jack said, "If we're going to pursue any of these alternatives we need to prepare a detailed plan. Then we can review it and decide whether we are going to do it. If we are, then we need to follow up to make sure we stay on plan or course correct."

"Good," Brenda said. "Then I support developing a detailed plan and reviewing it before we move forward. Okay, I support developing a plan for number six, moving people from Automotive to the other businesses. On number seven, how large a new business creation group are you thinking about?"

"Fifteen people from across the different departments and roughly a half million dollars per year," Jack answered. "We've never taken the time to take a hard look at where the future opportunities are, and we've missed out because of it."

"Sounds good," Brenda said. "When can you have plans for all these?"

"That depends upon when you cancel the cost reduction," Jack replied.

"Let me tell you where I am," she said. "I had two concerns before this meeting. First, what is Manufacturing's involvement and, second, what to do with the Automotive Business. G&K relieved most of my concerns about Manufacturing, and we have what appear to be viable options for the Automotive Business." She smiled. "The cost reduction is canceled. However, I'm not saying we will never cut costs, nor am I saying we will never have a workforce reduction. What I am saying is that we, including me, have to give top priority to the development and deployment of this knowledge asset. The upside return on this investment is too large to risk undermining it with cost reductions. For now, we need to apply all our energy to making Learning-First Product Development successful, and that starts immediately."

Jack and I exchanged glances with joint sighs of relief.

After a short, but very obvious pause, Brenda said, "A week ago, I knew the answer for IRT's future direction. Actually, that's not right, I assumed the answer based on my prior experiences. To be honest, I didn't know enough. Actually, I still don't. What I have learned is the power of LAMDA thinking. It is fine to be decisive, but it must be done so after the learning is complete. I do now believe that knowledge is the answer for sustained business growth — knowledge of what the customer wants now and in the future — knowledge of our technology gaps to meet those needs — and the knowledge within our people to remove those gaps. Any business strategy, whether focused on increased revenue, acquisitions, off shore manufacturing, or cost reductions must be done so with the impact on knowledge factored in."

"What can I do?" Al asked.

"I'd like you, Brian, and Jack to meet with me tomorrow at 8am to start putting the details of the plan together. Specifically, I want to validate that it will meet Jack's and my three-year goals. I already have my five whys prepared for you. By the way, bring it on an A3; let's do this right. Oh, and we'll work on the detailed implementation plans for the Automotive Business too."

After nods from Al, Jack, and Brian, Brenda looked at me. "Jon, you have taken the blame for our slow start many times over the last week. Stop it. That is the beauty of LAMDA thinking — it's a journey of learning. That's why it is called a cycle. We have completed one cycle of learning over the past year. We have looked at the results, asked and understood why, we have discussed it thoroughly, and in a few minutes we are going to act on the second cycle. Then we are going to do it again."

She added, "So, what do we change to get this restarted as a system? By the way, I do like the Learning-First Product Development name for the system and the model of the two value streams."

Jack said, "It is clear that the leaders of both companies made an unwavering and visible commitment to the system. We need to make a visible commitment to lead this transformation. As you and I have discussed, I need to make two organizational changes that will make my personal commitment clear. I'm talking to Ray about it tomorrow. I want my new organization in place on Monday."

"Good," Brenda said. "I mentioned it to Ray on Tuesday when I called to tell him I delayed the decision on the workforce reduction to explore this more fully. You won't get any resistance this time."

Brian then added, "Jack, this Learning-First System is bigger than product development — larger than Finance too. Marketing, Manufacturing, and our supplier base are all rich with knowledge. We have all been largely left out and we are a huge part of the Knowledge Value Stream."

"Yes, I agree," Brenda said. "Visible management commitment must be made and it needs to come from Ray's level but what will be the form of that commitment? I know we are going to visit the two companies but I would like to discuss it more now. What are the possibilities?"

I thought it was interesting that Brenda said Ray's level, not Ray. I said, "Let me show the implementation slide I showed a couple of days ago." I plugged in my laptop and turned on the projector. Luckily, the projector cooperated and the slide popped on the screen.

Learning-First Product Development Implementation Plan

	Step	Status / schedule / actions
1.	***Robust Visible Knowledge Development*** ➢ Train everyone on LAMDA / A3's ➢ Use for all problem solving and decision-making ➢ Management leads by example	➢Training and implementation complete in Security Systems ➢Training complete and implementation in-progress in Civilian Avionics
2.	***Knowledge-Based Product Development*** ➢ Test-then-design ➢ Identify Chief Engineers (Project Owners) ➢ Define and schedule Integrating Events ➢ Establish the Knowledge Value Stream: Knowledge Owners and Checksheets ➢ Capture what is learned in Set-Based Knowledge ➢ Lead creation of new knowledge and establish cadence of innovation	➢Integrating Events need to be defined and scheduled ➢Establish new roles / responsibilities ➢Identify knowledge owners and train in all businesses ➢Train in Checksheet development and defining sets of possibilities ➢Implement knowledge management system
3.	***Set-Based Concurrent Engineering*** ➢ Sets of possible design solutions are defined using trade-off curves generated from the Knowledge Value Stream ➢ Chief Engineer leads elimination of weaker solutions until optimal product and process design is found	➢Train in defining / seeing / utilizing trade-off relationships for Set-Based Design

IRT Infrared Technologies Corporation (Figure 9a)

I said, "The first step we have largely accomplished, as the principles of LAMDA problem solving and A3 documentation are well established in engineering. Jan and I agreed that this is really a necessary first step. LAMDA learning must be the base to build on."

Brian challenged, "Jon, I disagree with that statement. We are not done. It has not been established in the Sales and Marketing, or in Manufacturing. And it should be if this is a system of knowledge flow."

"Agreed," I said. "We need to do that. The benefits are immediate."

"Okay, let's stop there for a moment," Brenda said. "What is the commitment we need from management to make that happen. Everybody must take the training?"

"No," Al said emphatically. His challenging tone surprised us all. "You, have to practice it and demand that problems be solved via LAMDA and reported on A3s. By the way, I prefer Knowledge Briefs. I don't think we should imply a size of paper or paper at all."

"I agree," Jack replied with a knowing nod from Brenda. "That was a good lesson from Ron."

I said, "The first step is about the people — giving them the tools, authority, and process for learning. As Brian says, we need to extend it to other organizations, but we have proved our culture will and has adapted to it. I think we are ready for Step rwo."

"Knowledge-Based Product Development," Brenda said.

"We have to nail this to meet the 2009 goals and we don't have much time," Jack said. "Jan and Ron know how to do this. Jon, we need Jan out here next week — Ron, too, if possible. We need to figure out the new roles and responsibilities." Jack laughed. "And when Jan is here, let's talk her into rejoining us."

"Also," Brenda said, "set up a time for us to go to visit G&K in the next month — you, me, Jack, Brian, Al, and the right person from Manufacturing."

"Step two is also about the organization's ability to use the knowledge effectively," I said. "It is about the generalization and reuse of the knowledge. Jan and I discussed this a lot yesterday. We included Mac from G&K in on the discussions. We looked at what they had done at their companies and how best to replicate it. We decided that we needed to pull the right organizational behaviors and not push them. For example, we need to figure out the right way to manage our projects. Ron played both a quasi-Chief Engineer and quasi-knowledge owner role for Sonic. G&K has more of a Toyota style organization with clear organizational separation of project and knowledge ownership. We need to set up our development system to pull the behaviors needed while still retaining our company culture. We can do this by focusing on defining and using Integrating Events and Knowledge Checksheets to pull the knowledge into the products. It will also pull the right behaviors of the Functional leaders who own the Knowledge Value Stream and the project leaders who own the Product Value Stream."

"Okay, Jon," Brenda said, "I understand Step one. I am also fine with my role to lead by example. I think you are saying that Step two is about establishing the behaviors of the leaders by establishing how we review projects — and that being Integrating Events and Checksheets. Is that right? If so, you need to define both a little more for me, and what would be our role for top level commitment?"

"Yes, that is right," I said, "and I will try to explain better. We discussed Integrating Events some yesterday. They are simply the review points on a project where the project leaders and the functional leaders are making final product decisions. The difference is that the decisions are based on integrating the knowledge into the product decisions, and not on the status against process tasks. You are visibly looking at the knowledge, not at the project plan, for status. Traditional scheduling systems, such as Microsoft Project, are great at keeping track of tasks that need to be done. These are still important, particularly in the detailed design part of the project, which does focus largely on the execution of all the tasks required to bring the product to market. But early in the project, the emphasis should be on learning and the integration of knowledge — not tasks."

"And the A3s are the documentation of the knowledge that is used at these Integrating Events, right?" Brenda said.

"No, not exactly. The A3s are really the documentation of the LAMDA learning process, and while they might well be used at the Integrating Events, they are not the basis of the reviews. That is the role of the Knowledge Checksheets, which simply contain the learning from past projects and are the knowledge standards for the subsequent projects. At Toyota, the standards, or Checksheets, are updated at the end of every car project. The Checksheets can contain, for example, trade-off curves showing the range of possibilities and trade-offs, and they can contain rules for ease of manufacturing. They are organized around design decisions."

Brenda continued probing. "Why do you call them Checksheets rather than standards?"

I said, "The Checksheets contain the knowledge standards, but they are more than that, they are a tool designed to support the Integrating Events. The Checksheet is a deliverable of the Knowledge Value Stream and key tool of the Product Value Stream. Hence it is a key element of the integration of the two value streams."

I took a breath and said, "Step two is putting the Checksheets and the Integrating Events in place at IRT. It includes defining the product vision in terms of targets, understanding the knowledge gaps, and defining the Integrating Events specifically for resolving the gaps. Knowledge gaps are resolved using LAMDA. The design standards incorporate new knowledge, which the Checksheets pull out for the next project. We are ready to do this, and it will pull the management behaviors."

"Jack?" Brenda said, passing the decision to him.

Jack got up and walked to the board. Over his shoulder he said, "Everybody knows I am just an old country boy, but let me show you how I am thinking about this." He started erasing the board.

I smiled to myself. I knew the 'old country boy' beginning. This normally meant the old marine was taking charge. I leaned back and waited as he began drawing.

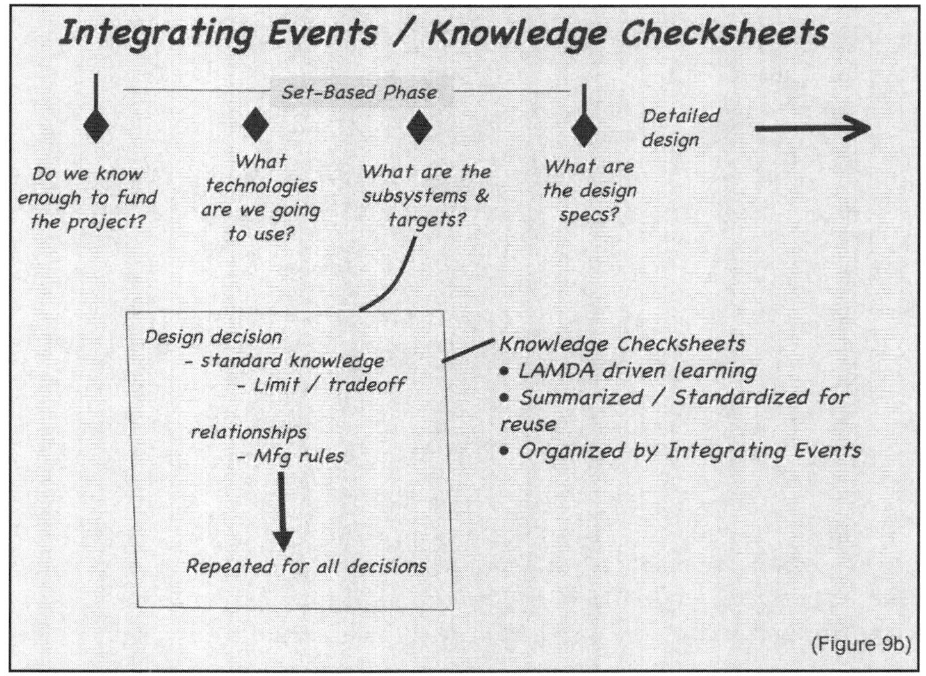

(Figure 9b)

When completed, he pointed at the top line and said, "If I understand right, we have Integrating Events within the Set-Based Phase where decisions are made, and I emphasize," he looked at me like he was preaching, "not where prescribed tasks are completed. The Integrating Events are organized by the decisions that must be made. These are knowledge gates, not task gates. The decisions to be made are concrete and the schedules set. We should never have started unless we knew we had at least one possible solution to meet our customer interests." He pointed at the first Integrating Event diamond. "Now when we start detailed design with validated specs," he turned to look at me again, "we better not have any loopbacks. Actually, our task-based scheduling system should work from there on. Right?"

Without waiting for a response, he said, "The Checksheets are simply a visual list of the knowledge needed to make the decisions at that Integrating Event. It ideally has trade-off curves to show the ranges of solution possibilities, but it also needs to include manufacturing rules, or best practice rules from anywhere. The knowledge needed to make those decisions is in our face."

Jack looked straight at Brenda. "Let's do it. As Ron told us, what do we have to lose? Using our current process, whatever design project we pick will probably not meet schedule and we'll have loopbacks all the way into production."

"Amen to that," Brian said, sarcastically.

"I agree," Brenda then decreed. "But I don't want safe projects that appear to be easy pilots. I want highly visible projects that are key to our future. I want the Checksheets coming out of these first products to start our road to dominating all the businesses. This will also show our commitment."

"Actually," Jack said, "I have to think about this more, but why would I not start this on every project we're working on including those already in detailed design? We know the integrating decisions needed, we can define the knowledge gaps and ensure that LAMDA and A3s are developed on all knowledge gaps. As Ron did at Sonic, the K-Briefs to remove the gaps will be the initial Checksheets for Integrating Events. We will turn them into standards — real Checksheets at the end of each project. Brian, we need to meet tomorrow with Jim Peters. (Jim was the Operations VP.) I want to know where all the projects are in all divisions. This thinking and my presence at all Integrating Events will be my priority. Brian, I want to beat all of your goals so you deliver more than six hundred million in revenue and more than seven percent profit in 2009."

This was a point of euphoria for me. Jack had just taken over my job. He had just taken real ownership.

"So, Jon," Brenda said. "I am becoming more comfortable with this. I now believe Step two is in good hands. What is your Step three?"

"Step three is really maturing the engineers to achieve Set-Based Concurrent Engineering. The ability to understand the interactions of knowledge through rather simple rules and trade-off curves will grow over time to very sophisticated optimization, looking at curves relating many variables on the same chart. It is really the continuous development of Set-Based Concurrent Engineering. I am not sure Step three ever ends — it just keeps evolving. However, I think it needs to be planned and encouraged, not just left to evolve on its own. We already have some instances of our engineers doing some really sophisticated problem solving using multi dimensional trade-off curves. This capability must be nurtured and developed."

"Okay, let me summarize," Brenda said. "I think we are in the midst of several LAMDA cycles to make this complete business transformation. We have just finished over the last couple of weeks the second LAMDA cycle on Step one. The first cycle was during the last year as we piloted the four cornerstones in the businesses. Although we did not reach our goals, we have learned to use LAMDA and K-Briefs effectively for learning and communication. We are now going to expand it for use outside engineering, and Jack and I will begin using it at our levels to solve our problems and make proposals. I also want to use it for removing engineering tasks that do not create knowledge. Jack and I will lead that effort as we are likely the cause of it.

Achieving Step two is another LAMDA cycle. There is no prescription for how we need to standardize and reuse our knowledge effectively. I think using Integrating Events and Checksheets are a good model to follow. Let's try it and we will look at the results. Jack and his business managers will lead that effort.

Another LAMDA cycle is the integration of an acquisition strategy and a supplier strategy that is based on the growth of product knowledge as the basis for business strategic growth. Al, you made a proposal yesterday. We will start the 'A' part of the LAMDA process tomorrow.

Brenda summed up: "Here is what I have learned — the road to business domination must be paved with the knowledge of all of our people. Anything less will not stand the test of time. The fact that I can't see the entire road ahead is somehow reassuring — although a few days ago, it would have been unacceptable."

She concluded with, "Let's get on with it!"

DISCUSSION

We would have loved to have ended the fictional story with IRT having achieved Toyota level capabilities. Nevertheless, IRT is well on its way. The company's top managers are leading the change as opposed to just being supportive. The change plan is based on some history of companies actually making the transformation to a Toyota system of set-based learning. The two companies discussed above in the fictional part, Sonic Solutions and G&K appliances, are fictional only to a degree. In actuality, the experiences are real. The following chapters will highlight case studies of two real companies and their experiences.

This entire book has been about implementation of the learning from Toyota into companies in other industries and other cultures. Toyota did not transform itself into a superior development system. Kiichiro Toyoda formed his car company with that philosophy and has been continuously improving it ever since — with some huge help along the way from people like Dr. W. Edwards Deming. Our job is harder as most manufacturing firms have evolved quite differently and must be transformed. Many of the approaches we defined in the first book for implementation were mostly theory as there were no good examples of significant change. The approaches outlined in this book are based on the real experiences of many companies, and these experiences have been quite varied. However, we have seen considerable common ground every company ought to be able to use to its benefit as each plans its own journey.

Part II will take a closer look at some of those real companies.

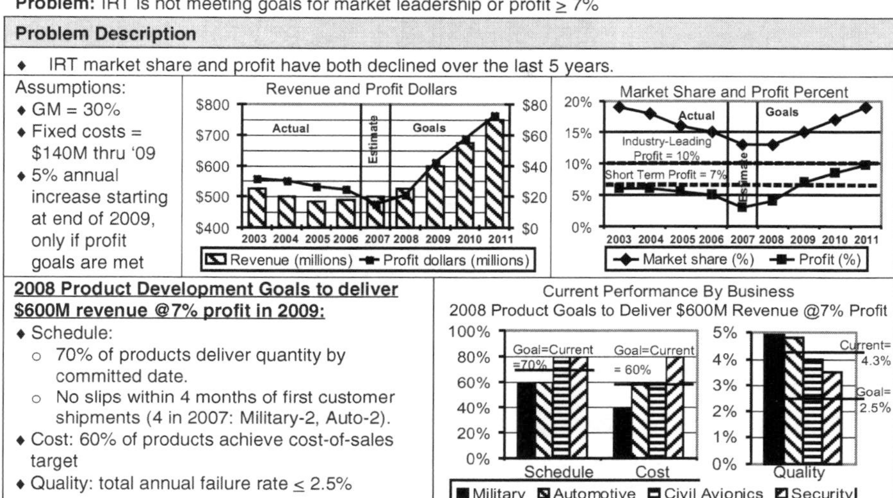

Problem: IRT is not meeting goals for market leadership or profit ≥ 7%

Problem Description

- IRT market share and profit have both declined over the last 5 years.

Assumptions:
- GM = 30%
- Fixed costs = $140M thru '09
- 5% annual increase starting at end of 2009, only if profit goals are met

2008 Product Development Goals to deliver $600M revenue @7% profit in 2009:
- Schedule:
  - 70% of products deliver quantity by committed date.
  - No slips within 4 months of first customer shipments (4 in 2007: Military-2, Auto-2).
- Cost: 60% of products achieve cost-of-sales target
- Quality: total annual failure rate ≤ 2.5%

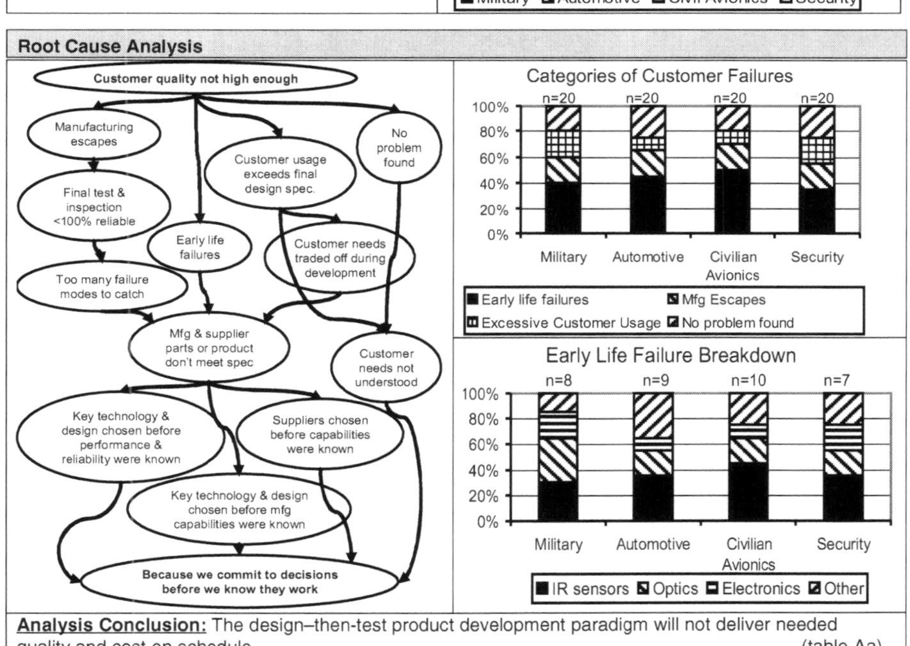

Root Cause Analysis

Analysis Conclusion: The design–then-test product development paradigm will not deliver needed quality and cost on schedule. (table Aa)

Assigned To: Jon Stevens	ID: 000375
Team: KBD Team	Last Edited Date: 10/22/2007

Alternatives

Alternatives Considered		1 year ROI	3 year ROI	Recommended
1.	Stay the course	-	-	**No**
2.	Cost reduction	++	+	**No**
3.	Learning-First Product Development	+	+++	**Yes**

Current: Point-Based Product Development Design-then-Test

Fuzzy Front-End Wishful Thinking

Unplanned Loopbacks

Few Concepts

Select Design

Detail Design

Test

Launch Sub-optimal Design

Recommended: Learning-First Product Development Test-then-Design

Look • Ask • Model • Discuss • Act

Learning Process

Trade-off Curves

Knowledge Briefs

Knowledge-Validated Design

No Unplanned Loopbacks

Create & find knowledge to develop feasible product & process designs

Detail Design

Test

Launch Optimal Design

Action Plan

Action		Responsibility	Timing	Target
1.	Learn from Sonic and G&K	J. Stevens	♦ Sonic -10/26/2007 ♦ G&K – 11/30/2007	100%
2.	Train step #1: Robust Visible Knowledge Development	J. Stevens	11/9/2007	♦ 100% of product development people ♦ All managers
			2/1/2008	All employees
3.	Train step #2: Knowledge-Based Development	J. Stevens	11/16/2007	20% of product development people
4.	Train step #3: Set-Based Concurrent Engineering	J. Stevens	2/1/2008	30% of product development people
5.	Implement Knowledge-Based Development	J. Holder	11/30/2007	100% of 2008 products
6.	Implement Set-Based Concurrent Engineering	J. Holder	10/31/2008	100% of 2009 products

Follow-up Plan

Action		Responsibility	Timing	Target
1.	Track and report performance versus schedule targets	J. Holder	10/31/2008	♦ 70% of 2008 products delivered target quantity on schedule ♦ No slips within 4 months of 1st customer shipment
2.	Track and report performance versus cost-of-sale targets	G. Rogers	10/31/2008	♦ 60% of 2008 products meet cost of sales goals
3.	Track and report versus total annual return rate target	Quality Director	10/31/2008	♦ ≤ 2.5% average for each business

Results

Action		2007 Baseline	2008	2009	2010	2011
1.	Schedule compliance (%)	70%				
2.	Schedule slips w/i 4 months	4				
3.	Cost-of-sales (%)	60%				
4.	Total annual return rate (%)	4.3%				

(table Ab)

Part II
The Journey to Domination

Chapter 10
Introduction to the Journey

The authors have had the opportunity to observe the journeys of dozens of companies toward superior product development as inspired by the Toyota Product Development System. Many are reflected in the fictional companies written about earlier in this book. From our interactions with these companies, we have learned that there are a number of possible paths to many different degrees of transformation, and that the best path for any particular company will differ. The transformation is not an overnight exercise — it is a journey. But it is a journey that can deliver significant value to the business at every step of the way.

The next two chapters will detail the stories of the two companies we believe have gone the farthest in understanding and implementing Learning-First Product Development. Neither had a goal of copying individual Toyota practices. Rather, their common goal was to put into place a superior product development system, borrowing tools and inspiration from Toyota.

We believe the lessons learned from these two companies, combined with the lessons learned from Toyota and the collected lessons from the other companies we have work with, provide all your company needs for you to confidently move forward on your own journey to domination. The lessons learned are collected and presented in the final chapter of this book.

Before we begin the case studies, in order to set the stage, we would like to discuss the challenges and questions that face a company embarking upon this journey.

Does it work in the real world?
Would it work for my company?
What must we do?
How long until we see results?

No doubt as executives, product managers, engineering managers and product developers around the world followed the fictional company IRT in its journey to a Toyota-inspired system of product development, they were asking these questions. Many are able to relate to IRT's struggles as they face similar challenges in their organizations. Yet there is much in IRT's solution to give pause. The philosophy behind what has become known as Learning-First Product Development and the practices that give it substance are, to say the least, unconventional.

First, there is the principle of 'test-then-design.' To see testing as a value-added activity and, what's more, to perform it before design, are in polar opposition to today's norm. Most organizations are constantly seeking ways to reduce the amount and the cost of post-design analysis. Their objective is to find the least expensive means to validate that the design meets the desired specification. At the same time, there is a reluctance to invest more than the absolute minimum in prototyping, usually limiting it to the final design of the critical components just prior to tooling release. These seem to be reasonable and necessary measures for maximum utilization of limited development budgets.

Yet the 'test–then-design' principle, adopted from Toyota practices and espoused in Learning-First Product Development, turns convention on its head. It moves most of the testing from the end to the beginning of the product development process. It changes the purpose of the testing from validation to learning. And further, it increases the amount of testing performed. In addition to the understandable doubts about how this could actually increase development productivity is the question, "How can this be implemented to practical effect?"

Furthermore, in the age of sophisticated software for engineering analysis and design, the notion that simple graphs of performance limits and of the trade-offs between performance and design parameters are powerful tools for design optimization seems antiquated. This is not to say that graphs aren't prevalent in product development today. With spreadsheet and graphing software available to everyone, graphs may be more widely used today than ever before. However, their primary use today is the display of supporting data for decisions already made, as opposed to their role as a primary analysis tool and the linchpin of product optimization at Toyota.

Perhaps the unconventionality most difficult to come to grips with is Set-Based Design. Typically, product developers seek to narrow potential design solutions to the best alternative, or at most to two alternatives, at the outset. There is also the early push to finalize detailed specifications for the future product because Marketing wants to know what they will be getting and engineering wants to know the expectations. Convention holds that decisions should be made as soon as possible so that developers can complete their work at the earliest date so that schedules will be met. The belief is that starting sooner on a specific product design always means finishing sooner.

The logic appears sound. However, Toyota and others that we will meet later in the following chapters have proven the opposite approach yields faster, more predictable results. Set-Based Design evaluates as many feasible alternatives as possible for as long as possible. Instead of actively seeking to guess the best solution at the outset, the weakest alternatives are systematically eliminated after careful evaluation, allowing the optimum solution to emerge as the process progresses. Decisions about components, materials, geometries and other design factors are delayed as long as possible. How can this be affordable, much less improve engineering productivity while producing better results faster?

Behind it all is the principle that knowledge is 'coin of the realm' for product development — the fundamental asset that must be managed, guarded, shared, optimized, increased, reused and never wasted. Problems are solved only once. Knowledge acquired is only paid for once. Lessons learned are permanent. Most, if not all leaders of companies will say that their people, and the knowledge in their heads, are their most important asset.

Many companies, but not all, have attempted to tackle this issue, sometimes referred to as "knowledge management." Lessons Learned databases, After Action Reports, Design Checklists, 8D Reports, and file after file of Evaluation Reports fill terabytes of server space around the world. Phase gate processes and quality standards often dictate their use. All these methods are logical, well meaning and, unfortunately, less effective than desired.

For example, Lessons Learned databases become black holes into which knowledge is pushed, never to escape. Developers, of their own volition or in compliance to company dictates, search the databases using the keywords they hope they share with the report author. A keyword that is too specific means no results. A keyword that is too broad means reading through dozens or maybe hundreds of reports with little or no relevance to the problem at hand. Even when successful in finding a potentially relevant report, developers often discover the report is too specific to apply to their situation or too broad to be useful. The accuracy and validity of the report may also come into question.

The potential of doubling, maybe quadrupling product development performance to the level of Toyota is alluring — and for some, imperative. And perhaps, all these unconventional and even counter- intuitive practices make the task of transforming a product development organization seem daunting, maybe impossible. For an individual, understanding and belief requires study and reflection, but it is within the reach of most. Transforming an entire organization is a different matter.

The transformation journey must lead the product development organization through the exploration of new methods, the understanding of the concepts, the acquisition of new skills, and the building of confidence in their ability to be successful using them. Engineers, designers and scientists are by nature a skeptical lot. There will be questions to answer concerning roles and responsibilities, changes to existing procedures, the specifics of the new methods, and new tools and resources. Most important, they must believe that their leadership is committed and willing to help them be successful.

Complicating the journey are the practical necessities of existing commitments. Sales forecasts are predicated on the new products already in the pipeline. Schedules must be met. There are urgent problems to solve on existing products. Development resources are tight. There are limited time and resources to invest in the transformation.

Product development practitioners have been intrigued by the opportunity and puzzled by the means of realizing the benefits ever since Dr. Allen Ward, Dr. Durward Sobek and others first disclosed Toyota's product development practices over a decade ago. Many more joined the ranks of the curious, the explorers, and the early adopters after reading our coauthor Michael Kennedy's book, *Product Development for the Lean Enterprise,* that introduced the concepts of Learning-First Product Development using the fictional story of IRT. Today, the stories of their journey, some successful and others less so, are beginning to emerge, and they provide a roadmap for transformation to Learning-First Product Development.

In the following pages, we will reveal the journeys of two real companies on their way to domination. One company is small; the other large. One company's products are very high tech, the other's less so. One company sells its products to other companies and governments; the other sells to consumers. One company is located in the United States; the other is half a world away. Through their stories, interspersed with anecdotes from other companies, we will answer:

- *How do these principles work in the real world?*
- *How do companies other than Toyota successfully implement these practices?*

- *What obstacles may be encountered and how can they be overcome?*
- *What can be gained and how long does it take to see the benefits?*
- *What are the lessons that can be applied to transforming any product development organization to Learning-First Product Development?*

Why would these two companies agree to publicize what they are doing? The answer is good corporate citizenship. The leaders of both these companies believe in a duty first to their company and then to the community at large. They are confident in their ability to deliver both. So they have agreed to share their stories with some reasonable restrictions on revealing real names and intellectual property. For this, we are thankful.

Even so, aren't they risking giving away their advantage to the competition? We posed this question to a Product Center Head at one of the companies. He responded, "We are on the right track. We have a head start. We have momentum. No one is going to catch us!"

Chapter 11
The Journey of Teledyne Benthos / Teledyne TapTone

Who They Are

South, then east, then north, the 115-kilometer peninsula curls into the Atlantic Ocean. Along the southeastern most tip of the northeastern state of Massachusetts, the 960-kilometer coastline of Cape Cod is dotted with marinas. It is a magnet for weekend boaters, beach vacationers and commercial fishing. Since the earliest North American colonists landed near here 400 years ago, life on the Cape has revolved around the ocean.

The community of Falmouth, in the southwestern corner of the Cape is home to one of the world's premier research organizations, the Wood's Hole Oceanographic Institution. It is not surprising to find a short distance away, in the community of North Falmouth, a company that for 45 years has been designing and manufacturing instrumentation to explore the ocean depths, Teledyne Benthos. The name itself is from the Greek for "depths of the sea."

Over the decades, the instruments and remote controlled underwater exploration vehicles of this company have provided governmental agencies and geophysical exploration organizations with the ability to safely image the ocean bottoms and to remotely measure temperature, current, salinity and other properties of the sea. Teledyne Benthos' remote controlled submersibles and side-scanning sonar played pivotal roles in locating the wrecks of the battleship Bismarck and the ill-fated Titanic.

Early in the 1970s, leaders of Teledyne Benthos discovered that their technology for sensing and signal processing could be applied to a terrestrial and less exotic problem. Packagers of liquids for the consumer markets needed a fast and reliable means of identifying leaky containers. Leaks are messy for packagers, distributors and retailers. And no one likes the taste of flat soda, stale beer or sour milk. Benthos developed a product line of instrumentation and sorting machinery called TapTone[1] to provide packagers with automated quality inspection.

The Business Imperative

Over the years Benthos had steadily advanced the technologies for their products, staying at the technological forefront of the company's markets. But when a new President, Ron Marsiglio, arrived on the scene

1 TapTone is now Teledyne TapTone, a wholly owned subsidiary of Teledyne Techonologies, Inc. It continues to be co-located and jointly manged with Teledyne Benthos.

in 2001, all was not well. In fact, the situation was dire. The ship of business was leaking cash and it was not a small leak. A gush of cash was leaving the company. There was a real possibility Benthos would not stay afloat.

Ron's first task as the new president was to plug the cash leaks, and the biggest leak was in manufacturing. Ron called on the Center for Competitive Change at the University of Dayton, an organization he had partnered with previously to turnaround other operations he had managed. Together they began a complete overhaul of the manufacturing operation using Lean Manufacturing Techniques. Assembly lines were optimized and redesigned. Workstations were 5S'd. Inventories were reduced. Quality was improved.

By 2003, the manufacturing operation occupied one-third the floor space it previously had. Inventory levels had been reduced to optimum levels. Productivity and quality were way up. Manufacturing had transformed from a cash sink to a cash source. It was time to turn attention from cost reduction to revenue generation.

Competition was intensifying. The company's oceanographic customers increasingly requested custom products with shorter delivery lead-times. While TapTone had recently released the most accurate instrument on the market, pricing competition was squeezing profit margins. And there was a cloud gathering on the horizon, as field service calls on their latest product were increasingly frequent. Smaller, faster, more accurate, easier to use and less expensive was the trend in all Teledyne Benthos' businesses.

Product development was in no position to help. Being a small company, product development had always depended on long tenured, highly knowledgeable experts, rather than on a product development process. The turmoil and uncertainty of the recent financial difficulties had motivated many of the experts to move to greener pastures. They had been replaced with skilled engineers who lacked the institutional knowledge of those that had left. By 2003, the organization was in a state of disorder. Only a few individuals possessed knowledge of what had gone on before and there was no process in place to guide the others.

President Marsiglio, along with the Center for Competitive Change, went to work to implement a traditional stage-gate product development process. Over the next two years the situation improved, at least somewhat. As Marsiglio recalls, "We got better results, but the product would still be late and our success rate was close to zero in terms of hitting all the specs without expensive loopbacks."[2] Furthermore, morale in the development organization had not improved significantly, and employee turnover was still too high.

By the spring of 2005, it was clear to Marsiglio and to most of his management team that the traditional stage-gate process was not enough. Marsiglio again turned to the Center for Competitive Change with the question, "Is there a better way?" Some of the consultants at the Center had recently heard Michael Kennedy speak at a conference. They suggested Marsiglio take a look at Kennedy's book *Product Development for the Lean Enterprise*. As Marsiglio read, he became more intrigued. He had begun his career as an engineer designing electro-mechanical parts. From his experience, the counter-intuitive approach derived from Toyota practices was not only interesting, but he believed it might work. As Marsiglio says, "It just made sense."

He passed the book around the company to other individuals involved in product development. At the beginning, there was little enthusiasm in the ranks for another product development improvement initiative. They had invested considerable effort in establishing their stage-gate process, only to find it increased the bureaucratic burden on the engineers without significantly improving their ability to meet schedules or develop better products. Everyone in the development organization was working overtime just trying to keep up with the projects already committed.

Furthermore, the cloud of increasing service calls on the most recently released TapTone product had grown into a full-fledged storm. An increasing dissatisfaction among customers was more than matched by increasing conflict between Engineering, Marketing and Field Service. Emotions, all negative, were running high, and signs of civil discourse and cooperation between functions were hard to find. Despite the poor organizational climate for change, slowly the ideas in the book gained some momentum and product development management agreed to at least investigate the concept.

Beginning the Journey

The journey began with a conference call. Benthos management, the National Center for Manufacturing Sciences, the Center for Competitive Change and Michael Kennedy discussed the situation and decided on the next steps. All members of engineering would first read Product

2 Patricia Panchak, "Teledyne Benthos Adapts the Toyota Product Development System," *Target Magazine*, Volume 23, Number 3, third issue, 2007.

Development for the Lean Enterprise to become familiar with the concepts. After this, Kennedy would meet with the engineering organization to further explain the concepts and answer questions.

In August 2005 the entire engineering organization and Benthos' top management assembled in the company cafeteria. A lengthy question and answer session followed Mike Kennedy's presentation on the Learning-First system of product development. Despite the communications, most of the organization remained very skeptical.

"It wasn't like a big light bulb went on," recalled one engineering manager. "It was apparent that we would be one of the early adopters of the concepts. There were no detailed processes of how to do this. We had no roadmap and no time available from already committed work."

Later they would admit that there was probably only a twenty percent buy-in after that first meeting. But the business imperative remained the same. "We needed to grow the top line and the best way to do that was to improve product development," said Marsiglio. "We needed to create more new products, better meet customer interests, meet engineering schedules, and end up with products that the customer wanted." So the 'thou shalt' approach was mandated, but the task of figuring out how to implement the concepts was not delegated down to the engineers. Everyone, including management, was to be totally involved. The entire company had to speak and act in a new way.

The goal was to increase product development productivity first by a factor of two and ultimately to the 4X level demonstrated by Toyota. The challenge was how to make the Toyota-inspired principles work at Benthos. The product correlation between Toyota and Benthos was significantly different.

"We wanted to develop a system based on their philosophy and principles, not their business nor their process," Marsiglio recalled.

Charting the Course

Marsiglio, The Center for Competitive Change, and Kennedy crafted a plan. The first order of business was not defining a new process. To begin with defining a process did not make sense for two reasons. First, to gain maximum buy-in to the new philosophy, every member of the organization needed to participate in its creation. The knowledge simply did not exist for the organization to create an effective process from the outset. Even if there was enough conceptual understanding, there was a second reason. Learning-First Product

Development and its model, the Toyota Product Development System, rely on a skill set and disciplines that were not highly refined in today's product development organizations. To have a process without the skills to execute it would have led nowhere. The first order of business was to build the fundamental skills.

So over the next twelve months, every member of the product development workforce would participate in four two-day workshops with a like number of coaching days from Kennedy's Targeted Convergence Corporation. The workshops focused on building the needed Set Based Thinking™ skills by applying them to Benthos and TapTone products:

The LAMDA learning process for building a deep understanding and a consensus on the course of action for any situation,

Knowledge Briefs (K-Briefs) for concisely capturing and communicating what has been learned,

Applying LAMDA and K-Briefs to effectively and collaboratively solve problems on new and existing products,

Applying LAMDA and K-Briefs to create a deep understanding of the customer and their interests across the development workforce,

Creating trade-off curves to understand and optimize total product performance, and

Set-Based Knowledge Mapping™ for connecting their knowledge from basic design decisions to the customer needs they are intended to satisfy.

After they learned the skills; after they built proficiency and confidence applying the techniques to real life situations; after they understood why the techniques worked, a formal process for developing products using the techniques would be defined. But real productivity gains would be realized long before a formal process was put on paper.

The first week of October 2005 marked the initial workshop for the three existing product development teams at Benthos. One of the development teams, known as the Geophysical Group, focused on the products that produce 3D images of the ocean floor using remotely operated submersibles and side-scanning sonar. The Communications Group developed instrumentation for sensing ocean conditions and communicating the data back to the surface via acoustical modems. The third was the TapTone team. The teams began the journey together, but would progress at different rates with some detours along the way.

Seeing the Ocean Floor — the Geophysical Team

The Geophysical team was the first to use the concepts and techniques as a remedy to an immediate need. The employee turnover during the past few years had left the organization with a wide range of design expertise and experience with its products. Individually, the team members were knowledgeable and skilled in their technical areas of expertise, but not all had worked in this industry before. Engineering manager Ron Allen knew individually they could design good subsystems, but how could they bring that piecewise expertise together to design an optimal system?

This team's product was an ROV (Remotely Operated Vehicle). It is a complicated system of sensors, data processing, control, communication, power, mechanical and propulsion subsystems. As they considered their product system, they came to the realization that the ocean itself was also a subsystem of their product. Although certainly uncontrollable and unalterable, nonetheless the ocean influenced and limited the performance of every subsystem in the product. Knowledge of that environment was critical to every subsystem designer.

For some time they had been seeking to develop a smaller, lightweight, and lower cost version of their current product platform. Yet each improvement proposed to one of the subsystems came with the unintended consequence of diminished performance in one or more of the other subsystems. For example, an increase in the tether length seemed to lead to increased power consumption, which in turn led to more power supplies that increased the weight that then led to even further undesirable trade-offs. It wasn't that the team couldn't predict most of the consequences. The questions were how much performance must be traded-off and would that trade-off be acceptable to the customer. The trouble was that until the advent of Learning-First Product Development concepts, the process for answering those questions was difficult, time-consuming and faith-based.

The established design process was basically a game of chase, pushing the problem around the system until it gave up or time ran out. An improvement would be made to one performance factor. Then an effort would be made to counteract the negative consequences to other factors caused by the first improvement, a chain reaction that would continue serially throughout the system with the hope that somewhere along the way the team would discover a combination of solutions that met the specifications and was affordable. The process was guided by experienced opinion and engineering intuition; but when pressed, no one could say with certainty when, where and how an affordable solution would emerge, or even if it was possible. The system was too complex for that. But engineering would work hard.

The Geophysical Team saw in the techniques of Set-Based Thinking™ an opportunity to improve this situation. First they listed the top dozen or so performance, cost and quality parameters their customers were seeking (referred to in LFPD as Customer Interests). Next they identified all the design decisions they made about components, materials, geometries, and so forth that influenced or limited the performance of the Customer Interest parameters. Finally, they described what they knew about how their design decisions, along with ocean conditions, affected — either individually or in combination with other design decisions — their Customer Interest parameters. This critical know-how, usually in the form of trade-off curves with explanatory text, was concisely captured on one-page Knowledge Briefs (K-Briefs).

This was not a full time effort. Most of the knowledge emerged from ongoing development projects. Knowledge would be captured when it was created or used. Engineers simply changed from summarizing their work in emails or as notes in personal design notebooks to the new K-Brief techniques. The task of developing some highly critical K-Briefs was assigned to experts who set aside a few hours per week to make their specialized knowledge visible in K-Briefs. The team met weekly to review progress, identify critical gaps in knowledge and to organize their knowledge in a Set-Based Knowledge Map™ allowing team members to see the interactions of all their design decisions.

Within six months of the first workshop, fifty K-Briefs, concisely describing why the team's product performed as it did and what its true limitations were, had been created. Knowledge was flowing across the organization. Furthermore, each developer could see on the Set-Based Knowledge Map™ exactly how the decisions they made affected other subsystems and overall system performance. Whereas before, when engineers understood only their area of expertise, the team now had greater visibility into how the system worked.

In addition, by using the trade-off curves and the interactions made visible by the Set-Based Knowledge Map™, the team could quickly analyze multiple sets of design solutions. For each potential design configuration, they could both predict the system performance and identify the factors limiting the performance. Decisions about which new business opportunities to pursue and which improvements to make to the product were now being guided by visible, factual evidence. While the exact improvements to the product resulting from this effort remain a trade secret, the game of chase was over.

Water Talkers — the Communications Team

Water temperature, current strength and direction, and salinity are just a few of the oceanographic conditions that are important to harbor masters, offshore oil production facilities and navies across the world. Benthos' Communications Product Team solves the problem of how to record these conditions and transmit that information to those needing it. Their products are battery powered electronic modules that sense the ocean conditions, process and store the data, and then on command from a command module on a boat, platform or dock, transmit the data to the monitoring station. Since radio frequencies don't work underwater and wires over the distances involved would be impractical and expensive, an acoustical modem based on SONAR principles is used to communicate between the submerged sensing units and the command module.

The challenge for the product designers is how to sense and transmit the most data before the sensing unit must be brought to the surface and the batteries replaced. More batteries would be a first reaction, but that increases the size of the sensing unit. And the larger the sensing unit, the harder it is to make a watertight container to protect the electronics. The surface command module has its own challenges. Since often these are portable units used on the deck of a ship, size and weight matter. And since the technician may need to operate the unit on rolling seas while wearing heavy gloves, the user interface requires special attention.

Rising oil prices and increased shipping had boosted the demand for this team's products in recent years, and their existing products were in a reasonably good, competitive position. To shore up and increase market share in the growing market, the decision was made to design a new command module called a Universal Deck Box that would communicate with and control all the team's models of submersible sensing units as well as some of those made by competitors. The goal would be to improve the user interface, size, weight and manufacturability over the current model.

Most of the solutions to the technical challenges were known to the engineering manager, Ken Scussel, and to a few technical experts. However, two-thirds of the engineers on the team had joined the company since the last deck box had been designed. Ken said, "Each day one of the new engineers would come to my office with a question about how some aspect of the system worked. I would go to the marker board, explain the concept, and then erase the answer to the question. Two days later another new engineer would come to my office with the same question and I would repeat the marker board explanation." Ken's first application of the LFPD principles was to use K-Briefs as a mentoring tool. Instead of going to the marker board to answer a question about the system, he would compose a K-Brief with the explanation. The K-Brief would then be sent to all members of the design team. Not only did this increase Ken's personal productivity by reducing the time he spent answering the same questions, but also it raised the entire team's understanding of the system.

Understanding some of the requirements for the system was a big issue for the team designing the Universal Deck Box. The sales force was telling them the new system needed to be 'easy to use,' 'highly reliable' and have an 'easy to read display.' But what did all that mean? And how would they know if their design was meeting those requirements? As they considered and discussed the issues, they decided that these statements were not actually the requirements, but rather, they were shorthand for sets of customer interests. To understand the real customer interests, they needed to discover the specific customer interests within these categories, so each of the broad categories of requirements were decomposed into specific customer interests. For example, 'easy to read display' was decomposed into readability in direct sunlight and aesthetics. A group of six displays were rated by the team. Each customer interest needed to be specific enough to be measured. For each customer interest a Customer Interest K-Brief was created that described the interest from the customers' viewpoint, why it was important and how it would be measured. The specific, measurable customer interests made it possible to objectively trade-off competing interests.

An even larger issue for the Communications Team was how trade-off curves could be applied to the embedded software in their system. The software processed and enhanced the signals from the sensors, packaged the data for transmission, and controlled the communication. There was also the software for the graphical user interface. Creating and using trade-off curves for mechanical housing and electronic components was fairly straight-forward. It was easy to see how trade-off curves could inform basic design decisions about geometries, materials and even selection of electronic components. Applying the same reasoning to software would suggest that trade-off curves should be created to inform decisions on the coding of the software at a very detailed level. The question was, was this the right approach?

The answer they came to was, "No." Applying trade-off curves to their software code, at least for most situations, did not seem practical. It would require a lot of effort without an apparent benefit. What did seem practical and valuable were trade-off curves between the use of either in hardware or software. For example, noise in the data from the sensors could be filtered out by adding special electronic components or through mathematical algorithms written into the software. More electronic components meant more space, more weight, more power consumption and more cost and could provide a certain measurable level of noise cancellation. The performance of implementing the noise filter in software could also be measured, and up to a certain point did not increase system size, weight, or cost. But at some point, a faster processor and more memory would be needed to run the software. Then the cost of the system would increase significantly. Where was the breakeven point between hardware and software? A set of trade-off curves brought objectivity and collaboration to the discussion between the hardware and software engineers. With the facts visible, the optimum trade-offs between implementing functions in hardware and software became apparent.

Righting the Ship in TapTone

While the TapTone Team's products had nothing to do with the ocean, their allegorical ship of business was definitely on the rocks by October 2005. Although their automated quality inspection system was as fast and as accurate as any product on the market, it was not meeting all customer expectations for uptime in their production lines. Further, the system was costly to manufacture, thus leaving little flexibility for sales to compete on price. Customers were expressing their displeasure to TapTone's sales force. The sales force, predictably, was passing along the displeasure to engineering with some amplification.

The development of this latest model had not been without issues. Sales contended that engineering had not delivered what the market needed and what engineering had promised them. Further they had taken too long. Engineering insisted that Sales had not taken their cautionary warnings seriously and that the product was released prematurely. In retrospect, the dialogue from both sides had been based mostly on opinion and wishful thinking. Nonetheless, decisions had been made and the product was in the market.

What had been a contentious relationship during development soon escalated after the product was released. Numerous field service problems and some lost contracts further increased the tension. Every cross functional discussion or email exchange on potential remedies seemed to quickly degrade into what industrial psychologists call 'fundamental attribution error,' the tendency to attribute the cause of any event to the personality traits of the actors rather than the circumstances of the situation. Non-psychologists call it the 'blame game.'

When the LFPD workshops began that autumn, TapTone engineering was working overtime to fix a long list of problems with their existing product. Yet each solution they proposed seemed to meet with an objection from Sales or Manufacturing or both — too late, too expensive or insufficient. The need to develop a new product was also looming on the horizon. Some technology development had begun, but they had little time to concentrate on it. And to spend time learning and implementing some new engineering methodology seemed out of the question. Furthermore, the engineering team was so besieged by that point that every offer of assistance felt like an accusation. They were in no mood for a major improvement initiative.

So for the next few months, the team went through the motions, doing just enough to get through the workshops but not applying the Set-Based Thinking™ techniques to their work. They continued working hard on their problem list in the same manner as before, and getting the same results. Marsiglio, patiently coaxed and coached the team during this period, but progress was slow. So finally in February 2006, Marsiglio decided to act.

In addition to his duties as president, Marsiglio had been acting as the Director of Engineering since the position was vacated a year before. Each week he held a design review with the engineering managers and top technical experts in which problems were reviewed, priorities set, resources allocated and decisions made. Marsiglio used that forum to inject some momentum into the adoption of Set-Based Thinking™. He issued an edict. From that point forward, the official format for presenting problems and status in that meeting would be the Problem K-Brief, and presenters should be prepared to discuss how they were applying LAMDA in solving the problem. This was of little note to the

Geophysical and Communications teams since, for the most part, they had been using these tools for a couple of months, but TapTone now had to join the movement.

The TapTone group had been holding to the misconception that a Problem K-Brief was a post event documentation tool. As they began using the technique, they discovered the true value of the Problem K-Brief. It was a living document to guide the team through the problem-solving effort, from definition through root cause analysis to the validation of the solution. On a single page, it concisely and visually communicated what the team knew as fact on that day and what they would do next. In conjunction with LAMDA, it sifted the facts from the sea of opinion and made them visible.

In a short time, the Problem K-Brief replaced the unending email threads as the focal point of discussion for the TapTone field service problems. A deeper understanding about the causes of the problems and a more objective evaluation of the alternative remedies emerged. As the vetted facts became visible on the Problem K-Brief, the dialogue between Engineering, Sales and Manufacturing slowly evolved from conflict to collaboration. Problems began to be solved. Over the ensuing four months, the team solved seventeen problems on their production model. "This was our first big breakthrough," recounted the TapTone engineering manager. "The engineers easily understood the benefit."[3]

With the issues on the existing top end model stabilizing, TapTone could now turn its attention to developing a new product.

Putting It Together — the Process

By June 2006, all the engineers had acquired the skills and practiced the techniques of Set-Based Thinking™. They had learned to apply LAMDA to various situations. They had created trade-off curves to describe the relation between interacting design decisions. They had captured the knowledge they had used or had created into Knowledge Briefs. The Knowledge Briefs had been organized into Set-Based Knowledge Maps. All three product groups had applied the techniques to assist in existing development projects. It was now time to define the new product development process.

Teledyne Benthos had a fairly traditional, well documented, phase gate style process. It included a detailed, multifunctional product specification phase, followed by system design, intermediate level design and

3 Patricia Panchak, "Teledyne Benthos Adapts the Toyota Product Development System," *Target Magazine*, Volume 23, Number 3, third issue, 2007.

detailed design phases. A formal prototype build, beta build, and pilot build integrated the design phases into the manufacturing releases. Their process was clearly a design first and then test until done paradigm.

The entire management and engineering teams attended a two-day facilitated session to define the new process. There was no blueprint to follow; there was the Learning-First Product Development model as a high level guide. Kennedy's role was much more of a coaching role than a teaching role. The goal was not to copy the Toyota system, but also not to break the DNA that made Toyota so successful. The workshop was primarily a LAMDA cycle; everyone was learning together. The teams looked at the problems with the current process, they asked and dug into the root causes, and finally they broke into their different teams to define their new process model. One team defined a very creative multiple LAMDA process — the first cycle was to determine if the team knew enough to commit the dollars; the second cycle was to determine if the team knew enough to set the specifications. It was clearly a learning-first approach; the knowledge was the promotion to the next LAMDA cycle. It was rough, but a great start. After discussion, all the teams adopted the concept. Over the next several months, the teams built the process out as the new standard. It not only defined the stages of visible knowledge for design releases, it also had a clear path for the continuous innovation of the functional subsystems across generations of new product. The concept of the core competency teams was born. The new product development road map poster now proudly hangs on the walls, the result of the collective learning and joint development from all the teams and disciplines. As are all good LAMDA cycles, the product development process remains a work in progress, along with defining the roles and responsibilities.

TapTone Sets Sail

TapTone's product line offered solutions at the top end of the price-performance spectrum and at the low end. The opportunity was in the middle. Some existing customers, plus an additional group of packaging companies that TapTone would like to have had as customers, were increasingly seeking leak detection systems at mid-price point with capabilities slightly different than other products on the market. The questions were, "What did these customers really want?" and "What could TapTone deliver?"

As summer on Cape Cod eased into autumn, engineering resources began to free up. The solutions to the problems on the existing model were taking effect. Additionally a technology development project was nearing completion for a new digital signal processing subsystem that would reduce the cost of the existing products and add some new capabilities. Engineering effort shifted to defining the new product.

Sales and Marketing had provided Engineering with a set of specifications and a target cost based on their discussions with customers and a market analysis. As the engineers discussed the proposed specification, they discovered that — while they knew what the customers were asking for — they did not fully understand why that set of performance parameters was important to the customer. This was going to be important. The desired specifications looked unachievable based on what they thought their capabilities were at the time. Trade-offs would likely have to be made, but the question was, which ones?

The training they had received on Set-Based Thinking™ had emphasized the importance of firsthand, objective observation of a situation and had provided several examples of the length Toyota would go to understand what was important to their customers. As the engineering team discussed the situation, they realized that only three members of the team had actually seen their product in use in a customer's production environment. And while the technical understanding of the different specifications was fairly consistent across the team, opinions on the role each played in customers' production lines and the relative importance of each varied widely.

So, with the active support of the president, a series of customer visits was arranged for the fall of 2006. For each visit, an engineer would be paired with a salesperson. These would not be courtesy visits. And they would not be searches for solutions. That would come later. The engineers would be applying LAMDA to understand the production and business problems their customers were seeking to solve when they purchased the product. And in a further departure from past practices, the findings would not be summarized in an emailed trip report.

Instead, for each specific customer interest identified, a K-Brief would be produced. The K-Brief would describe what that interest was, why it was important to the customer, and how the customer would know their interests had been satisfied. The K-Brief would also include a visual representation that communicated the concept behind the customer interest. The visualization might be in the form of a flow chart, a sketch, a picture or even an embedded video. Whatever best communicated the concept would be used. The Customer Interest K-Brief would be the joint product of the engineer and the salesperson. The two had to reach consensus on the content and therefore, the true customer interest. Moreover, the K-Brief had to be understandable to every member of Sales and Engineering so that the knowledge was transferable to all members of the team.

By November 2006, a consensus understanding of the customers' needs for the new product was emerging. There were still some questions to answer about the customers' interests, but the TapTone engineering manager, Rob Chevalier, could now begin to think about a solution. His colleagues in Geophysical and Communications had been using the Set-Based Thinking™ techniques of test-then-design and trade-off curves for several months. They had experienced some success with the techniques, but so far they had applied them only to derivatives of existing products, not to the challenge he now faced of developing a completely new product. Still, encouraged by their success using the Set-Based Thinking™ tools to solve problems and understand their customers, he wanted to give these other techniques a try. He just needed to figure out how.

Early one morning, Rob and the lead system designer huddled in front of a marker board. On the board they mapped the top five customer interests to the basic design decisions that determined the performance of each, looking for interactions between the different parameters. Discussion then turned to the physics and economics that defined the relationships between the basic design decisions about components, geometries, speeds, and so forth, and the top-level machine performance. They wanted to make sure they understood the 'why,' not just the 'what.'

The discussion focused on the design variables and customer interest performance variables. There was no discussion of the specific values that these variables might take in the design. From their existing product, they knew the performance that one set of values for the design decisions produced. However, their new product required different performance, and it was not clear which of the basic design decisions should be changed and by how much in order to produce that performance, or if it was even possible. They lacked the knowledge.

In the past, the engineering team would have met and, based on their collective experience, theorized the design values that had the best chance of meeting the specifications for the new product. To keep development costs and time as low as possible, they would have tried to propose as few changes to the existing product as possible. There was much uncertainty in this approach and that uncertainty would have engendered fear. So their project plan would have been as conservative as they could convince management to accept. Historically they would have forecasted an 18-month development schedule and historically the actual development time would probably have been closer to 24 months.

This time things would be different. Rather than design then build and then test the new product, they were going to test first. From their map on the marker board they could see the relations between design decisions and customer interests where they needed to understand the limits and trade-offs. By lunchtime they had a test plan. Using their standard test jigs and some minor modifications to their existing product, they could develop the knowledge they needed. It would take four or five weeks to run the tests and summarize their learning in K-Briefs, but at the end they would know the full range of capability of their current technology. More importantly they would be able to see specifically which technologies would limit their ability to meet the new product objectives.

When Benthos employees returned from their Christmas holiday in January 2007 they noticed something remarkable. The newer employees confided that they did not think it was possible. More tenured employees claimed they had seen it years before, but had not expected to see it again. The TapTone engineering manager was smiling, constantly.

Test-then-Design

At first mention, the principle of Test-then-Design often conjures images of huge time devouring experiments and costly full product prototypes. In practice this is rarely the case. Once what is already known is made visible, the critical knowledge gaps are usually much smaller and more focused than originally imagined.

Further, creating prototypes for test purposes is much easier and quicker than creating full designs intended for the marketplace. The vast majority of the design can be ignored; only the issues that affect those being tested needed to be considered.

For example, important knowledge leading to a major breakthrough on the TapTone product was gained by simply adding two $14 carpenter's clamps to the existing product and a few hours of testing.

The trade-off curves constructed from the testing had suggested that they could not only meet, but also exceed all the goals for the new product. Much work still remained, but there was hope. Chevalier conceded that, "The opportunity was there all along. But the complexity of the system kept us from seeing it until we had the trade-off curves."

Some in the organization were tempted to revert to past practices and start design immediately, but Rob, as guided by the new LAMDA based process, insisted they did not know enough yet. First, they had only looked at five of the customer interests and the design decisions that affected them. There were other customer interest and design decision interactions that had to be understood. Moreover, there was an indication that a minor technology change would produce the desired performance, but there was no proof. And Learning-First Product Development is about decisions made from facts, not guesses. So another round of LAMDA guided test-then-design was planned and executed as per the new process.

By mid-March the team was ready to validate their new-found knowledge. In a four-week period, a full prototype was built and tested. The prototype bore little resemblance in form and appearance to the final product. However, it was fully capable of demonstrating fit and function. It incorporated the knowledge the team had gained through the testing and the lessons they had learned from the previous model, which had been captured in Problem K-Briefs. The prototype worked.

Engineering was feeling very confident in the project at this point, but not Sales. Sales had purchased booth space at three trade shows in October to demonstrate the new product. It was now mid-April and engineering had yet to produce one single CAD drawing of the new product. Historically the angst of the Sales organization over the approaching deadline would have been shared by engineering. There would likely have been a discussion of reducing the performance goals to help meet the schedule. Not this time. Engineering's response was, "Don't worry. We will meet the deadline." And they meant it.

"There was no fear," said Rob. "We knew as fact what our customers needed and what our capabilities were."

More surprising still and underscoring engineering's confidence, they still did not start the detailed design phase despite the rapidly approaching deadline. Instead, using the knowledge they had gained about the feasible ranges of components, geometries and materials, they next created conceptual sketches of the final product. Armed with the conceptual sketches and test results from the prototype, they again visited their key customers for another LAMDA cycle on the customer interests. Their customers, presented with evidence that their primary interests would be satisfied, offered further suggestions on how the machine could be improved for easier cleaning and maintenance. Since detailed design had not started and no tooling had been ordered, the new enhancements were easily incorporated into the design concept.

On May 1st, 2007, detailed machine design began. The CAD/CAM design of the product, all the parts and all the drafting files, took only four weeks. Beta-build took another four weeks. Trial production began in August and in October the new product was introduced at the trade shows to the great satisfaction of Sales, Engineering and most important, TapTone's customers. The new model was less warmly received by the competition.

The new product meets customers' leak detection requirements with a 25% higher throughput rate and uses half the floor space — all for about half the price of the previous model. For TapTone, the new product meant greatly reduced field service problems, easier manufacture and higher profit margins. There had been no unplanned design loop-backs because of incorrect engineering or marketing assumption. Manufacturing start-up was smooth. In fourteen months, from beginning to fully understand their customers' needs, till production release, TapTone had created a win for their customers and a win for TapTone.

TapTone's engineering manager, Rob Chevalier, credits the project's success to this: "We acquired all the knowledge we needed to be successful before we started the final design...not after we released the product."

But TapTone's story doesn't end there. Over 180 Knowledge Briefs on their Customers' Interests and the fundamental limits and trade-offs between design decisions were created. "That is reusable knowledge," says Marsiglio. And it is already being used to design the next product in the TapTone line. The development schedule for that product is only nine months.

What Does the Customer Really Want?

A common discovery across the Geophysical, Communications and TapTone teams was the need to better understand the customers' interests. They had plenty of input concerning what the customers wanted. There was a steady stream of emails, phone calls, presentations, specifications and requests for quotes from the sales force. But somehow this was not enough to design products that fully satisfied their customers.

One engineering manager described a recurring situation. "We would often have a requirement that the new product be "easy to use" or "highly reliable." We would do our best in Engineering to meet that expectation. Yet when we released the product, we would discover that our interpretation of what was wanted was different than the sales force's. And neither of our interpretations exactly matched what the customer really needed. The requirements were too vague and our understanding too limited."

One of the other engineering managers faced the opposite problem. He described receiving specifications from marketing that were too specific. "It was like they were designing the product for us." Upon first consideration, those detailed specifications might have appeared beneficial, but there were serious unintended consequences. First, each requirement in the detailed specifications usually represented the most aggressive value requested by any customer. When considered in the whole, the specification became the ideal product for all customers. The problem was that the people setting the specification did not and could not know if the laws of physics and economics actually allowed such a product to exist.

The other problem was that once the desired specification was put on paper, it was viewed as an absolute requirement. No variance from the goal was acceptable. Since the requirements were not a variable, the only variables left were time and money. That meant missed schedules and cost overruns.

To get to a better understanding of their customers' interests, Engineering needed the assistance of Marketing and Sales. And they needed more time for face-to-face interaction with customers to fully understand the 'whys' behind the requirements being requested. Predictably there were concerns that Engineering was usurping the role of Marketing and that Engineering might somehow damage the relationship with the customer. Training the Marketing and Sales teams in LAMDA and Customer Interest K-Briefs helped to dispel many of the concerns. Some good experiences, aided by sound leadership, relieved more concerns.

"It is not perfect and may never be," according to the Director of Engineering, "but it is better than it was."

Now, when new product requests come in from Marketing and Sales, Engineering asks for a full understanding of the customer interest instead of just starting a design to some specification. LAMDA and the Customer Interest K-Briefs are the means to that understanding.

Benthos' Core Competency Teams

As Benthos' knowledge became visible in K-Briefs and the K-Briefs circulated around the various engineering groups, engineers saw an opportunity. They had always known that Geophysical, Communications, and TapTone each used power supplies, transducers, waterproof housing, digital signal processors and other core technologies. However, the form and fit that these technologies took in the various product lines differed. With those differences, engineers could not see how to leverage their knowledge about these technologies across the organizations. Of course, there were hallway conversations, emails and the occasional cross organizational meeting when the situation merited, but little in the way of organized knowledge sharing.

The K-Briefs with their trade-off curves and accompanying explanation of the function of the technologies caused the engineers to rethink their assumption. As the K-Briefs were shared across the company, engineers increasingly realized they had more in common with the engineers in the other business units than they had suspected. Furthermore, they were learning more about the technologies they were using and the best design practices for implementing them from the K-Briefs. They decided they could get even more beneficial knowledge sharing with a little structure.

Benthos organized twelve core competency teams around the technologies that were critical to product success. Each team was comprised of an expert representative from each of the three business units, plus other organizations as appropriate. The core competency team would first provide an expert peer review of any K-Brief created in the realm of their technology. Then they would act as the knowledge clearinghouse, ensuring that engineers were aware of K-Briefs that might be helpful in their projects. Finally, with the company's knowledge about their key technologies visible and collected in one place, they could see critical knowledge gaps and the specific areas where technology advancements could benefit the company. Technology development projects could be planned and prioritized. The core competency teams controlled the quality, distributed the knowledge and planned the strategic roadmap for the company's core technologies.

Rocks and Reefs — Obstacles Encountered and How They Were Overcome

Benthos' journey to Learning-First Product Development was not always smooth sailing. In addition to the difficult climate for organizational change described earlier, Teledyne Benthos faced issues common to all organizations converting to a new way of operating. Time was an issue — the time to get things done the old way while learning and implementing the new way. Some new development projects were delayed to create some capacity for the transition. Marsiglio admits that was the hardest part.

The engineering team agrees that the second hardest part, according to Marsiglio, was changing the culture from a "doing" culture to a "learning first" culture. There is a constant intense pressure to move quickly from knowledge-gathering to designing.[4] LFPD does not alleviate this tension. Instead, it relies on it to keep the learning from becoming an academic exercise. In LFPD, Integrating Events and the design decisions to be made at each event are firmly scheduled. The requirement for a successful Integrating Event is that the engineers present evidence that the design decisions being made will work. Together, a firm schedule and the requirement of proof create a check and balance system that pulls the right knowledge from the organization at the right time. The learning is focused on the project objective and the schedule doesn't proceed on wishful thinking.

Even so, it takes discipline to change the habit of beginning designs without the knowledge necessary for success. Under schedule pressure and the inertia of old habits, there is a tendency to design as before. Overcoming the inertia of the status quo required the intervention of Benthos' leadership.

A notable example of leadership's contribution to successful implementation occurred a few months into the transition. Periodically the entire engineering staff would meet in the company cafeteria to discuss progress and issues with implementing the new system. President Marsiglio regularly attended these sessions and sat quietly in the back of the room, listening to the discussions. On one occasion an engineering manager gave voice to a common concern: "I can see the logic and the long term benefit of the new methods, but I am afraid if we try to implement them on the current project, the project will be late and over budget."

---

4 Patricia Panchak, "Teledyne Benthos Adapts the Toyota Product Development System," *Target Magazine*, Volume 23, Number 3, third issue, 2007.

A silence filled the cafeteria as all eyes in the room turned to Marsiglio. After a moment that seemed longer than it was, Marsiglio rose and addressed the engineering manager. Without censure or recrimination in his voice, he said, "We are always late and over budget anyway. Who is going to know the difference?" In that brief statement, Marsiglio had restated the case for action, acknowledged there would be difficulties, and gave them the permission to invest in the change.

Leadership of the initiative did not end there. Management provided a buffer between the R&D teams and the Sales Force during the transition by explaining what the R&D team was seeking to achieve and why it was important. This gave the R&D team the space and time to transition. Second, management constantly challenged the engineers on the state and progress of their learning. Specific questions were asked about what the engineers knew, what they needed to know to be successful and how they were going to close the gap. The focus of the dialogue changed from activities to the learning that would produce results.

Bob Melvin, director of engineering, and his engineering managers were quick to point to another necessity for overcoming the implementation obstacles: "Training, training and more training." One of the cornerstones of Learning-First Product Development is an expert engineering workforce. An expert engineering workforce is characterized by its ability to understand the complex causal relations that link their basic design decisions to the full set of customer interests. LAMDA is the means for discovering the causal relations. And the ability to capture the knowledge clearly, concisely and visually in Knowledge Briefs is also critical. Together these foundational skills underpin the expert engineering workforce. The skills must be acquired and proficiency built through practice and mentoring.

Equally important to building proficiency in the foundational skills, is learning and confidently applying the concepts of test-then-design, fact-based decision making and set-based concurrent engineering where decisions are delayed as long as possible to allow the optimum solution to emerge. While simple in concept, these powerful methodologies are paradoxical to traditional practice. So understanding the practices and confidently applying them to real projects requires study, thought and perhaps some experimentation. Training and coaching in these areas also helps build both the understanding and the confidence.

Distance Traveled — Evidence of Progress

When the journey to Learning-First Product Development began, support for the initiative was less than twenty percent. Consistent leadership, training and experience have steadily increased support. Each of the three product lines took a slightly different approach to implementation. Each chose to first emphasize the specific techniques that provided immediate benefit to their unique situations. And having mastered and benefited from them, they added the remaining methodologies of Learning-First Product Development until the three product groups coalesced in a common process. Along the way, each of the product lines greatly increased their productivity with:

- *Faster and more effective problem solving,*
- *Capture and reuse of their knowledge, and*
- *More optimum design solutions in less time.*

Today the engineering managers report that the organization's support for the Learning-First Product Development exceeds eighty percent. Before LFPD was adopted, engineering turnover was a significant issue. Eighteen months into the LFPD deployment, it was noted that they had not lost a single engineer since they had started the journey.

When asked to describe how behaviors have changed, the engineering managers summarized it this way:

- *"We are gaining knowledge about our customers' real interests and more design decisions are now based on those interests rather than pure engineering."*
- *"We are spending more time developing the knowledge necessary to be successful before jumping into the design. Our designs are now based on knowledge, not the fear of the unknown."*

Marsiglio, among his other talents, possesses an ability to boil a situation down to its essential elements and to state it in the simplest terms. He sums up the journey's destination this way, "You must know what your customers want. You must know what you can do."

The operative word is 'know.'

Chapter 12
The Journey of Fisher & Paykel

Who They Are

A full 19,500 kilometers southwest of Cape Cod, lies the island nation of New Zealand. Like Cape Cod, the ocean is ever present in the lives of the Kiwis, who won the 2000 America's Cup yacht race. And like Cape Cod, there is a company in New Zealand on the journey to Learning-First Product Development, Fisher & Paykel. Unlike Teledyne Benthos, however, Fisher & Paykel's products have nothing to do with the ocean.

Fisher & Paykel designs and manufactures premier home appliances: cook tops, ovens, dishwashers, refrigerators and freezers, washers and dryers. Since starting in business in 1934, F&P has steadily grown to be the leading appliance manufacturing in Oceania and a globally recognized brand. Innovation in technology, manufacturing and product design has fueled the the company's growth. It was the first to use plastics and polyurethane foam in appliances. In the 1960s its people developed their own flexible factory machinery to economically enable short production runs of different models. They were also the first to develop a method for forming pre-painted sheet steel, further increasing factory efficiency. And products such as their DishDrawer™, a dishwasher in a cabinet drawer, have won numerous design awards around the world.

At Teledyne Benthos, the product appearance is always subservient to the product's function. Not so at Fisher & Paykel. The consumers of top-end appliances not only demand the best performance from the products, but also insist the products look good doing it. When you look at an F&P appliance you can see the best of New Zealand. Kiwis are justly proud of their national rugby team.

The All Blacks are perennial contenders for the Rugby World Cup. The team embodies the spirit and ruggedness of a nation of seafarers and ranchers. Of equal pride to Kiwis is the natural beauty of New Zealand. From the tropical flora and beaches of the north through the peaks of the Southern Alps to the rugged coastlines in the south, New Zealand is a visual feast. Fisher & Paykel's product designers have created a style that captures the essence of New Zealand and projects performance, reliability and beauty.

The difference between Fisher & Paykel and Teledyne Benthos does not end with products. F&P has ten times the number of engineers as

Teledyne Benthos. Furthermore those engineers and designers are distributed across multiple sites, some as far away from Auckland as Ohio and Italy. So F&P's journey to Learning-First Product Development would face a challenge of scale not to be found at Teledyne Benthos.

The Business Imperative

As the market leader and largest manufacturer of home appliances in the Oceania region, Fisher & Paykel could leverage economies of scale in both manufacturing and the sales channel. F&P's decision to expand into the global market changed that. No longer was all manufacturing done in New Zealand. By 2006, the company had manufacturing operations in North America, Europe and was planning a new manufacturing operation in Thailand. Instead of the products being sold primarily through small franchised retailers, F&P was now competing for floor space in the large home improvement retail chains against appliance manufacturers ten times the company's size. Moreover, consumers' preferences for style, performance and reliability differed across the globe.

All this placed new pressures on the company's product development process. F&P's engineers and designers had always been innovative, but now they needed to innovate faster to stay ahead of the global competition. Further, new products needed to incorporate the differing architectural standards and consumer preferences of the global marketplace. And the personal service of small retailers and the reputation for quality they enjoyed for 75 years as a regional supplier could no longer be counted on to mitigate any product reliability issues.

Like most companies, F&P employed a gated product development process. And like many companies, they found the results to be unpredictable. Most development projects were late due to unplanned design loopbacks. Some new products remained in the pipeline for years. The project managers were frustrated and engineering morale was eroding. F&P's small regional distributors were somewhat forgiving of missed schedules. Large global retailers were not.

Under the leadership of CEO John Bongard, improving product development became a priority. According to F&P's Vice President of Engineering, Christian Gianni, "Our hallmark has been innovative products. We needed better schedule predictability without sacrificing innovation. Our current process didn't seem capable of delivering that." Fisher & Paykel needed a different approach to product development — one that predictably delivered innovative, reliable, market leading products.

Beginning the Journey

Fisher & Paykel began by appointing a full time champion. For this role the New Zealand company turned to a Scotsman. Colin Gilchrist had emigrated from Scotland years before with his Kiwi bride. In his many years with Fisher & Paykel, Gilchrist had at one time or another managed every major department in engineering and manufacturing. Experienced, practical, tenacious and a respected leader, he was the natural choice. As for Gilchrist's perspective, he had been looking forward to easing into retirement in a year or so. But he had believed in the need for such an initiative for many years, and he accepted the challenge.

Gilchrist's first act was to form a team of thought leaders from engineering and project management. The team would meet weekly to discuss the product development improvement challenge and what could be done about it. The team agreed fairly quickly on the need for a change, but the question of what to change to was more difficult. So team members began researching what other companies were doing.

"When the team was discussing what we could do, we kept coming back to the Toyota-inspired methods described in Kennedy's book," says Gilchrist. "It just seemed to have an affinity with our overall philosophy."

Gianni added, "It just made sense."

The next step was to learn more about what it would take to implement Learning-First Product Development. So Gilchrist began a series of phone calls with Mike Gnam of NCMS and our coauthor, Kennedy. With the knowledge gained from the discussions, Gianni and Gilchrist became more comfortable with the methodology and how to implement it. But Fisher & Paykel was a large organization and to be successful, the rest of the management team would need to be on board.

So with CEO Bongard's support, Kennedy traveled to New Zealand in August 2006. He spent a week at the New Zealand offices where he met individually with the engineering managers, thought leaders and key people from manufacturing, marketing and finance, representing both key sites in Auckland and in Dunedin. At the end of the week, he presented an overview of LFPD to the assembled engineering and industrial design organizations at each site. According to Gianni, "Those presentations were received even better than we expected. Our people were quick to embrace a system that allowed them to capture and share knowledge."

"The biggest problem," recalls Gilchrist, "was coping with the impatience for change."

Organizing for Learning-First Product Development

Gilchrist was quick to take advantage of the wave of enthusiasm. The first task was to get the management team trained. "Bongard had communicated his unreserved support for the initiative to the executive leadership team. Everyone would participate. If we were going to lead the change, we needed to fully understand all the principles," said Gilchrist.

In November, all engineering management in New Zealand, plus key managers from operations, marketing and finance participated in a one week accelerated course in LFPD. The course covered all the principles and included practice on the techniques. With the management team trained and on board for the change, a full deployment was planned for early 2007.

In addition to an extensive training program culminating in the definition of a new product development process, the deployment would also include a complete reorganization of the product development department. The existing organization, which had been in place for over a decade, consisted of product area managers with development project teams reporting to them. Shared functions such as industrial design, tooling design and product evaluation were in separate organizations. The extensive discussions held with members of the organization at all levels during the preparation for the change had surfaced several concerns with the existing organization.

The foremost concern, according to Gilchrist, was that "nothing would change with the same structure and managers in place. When things got tough, the fear was that we would revert to previous practices." The project managers had also expressed a lot of frustration with unclear priorities and resource allocations in the shared functions. Finally, the existing structure of project teams had been designed to speed execution, but that was clearly not working. Further, there was no clear responsibility for building engineering expertise and owning the knowledge created in the present organization.

So the product development executive leadership team designed a new organizational structure. Reporting to VP of Engineering would be Centre Heads for each of the major product areas and for electronics and industrial design. Reporting to the Centre Heads were Functional Managers and Chief Engineers. The Chief Engineers would act as project leaders, system engineers and surrogate customers all rolled into one. They would be responsible for the success of the projects.

Reporting to the technical functional managers were functional leaders for each of the knowledge subsystems of the product. A knowledge subsystem is all the technical knowledge needed to provide a specific function in the product such as Structures and Dynamics, User Interfaces, or Ice Making and Water Dispensing. The leaders of the knowledge subsystems would be responsible for providing solutions for the development projects, creating new expertise and knowledge, and capturing that knowledge for reuse. They would be responsible for the performance, cost and reliability of the solutions they developed.

This structure was intended to provide a better balance between market driven and technology driven development. And since both project leadership under the Chief Engineer and technical resources under the functional managers reported to the Centre Head, prioritization and resource allocation should be improved. More important, the ownership of knowledge clearly resided with the functional managers and leaders. However, they still needed to address the concern that "nothing would change with the same . . . managers in place."

Fisher & Paykel's executive team decided every position in the new organization would be open. They would post a notice of the openings internally and any employee who felt he or she was qualified could interview for a position. "We believed we had to do this," said Gilchrist, "but it was not without its risks. First we needed managers and chief engineers that not only could help us transition to the new product development philosophy, but also thrive using it. We weren't sure if we had enough in-house talent. And there was a risk that some of the existing management would leave, upset that they had to compete for their positions."

Despite the concerns, F&P pushed ahead and began interviewing candidates for the new positions in January. They began with the Centre Head position and worked their way down the organization chart. The process of filling dozens of open positions took considerable time and effort, but by the first of May the new organizational structure was in place. Along the way, the company did lose a couple of individuals who were not satisfied with their personal outcomes. However, the concern over having enough talent never materialized. In fact, the opposite was the case. According to Gilchrist, "Our problem became what to do with all the talent we discovered."

Building the Skills

F&P did not wait for the organizational change to be complete before moving ahead with the other elements of deployment. Regardless of how the org chart evolved, the organization would still need the skills to be successful. So in February, in a training blitz, the entire product development organization was trained in the foundational skills of LAMDA, Knowledge Briefs and trade-off curves.

The training was conducted by Targeted Convergence Corporation in two-and-a-half-day workshops, where small teams learned the foundational skills by applying them to real problems and real situations they were experiencing on the job. At the end of the workshop, the teams would present the Problem K-Briefs and trade-off curves they had produced to the product development leadership team.

"We believed leadership participation in the workshops was very important," said vice president Gianni. "It demonstrated our support for the program and gave us visibility into how well the techniques were being adopted by individuals and teams."

Gilchrist added, "We were pleasantly surprised at how fast the teams were applying the concepts and the results they were getting. We knew we would see results, but we hadn't expected them so quickly. Teams were actually solving some long standing problems during the workshop."

For six weeks the organization practiced applying the foundational skills in the workplace. Then it was time to put the skills in place to generalize the knowledge for reuse and build knowledge ownership. These skills would be needed by the chief engineers, functional managers, functional leaders and subject matter experts in the new organization. By this time, the potential candidates for these positions in the new organization were beginning to emerge. Those individuals were trained in how to capture the knowledge being created into Set-Based Knowledge Maps™ and to use the maps in the design of products. Like the earlier workshops, the attendees learned by applying the techniques to projects they were currently working on. And like the earlier workshops, they saw immediate results.

In one case involving a refrigeration product, the SBKM™ revealed a component that was not adding any additional performance. It could be removed from the design immediately at a substantial cost savings. Critical knowledge gaps were identified on other projects and those were targeted for test-then-design. One particularly beneficial finding involved a washing machine that Gilchrist described as having been in development for "an embarrassingly long time." The objectives for this project had included a twenty percent increase in one of the technical performance factors over the value advertised by competitors. This would be a selling advantage in the showroom. Also included in the project was a decision to use a technology in another subsystem of the washing machine that was of strategic value to the company.

Two decisions in two subsystems of the product had been made to improve performance. Both seemed achievable alone. What the SBKM™ and trade-off curves revealed was that those two decisions imposed a constraint on a third subsystem of the machine. They also showed that the physics and economics of the situation prevented that constraint from being removed without a significant cost increase. Much development time and money had been spent trying to solve an unsolvable problem imposed by the earlier design decisions. With the system interactions and limits now visible, a consensus on the best trade-offs could be reached, and development could proceed.

F&P's Process for LFPD

By June, the new organization was in place. The organization had been trained, and more important, they had experienced success applying the techniques to localized problems. Now it was time to define the process for Learning-First Product Development.

Upon reflection, the process effort should have started earlier. F&P, under the aggressive guidance of Bongard, Gianni and Gilchrist, had moved very quickly in training, implementing the principles, and installing the new organization's structure. Yet it was clear that more thought needed to be given to the new roles and responsibilities. For example, the roles of marketing and manufacturing in the new process had not been well defined. The existing phase gate system was still in place — how and when this was going to be revised to the LFPD principles were still open questions. It seemed that most parts of the new system were being developed while running full speed toward implementation. Gilchrist said, "Kennedy used to warn us about loss of momentum. We were determined not to have that happen."

Gilchrist and Kennedy devised a way to bring all this together quickly. They jointly organized a large group session of key leaders from both sites and all organizations to pull it all together into a complete business system. Kennedy had learned at Teledyne Benthos that the best approach is to let the teams build their own system to support the LFPD model. This fully supported the John Bongard edict that this must be a participative change. This again was primarily a two-day LAMDA cycle. Process modifications were made to the phase gate process to allow early learning. The key Integrating Events were designed, and the roles of all the impacted organizations were discussed and initial changes defined. However, as are all LAMDA cycles, the changes are an ongoing work in progress. A second round is planned about the time this book will be released. However, there is no doubt it will be successful — the guidelines are in place, and the leadership is engaged.

Overcoming Obstacles with Style and Innovation

The beginning to Fisher & Paykel's journey was smoother than Teledyne Benthos'. There was not a high level of initial resistance to changing the product development practices to be overcome. Even so, as with any change, no matter how positively it is perceived, issues and reasonable doubts arise. One of the first to raise its head at F&P was a fear that test-then-design and LAMDA would lead to 'paralysis by analysis.' The experiences in the workshops and shortly thereafter relieved those fears as the new approach generated robust solutions in the same or less time than before.

More challenging was demonstrating management's commitment to stick with the new approach when times got tough. "Our culture was definitely action oriented," said Gilchrist. "Before we would do about half a 'Look' then jump straight to 'Act' . . . and management was the top offender."

So for a successful transition, management was going to have to change its habits. "For the first months of the transition, we concentrated just on doing LAMDA right," said VP Gianni. "That meant that we had to have the self-discipline to do it ourselves and then to ask the right questions during reviews to pull the use of LAMDA in the organization."

The most interesting issues during deployment concerned the use of trade-off curves. Fisher & Paykel defines its DNA to be equal parts of Innovation, Style, Integrity and Care. To many, the notion of trade-off curves seemed antithetical to innovation and style. The industrial designers were particularly concerned that trade-off curves of technical performance meant limits on their creativity. Mark Elmore, the Industrial Design Centre Head, was quick to understand the benefit of trade-off curves to industrial design and to relieve the concern of his charges.

Elmore said, "Our job is to create stylish designs that appeal to our customers, but the design still must work and be manufacturable. By understanding our current capabilities from the trade-off curves we can try to find styles that fit within that capability. And when we can't, we can work with manufacturing and engineering early in the project to have those capabilities in place before design release."

A significant minority of the engineers held a similar concern about trade-off curves and innovation. Trade-off curves and innovation interact in three ways. The first is when a more optimum set of trade-offs is discovered among an existing set of trade-off curves. This means finding a better solution for performance, quality and cost using existing technologies. The second is when a better solution is enabled by moving a small number of trade-off curves. This happens through the incremental improvement of existing technologies. The third type of trade-off curve relationship with innovation is when existing technologies can no longer provide the needed performance. Then a new technology solution must be discovered and trade-off curves created to describe its performance. In other words, a technological breakthrough is required that is understood through the creation and use of trade-off curves.

Most of the exercises in the workshops had focused on optimization and incremental type innovations because they tended to have a scope that was manageable within the context of a workshop. The F&P engineers had been very successful in the workshops employing these techniques. Some teams had discovered cost savings on existing products representing $100,000 per year or more. Others had discovered how to use existing technology to penetrate new markets. So when the discussion on this topic first arose, it was thought that these engineers had misunderstood some aspect of the concepts. Further discussion revealed that they fully understood the concepts. Their point was that their management only recognized and rewarded breakthrough innovations. Therefore, they should only be focused on creating those. And since every project should involve breakthrough technology, there would be little or no reuse of trade-off curves — so why bother creating them.

The existence of this strong perception came as a surprise to management. "We don't know how they came to believe that management didn't appreciate a $50,000 a year innovation," said Auckland Centre Head Ant Belsham, "but we are going to convince them that management appreciates all innovation — big and small."

Distance Traveled — Evidence of Progress

As of the writing of this book, Fisher & Paykel is in its first wave of products developed under Learning-First Product Development. The sample size of projects is still too small to provide meaningful statistics on metrics such as time-to-market and productivity. However, strong anecdotal evidence is emerging that the investment is paying off. Dan Witten-Hannah, the Dunedin Centre Head, describes one such incidence on a new model of one of their top dishwashers:

"We planned to incorporate a number of new innovative features in our latest model. Since we had just learned about test-then-design and trade-off curves, we decided to apply those techniques in the development of the features. What we learned is that one of those features would present a substantial warranty risk. In the past, before early testing and trade-off curves, our wishful thinking on the marketability of the feature would have outweighed any opinions about its viability. We would have pushed ahead with release.

"With the facts generated by testing clearly visible on the trade-off curves, reaching consensus on what to do was easy. Everyone — Bongard, Marketing, Engineering — agreed that we should release the model without this feature. Better yet, from the trade-off curves, we can see exactly what we must do to have this feature ready for the next model."

Witten-Hannah was also quick to credit the techniques for the progress on a revolutionary gas cook top now under development: "There is no doubt in my mind that we would not be this far along without these techniques."

Gilchrist added that all the soft measures — morale, involvement, generation of Knowledge Briefs, and the use trade-off curves, Set-Based Knowledge Maps™ and Knowledge Checksheets are all very positive. Management seems genuinely pleased with the results so far.

Gilchrist sums it up this way: "IT FEELS GOOD!!!!"

The Journey Ahead

Fisher & Paykel is presently deploying LFPD in their smaller development organizations in North America and in Europe. The company is also gearing up to extend application of the LAMDA, K-Brief and trade-off curves to cost and quality improvements in manufacturing.

"The techniques are fully applicable to those situations," said Gilchrist, "and we will be able to transfer the learning from operations back into product development."

Learning and Knowledge Reuse is Important Everywhere

Fisher & Paykel is not the only company deploying knowledge capture and reuse throughout the business. An international manufacturer of consumer products is deploying LAMDA, K-Briefs and trade-off curves throughout their planning, marketing and finance operations. Coupled with a performance measurement system, these techniques will form the backbone for their continuous improvement culture.

An Unexpected Benefit!

It came as a surprise to everyone when the Teledyne Benthos HR manager first made the observation. In the year and a half since the company began implementing LFPD, not a single engineer had left the company. Before, engineering turnover had approached fifteen percent annually. Several engineers were discretely asked why this might be the case. While they expressed it differently, the common sentiment was, "this is what we thought we would be doing when we chose engineering as a career."

One newly hired engineer went further. She said, "I love the Set-Based Knowledge Map™. I can look at it, see exactly what I need to do, how it affects other parts of the system, and who I need to talk to. At other jobs it took me six months to make a difference. With the SBKM, I feel like I can contribute immediately."

Fisher & Paykel also observed engineering morale increasing steadily with every success. During an early discussion on where to apply the techniques to get the fastest return on the training investment, John Wardrop, F&P's VP of HR declared, "From an HR perspective, I think the training has already paid for itself. I can not remember ever seeing R&D this energized, and I can't think of anything we could have done in HR to get the same result."

That is not to say there wasn't early skepticism among the technical community. But with an understanding of the techniques and experience applying them, the skepticism turned to confidence. They found the LFPD techniques improved the effectiveness of two things that most technical people derive job satisfaction from: learning and solving problems.

Importantly, leadership at both these companies had nurtured an environment where this was possible. A consequence of making visible what one knows is that what one doesn't know is also visible. Company leadership made clear that not only were knowledge gaps all right, they were important. Once they became visible, the knowledge gaps could be prioritized and closed. There must be no fear of recrimination for exposing a knowledge gap.

Chapter 13
Roadmap to Domination

Routes to the Same Destination

Teledyne Benthos and Fisher & Paykel are two very different companies on a journey to the same destination. They differ in size, products, technologies, markets, and culture. Yet they have the common goal of being a dominant force in their respective industries. They have both chosen Learning-First Product Development as a path to that destination. Yet each journey was somewhat different, accommodating their unique needs, capabilities and cultures.

In Chapter 10, we discussed how each company was implementing the principles in different ways that met their unique circumstances of needs and culture. While there doesn't seem to be an exact prescription, some common factors critical to success have emerged. It is informative to see how Teledyne Benthos and Fisher & Paykel addressed these essential elements in their own way.

First Critical Success Factor: Adopt a Simple, Visual Model of the Transformation

Learning-First Product Development is a fundamentally different paradigm for developing new products. Before beginning the transformation, the leaders of the organization need to understand the principles, why those principles produce better long-term results than traditional product development and the milestones of the journey. It is not necessary to know the details of each step at this point, but the leadership needs to share a common vision of the future state, why the journey is to be taken, and the general path to be taken. Visual conceptual models, such as Figure 9A, help to align the vision.

Teledyne Benthos and Fisher & Paykel both began their journeys with study. They read; they discussed; they consulted with experts; and once they understood, they communicated a shared vision of the destination and why they were making the journey.

Second Critical Success Factor: A Learning Process in Place Coupled with a Skilled Workforce

Learning-First Product Development is founded on the efficient and effective creation, capture and reuse of Set-Based Knowledge. Obviously this means continuous learning. Equally apparent is the need to concisely capture that knowledge. Then there is the need to make sure the knowledge is reused where appropriate. Specific skills are needed to do this efficiently and effectively.

In discussing how Teledyne Benthos and Fisher & Paykel built these skills, it may be helpful to group the necessary skills into sets around their predominant users. First is effective learning; LAMDA is the technique that enables this. And the knowledge gained from LAMDA must be captured. Knowledge Briefs and trade-off curves are the primary mechanisms. For this discussion, let's designate these as knowledge creation and capture skills.

The knowledge owners need an additional set of skills. These involve generalizing, organizing and optimizing the knowledge for reuse. They need to be able to take the knowledge created in their areas of responsibility, validate its quality, generalize it to fit more situations, and then organize it to fit how it will be reused. So they need to be able to capture the lessons learned in the form of design rules and limits and to create and use Set-Based Knowledge Maps™ for understanding the interactions of those rules and limits.

Finally, there is a third set of skills needed to effectively create and reuse knowledge within a development project. Functional Managers and Entrepreneurial System Designers must know how to schedule and execute Integrating Events, and to build and use Knowledge Checksheets.

The principles behind all of these are fairly simple and straightforward. However, they are acquired skills that must be learned and practiced to gain proficiency. At Fisher & Paykel leadership decided to train everyone on the foundational skills needed to create and capture the knowledge. Then only the newly designated functional knowledge owners and the entrepreneurial system designers were trained on the remaining skills for knowledge organization, optimization and the process for use in development. On the other hand, Teledyne Benthos is a small company where everyone wears many hats and may be called on to perform any job at any time. So Leadership decided to train the entire organization in all the skills.

Both these companies considered the skills their workforce would need to be successful and built those skills before converting to the new process.

LAMDA in Practice

"LAMDA has become the tool of choice at F&P. We have demonstrated that time spent understanding the current situation leads to faster, more robust solutions."

Christian Gianni, Vice President of Engineering, Fisher & Paykel

"Engineers are taking a more scientific approach to tasks. They don't jump to conclusions or propose solutions before looking at the problem."

Bob Melvin, Director of Engineering, Teledyne Benthos

Third Critical Success Factor: Functional Subsystems Are Defined with Clear Responsibility for Knowledge Growth and Quality

One common reason organizations are not effectively capturing and reusing their knowledge is that no one is formally designated with that responsibility. Equally ineffective is the case where everyone is responsible for knowledge management in general, but specific areas of responsibility are not defined. These conditions are likely, if not necessarily, the consequence of knowledge not being visible. With the advent of Knowledge Briefs and trade-off curves, this prerequisite is met. Still, responsibility for creating, capturing, generalizing, maintaining and reusing the knowledge needs to be explicit.

Products are made up of subsystems that perform functions that customers want. The language of design for Set-Based Knowledge Development includes trade-off curves that reflect known performance of design decisions against defined customer interests. This provides a natural architecture for allocating the knowledge management responsibilities. Often, as in the case of Teledyne Benthos, the structure of the development organization mirrors the subsystems of the product. In these cases, formal responsibility must simply be assigned to managers of engineering teams.

At Fisher & Paykel, most of the engineering resources were dedicated to project teams for specific products. While this focused resources on the projects, it did little to build the deep expertise synonymous with effective knowledge growth and quality. As part of their organizational restructuring they identified their major knowledge subsystems, staffed around them and assigned the knowledge responsibilities to subsystem functional leaders.

It is possible to over think the partitioning of knowledge subsystems in the product. The most important thing is what Teledyne Benthos and Fisher & Paykel did — clearly define some and assign responsibility.

Fourth Critical Success Factor: An Entrepreneurial System Designer Must Be Identified for Every Project

The role of the entrepreneurial system designer (aka chief engineer) has been fully discussed earlier in this book and in the earlier book Product Development for the Lean Enterprise. So we will not elaborate on it here other than to offer a reminder that every project must have one. Fisher & Paykel created chief engineering positions in their new organization. At Teledyne Benthos, the existing project managers took on the role. In both cases, the responsibility for business success, customer advocacy, and technical trade-offs was clear.

Fifth Critical Success Factor: Install a System for Generalizing, Visualizing, Managing, and Reusing Set-Based Knowledge

The system for managing Set-Based Knowledge is multi-faceted. It involves practice of the techniques by the Expert Engineering Workforce, the Knowledge Owners and the Entrepreneurial System Designers. It involves the processes of test-then-design, Integrating Events and knowledge based reviews. And importantly, how the knowledge now embodied in Knowledge Briefs will be stored and retrieved, either physically or electronically. Teledyne Benthos and Fisher & Paykel will both readily admit that the latter still needs work.

The authors of this book are all former engineering managers. As such, we have firmly ascribed to the principle that a new technique should be perfected manually before automating it. Otherwise there is the risk that automation will result simply in the ability to make mistakes faster. With this predisposition, we have not encouraged urgency in implementing an electronic system for managing the Set-Based Knowledge. Experience with dozens of companies implementing Learning-First Product Development indicates that is a mistake.

A product development organization can create and capture valuable, reusable knowledge at an astonishing rate. On average, LFPD organizations create 2.5 Knowledge Briefs per person per month. So in a six-month period, an organization of 50 developers would generate 750 Knowledge Briefs.

The first implication of this statistic is the realization of just how much knowledge is presently lost in organizations. This is knowledge that is presently being created or used, not knowledge that has just been regurgitated for the purpose of filling some quota of Knowledge Briefs (quotas are not recommended). Prior to LFPD, this knowledge had resided in the heads of the developers, with little sharing and a high risk that it walked out the door with the engineer.

The second implication is that if an organization waits even a few months before considering how the knowledge will be archived and retrieved, there will be a tremendous legacy of Knowledge Briefs that must be transferred into whatever electronic system is chosen as a solution. In addition to the effort of importing the accumulated knowledge into a system, there is the consideration that until the solution is in place, it becomes increasingly difficult to find and reuse the knowledge. For this reason, it is now our advice that the search for a solution should run concurrent to the training rather than sequential to it.

Although a detailed dialogue on the desirable attributes of a system for managing Set-Based Knowledge is merited at some point, for now we would like to offer two guiding principles:

> **Knowledge is an asset.** If an organization is considering implementing Learning-First Product Development, then it has recognized that knowledge is both the raw material and the tangible product of research and development. Depending on your industry, your company is investing anywhere from five to twenty percent of annual revenues to develop that knowledge. A system to manage this corporate asset deserves the same attention given to managing raw materials, inventories and other corporate assets.
>
> **'How will we store the knowledge' is the wrong question.** Knowledge will be created and captured once. The objective is for it to be reused tens, if not hundreds of times. No one would consider a materials inventory system optimized around putting material into inventory. What is important in an inventory management system is the ability to quickly see what is there,

what is needed, and get it to the right operation at the right time. The same holds true for managing Set-Based Knowledge. The right question to ask is: *"How effective is the system at helping us find, maintain and use the knowledge we have captured?"*

Sixth Critical Success Factor: Top Level Management Must Drive the Transformation

Many engineers upon completion of the LFPD training proclaim that they could employ the techniques of LAMDA, Knowledge Briefs and trade-off curves to their personal benefit, even if no one else in the company practiced them. Alone they are useful tools, but the greatest value is when they enable the entire organization to operate as a unified, Lean, productive workforce. Achieving this requires visible committed leadership.

The small size of the product development organization at Teledyne Benthos allowed President Marsiglio to personally participate in each step of the journey. His support was visible throughout. He took the training. He coached individuals and teams. He quickly addressed obstacles and solved implementation problems. And he changed the way he worked to pull the new behaviors from the organization. For example, he asked for Knowledge Briefs, not PowerPoint presentations, he asked for reviews and he questioned teams on their LAMDA results before allowing action plans to be implemented. Marsiglio stayed on message and walked the talk.

Fisher & Paykel's size dictated a different leadership structure. CEO Bongard invested in learning how the principles of LFPD would address the many issues to do with product development at F&P. He communicated his unreserved support to VP Gianni and to the organization as a whole. And he backed up his message by appointing Gilchrist as the champion. Bongard's visible leadership did not end at the beginning. Throughout the transformation, Bongard continued to demonstrate his genuine interest. He would stop in front of Knowledge Briefs and Set-Based Knowledge Maps™ posted on the walls in engineering and ask the engineers to describe their work.

The vice president of engineering, Gianni, was equally involved. He participated in the first training session and then attended the feedback session for every subsequent workshop. Like Marsiglio at Teledyne Benthos, Gianni also pulled the new behaviors from the organization by insisting on LAMDA and asking for Knowledge Briefs. As the new Centre

Heads were appointed, they too followed Gianni's example. And Gilchrist's role as champion cannot be understated. He planned and arranged the training, facilitated the organizational restructuring, and constantly solicited feedback from the organization, quickly addressing any issues.

While the approaches differed, the common component in these two successful transformations was knowledgeable, visible, and consistent leadership.

The Three-Step Transformation

Teledyne Benthos and Fisher & Paykel are two of an elite group of companies that have fully implemented the Learning-First Product Development process. Dozens of others are on the journey; their objective is achieving the full 4X productivity gains possible in the new paradigm. Interestingly, however, there is another set of organizations that have chosen an intermediate milestone as their near-term destination.

An important characteristic of LFPD is that each step of the journey, each technique learned and implemented, enhances the productivity of the organization. Alone the techniques do not provide the same magnitude of productivity improvement as when they are implemented as a complete and complementary system, but the gains can nevertheless be significant. A number of organizations have made the strategic decision to implement only the foundational skills and forego, for the present, implementing the full LFPD process. The reasons vary. Some based their decision on the amount of change they felt their organization could absorb in the near term. Others decided to make a slow transition and to entrench the basic skills before advancing to full LFPD. Some decided that the foundational skills met all their objectives. And one recognized that those basic knowledge management skills applied not only to product development, but also to their entire organization. They chose to deploy them across the entire company as the foundation for a continuous improvement culture, before implementing the rest of LFPD in the development organization.

To understand their thinking and to provide a framework for discussing the implementation journey, we would like to propose a three-step implementation model.

Step 1: The first step is about effectively and efficiently learning and capturing the knowledge from the learning. We call it *Robust Visible Knowledge Development.*

Step 2: The second step is establishing the abilities to optimize and organize that knowledge for reuse in all future development projects, to effectively manage the flows that create and reuse that knowledge, and to effectively use the knowledge in product designs. This second step we call *Knowledge-Based Product Development.*

Together, these two steps enable the full Knowledge Value Stream from creation to use and reuse. And for reasons we elaborate on in Appendix A, the techniques by which the Knowledge Value Stream is optimized in these two steps can be described as Lean Knowledge Management (LKM).

Step 3: The third step we call *Set-Based Concurrent Engineering* (SBCE). In this step Set-Based Knowledge Mapping™ and other techniques are learned and applied to identify and trade-off alternative solutions. Techniques for finding existing knowledge and closing knowledge gaps are implemented. This phase culminates with formally integrating the LFPD methodology into an existing product development process or creating an entirely new one.

Summary and Overall Conclusion

In business novel format and through case studies and discussion, we have set out to explain the concepts and benefits of a different approach to product development that we call Learning-First Product Development. The methodology, inspired by practices of Toyota Motor Company and refined through application to a wide variety of industries across the globe, is based on some simple, but powerful principles:

1. Knowledge is both the raw material and the output of product development,
2. Set-Based Knowledge is infinitely more valuable than Point-Based Knowledge,
3. Knowledge must be visible to be used and managed,
4. The product development organization must be skilled at creating, capturing and using the knowledge,
5. The knowledge needed to be successful is a deep understanding of the interests of all the customers in the operational value stream, how decisions made in design affect them and how those design decisions interact with each other,

6. The knowledge needed to be successful should be learned before the decision, not afterwards,
7. The decisions should be delayed as long as possible to allow the maximum learning within time and budget,
8. Mechanisms must exist within the product development process to pull the reuse of existing knowledge and the creation of additional knowledge before the decision deadline,
9. That knowledge should enable and be systematically used to eliminate the weakest alternatives from the set of all feasible solutions allowing designs to converge to the optimum, and
10. The organization must manage the process of creating, capturing and using the product development knowledge with the same diligence given to other corporate assets.

A profound and fundamental change occurs when these principles are implemented. Knowledge, the true value of product development, once invisible and scattered, is now visible and concentrated. Knowledge has become material. And as such it can be truly managed as a corporate asset.

Hopefully we have conveyed that the skills and tools needed by the organization to implement LFPD are simple, easy-to-learn and powerful. What is difficult is that some of the principles are opposite to today's practices and even seem counter-intuitive. Further, some roles in organizations may need to be created or modified for better knowledge management. And, as with any initiative, there is the need to lead the organizational change.

As these principles and capabilities begin to fall in place, engineering productivity and schedule attainment increases rapidly:

- *Less time solving problems,*
- *Better problem solutions,*
- *No repeat problems,*
- *Greatly reduced design loopbacks,*
- *Less time recreating knowledge that has walked out the door,*
- *More optimum product designs,*
- *Fewer manufacturing start-up problems,*
- *And more satisfied customers.*

And the news just gets better, because the captured knowledge grows like compound interest in a bank account. As knowledge is captured and reused, more resources are available to create new knowledge. Instead of resources going into repeatedly learning the same lessons and firefighting at the end of projects, they are being used to discover new technologies, to improve the existing ones, and to better apply those to new products. And as that knowledge is captured and reused, even more resources become available for advancing the organization's knowledge and products.

This is not good news for the competitors of Toyota, Teledyne Benthos, Fisher & Paykel and the competitors of others that are well on their journey. These companies started first; they have been making steady progress; and their reserve of captured knowledge is extensive. They have established a lead in building their knowledge equity and that lead will be difficult for their competitors to overcome.

But this is good news for everyone else. You don't have to be as good as Toyota or even the other early adopters. You couldn't start there even if you wanted to. You just have to be better than your competitors by starting first and keeping a good pace. And that is your journey to domination.

If you would like help along your path, or would like to share what's worked for you, we would love to hear from you. You can find us at:

http://www.TargetedConvergence.com

or email us at:

Answers@TargetedConvergence.com

Appendix II.A
Lean Knowledge Management of the Knowledge Value Stream

In Chapter 13, we identified three steps involved in the transformation to Learning-First Product Development. We also asserted that the first two steps enable the management of the Knowledge Value Stream using 'Lean Knowledge Management' principles. That assertion may raise a few eyebrows, so some explanation is probably merited.

From the initial understanding of Toyota's product development system, it was clear that visible knowledge played a critical role. It was equally clear that the techniques employed by their expert engineering workforce were integral to creating, capturing and reusing that knowledge. As we have partnered with organizations on their implementation journey, our understanding of why LAMDA, the process of writing Knowledge Briefs, trade-off curves, and the role of the knowledge owner are so vitally important has deepened. With the increased understanding came the need to be able to explain it in a framework and context relatable to others.

The decision to describe the collection of these techniques as an approach to Lean Knowledge Management was not made without deliberation. First, 'Lean' seems to be the current marketing adjective of choice for every improvement initiative that comes down the pipe. So many people have developed an immune response to the word. Yet when the needs of knowledge management in product development are examined, the fundamental principles (not the manufacturing techniques) of Lean address each and every one of those needs. Second, 'knowledge management' is another term that meets with mixed reception in the corporate world. Many knowledge management initiatives have not delivered on their promise. Often these initiatives have really targeted data and information management, not knowledge. There is a difference. And those that have focused on knowledge have not addressed both the human and non-human elements of the knowledge system from creation to reuse. Still, this first phase is about learning, capturing the knowledge and reusing it. That is managing knowledge. So while the term Lean Knowledge Management comes with some baggage, we found it to be the most descriptive name for a major milestone on the journey to LFPD. It establishes the critical

Knowledge Value Stream introduced within the IRT storyline. Whether a company chooses to use the phrase Lean Knowledge Management is unimportant; understanding the importance of the principle is critical for eventual success of the LFPD environment.

Allen Ward described the state of knowledge in most organizations as "scattered." It resides in the heads of individuals, in personal files, in notebooks, in presentations, in databases, and elsewhere. It is not in a concise form that can be discussed, validated, generalized, made relevant and ultimately applied. Its existence is often invisible to those that need it. Its accuracy and relevance is questionable. In this state, knowledge is virtual and unmanageable.

A colleague on a project management process initiative once stated that "a true project deliverable must have mass. You must be able to hold it in your hand and when you drop it, it will hit the floor." Knowledge Briefs and trade-off curves bring the same quality to knowledge. It makes it visible and gives it mass. Knowledge becomes material. And that provides us with an analogy to help explain the concept of Lean Knowledge Management.

Knowledge is both the raw material and the output of product development. The process takes in knowledge about markets, customer interests, technology and manufacturing capabilities. New knowledge is created to fill any gaps. All that knowledge is transformed by the collective intellect of the development organization into knowledge that manufacturing can use to make a product that customers will buy at a profit to the firm. That output knowledge is often encoded and made visible in the form of drawings, bills of material and process instructions. The analogy of visible knowledge in product development (and other business processes) to material in manufacturing is not perfect, but it is instructional.

The objective of Lean Manufacturing may be described as the ability to get the correct things, to the correct places, at the correct time, and in the correct quantity with minimal waste. Following the same logic, the objective of Lean Knowledge Management is to get the correct knowledge, to the correct people, at the correct time and of the correct quality with minimal waste.

Correct Knowledge

So the first question is 'what is the correct knowledge?' The first principle of Lean is to understand value from the customers' perspective. (Remember the consumer of the product developer's work is not only the end user of the product but also manufacturing, sales, sometimes regulatory agencies, and maybe others. Dr. Ward described the customer as the operational value stream.) Customers derive benefit from the work of product development when their interests are satisfied. You may have noted in the case studies the effort invested in truly understanding the customer interests. So understanding the customer interests and why they perceive value in them is one important category of knowledge, but not the only one.

The act of developing a product is about making design decisions that satisfy those customer interests, hopefully in the most optimum manner. The design decisions may be about materials, components, geometries, process parameters and anything else that will eventually find its way into a drawing, bill of materials, or processing sheet and ultimately the product. Those decisions will vary in size and significance from choosing the fundamental technology to the thread count on a bolt. Developing even the simplest product involves hundreds of such decisions. For a developer, knowing how each decision influences, either directly or indirectly, the customer interests is critical.

Design decisions are not independent. Each design decision made places constraints on other design decisions. A third critical piece of knowledge for developers is to understand how and to what degree the decisions they make influence other design decisions in the product.

So the correct knowledge in the product development application of Lean Knowledge Management is that knowledge that informs us about our customers' interests, how our design decisions serve the interests of our customers, and how our design decisions interact with other design decisions.

Correct People at the Correct Time

The correct time for knowledge to arrive at the correct people is, of course, when those people need to make a design decision, and there are a couple of elements of timing that are fundamental to Lean Knowledge Management and the lean principle of 'pull.'

One basic approach sometimes used in an attempt to manage knowledge in product development is trying to push the knowledge through the organization. For example, requiring that lessons learned reports be generated and sent to all parties that might be interested. Or alternatively, requiring they be presented at lessons learned reviews.

The problem with these approaches is that the knowledge may arrive at a user so far in advance that they do not recognize its significance or forget it before the need arises. At that time, they may not even know that they are (or going to be) the correct people for that knowledge. There is also the possibility that it does not arrive in time, so decisions are delayed or are made without the best knowledge. A push system also requires the user to sift through all the information sent to them or put it in a big knowledge box to find what they need. As the amount of captured knowledge increases, the inefficiency of this type of arrangement increases geometrically.

In knowledge management as in production, pull is leaner than push. The decision maker needs the ability to see specifically the best knowledge the organization has captured about that decision they are currently trying to make. The design decision is the trigger for the pull. The inventory is the organization's existing knowledge specifically related to that decision. And the lead-time is the time needed to close any knowledge gaps.

Finally, another important timing aspect of Lean Knowledge Management is accessibility. For people to be willing to search for and reuse existing knowledge, they must perceive that they can find and understand existing knowledge quicker than they can recreate it themselves. This is one area where traditional attempts at knowledge management have fallen woefully short. Keyword searches of lessons learned databases can produce a long list of documents related to the subject. Since the knowledge is organized by topic, rather than by being linked to the specific design decision, the designer is forced to review each document to determine its relevance. And those documents can be long. To the designer this can appear to be a lot of work with no guarantee of a result. Concisely capturing knowledge in one-page Knowledge Briefs and linking them to the design decisions they inform solves this problem.

Correct Quality

Perhaps the number one impediment to the reuse of knowledge is poor quality of the captured knowledge. Those that might reuse it simply don't trust it. Fully discussing all the issues surrounding the quality of knowledge would likely fill a separate book. So for now we will limit the discussion to a few of the major quality attributes and the solution.

Some of the important quality attributes of knowledge are:

Accuracy: The knowledge is correct and with the precision sufficient to the need. It doesn't have to be perfect, but the user needs to understand to what degree they can trust the knowledge.
Credibility: How was the knowledge obtained? Is it sound? Is it based in fact?
Robustness: The knowledge must be insensitive to minor variations in situation. Set-Based Knowledge and trade-off curves excel in this area.
Comprehensible: The reader must be able to understand the documented knowledge, so good technical writing and graphics are a must.
Current: Is the knowledge obsolete? Knowledge must be cur-

The most important quality characteristic of knowledge is this: knowledge must enable good decisions. Knowledge is never perfect. The late Dr. Richard Feynman, the famous Nobel Laureate in the demanding science of quantum physics, frequently stated, "Everything we know is only an approximation." So for the knowledge to be of useful quality, the approximation must be good enough to result in a good decision. Therefore the quality of any specific piece of knowledge is inextricably linked to the decision it serves and the importance of that specific decision to the overall project.

There are other quality attributes of knowledge. The point is that for knowledge to be reused it must be of good quality. And the way to get high quality knowledge is to build in the quality when it is created; quality-in equals quality-out. LAMDA, Knowledge Briefs and Knowledge Ownership, working in concert, build in that quality.

Minimal Waste

When Lean is mentioned the focus of management seems drawn to the elimination of waste, often to the detrimental lack of attention to the other Lean principles and the overall philosophy. So we want to enter a discussion on knowledge waste with the recognition and reminder that the elimination of knowledge waste is only part of a Lean Knowledge Management system.

In his discussion of knowledge waste in the book Lean Product and Process Development, Dr. Allen Ward identified three primary categories of knowledge wastes: scatter, hand-off and wishful thinking. For

those interested in exploring this subject further, Dr. Ward's book should be on the reading list. However, since most readers of this book are more familiar with the seven types of waste normally associated with manufacturing Lean, we will provoke thinking on the concept by analogizing waste in knowledge management to those in manufacturing:

Overproduction: In production, this means building product in excess of demand. For knowledge management in the product development arena, this means creating knowledge for the sake of knowledge. Knowledge must serve the objective, and that means informing design decisions that satisfy true customer interests. An important caveat, however, is that knowledge that informs us as to what will not work is equally important as knowledge that tells us what will work.

Transportation: In a production environment this refers to the unnecessary movement of material, inventory or finished product. In knowledge management, once the knowledge is visible and tangible, how can it be most efficiently transported (or made accessible) to the user? There is also an issue of transportation unique to knowledge and its use. Dr. Ward described this issue as one of hand-offs. This inefficiency in the creation and use of knowledge occurs when responsibilities for knowledge, decision-making, action and feedback are separated. The knowledge flow is broken in this situation and inefficiencies result.

Motion: Whereas transportation deals with the flow of knowledge, motion deals with the work required by developers to create, find and reuse the knowledge. Sifting through a lot of irrelevant knowledge to find the needed knowledge is wasteful motion. The knowledge logistics must be optimized for the efficiency of the developers during creation and especially during reuse.

Waiting: In production this refers to machines or people waiting on material to arrive at the workstation. In knowledge management, it is not having sufficient knowledge available to make a good decision in a timely manner. One form of this is not being able to find the knowledge when it's needed. The most insidious form is discovering the necessary knowledge after the product has been designed and tested, thus necessitating a design loopback.

Inventory: Keeping inventories of raw material, work in progress and finished goods above demand and the minimum necessary to keep the line flowing in production is wasteful. When applied to knowledge there are two issues: clutter and obsolescence. Clutter is the accumulation of knowledge that is not directly relevant to supporting design decisions that serve the operational value stream. Obsolescence is knowledge that has been superseded by new learning. These at best can cause users to be inefficient and at worst to make incorrect decisions. One role of knowledge owners is to manage the knowledge inventory.

Over Processing: In the manufacturing environment, this refers to unnecessary activities required to produce the product as a result of poor machine or product design. In product development, the most common over processing waste is in the effort required by the user of the knowledge to understand the captured knowledge. Ironically, this is often the result of under processing by the creator of the knowledge.

Defects: It is important that a knowledge gap not be considered a defect. Rather it is an opportunity to be prioritized and acted upon to increase value to the customer. Likewise, as discussed earlier, an imperfect approximation is not a defect so long as it enables good decisions to be made and does not limit the ability to provide value to the customer. The most prevalent defect is information, not validated by observed evidence, which is put forward as knowledge. In other words, defective knowledge is opinion and wishful thinking masquerading as knowledge.

However, the analogy of waste in Lean Knowledge Management to those in other Lean processes comes up one waste short, and it is probably the most predominant knowledge waste. The reason this waste isn't recognized in Lean Manufacturing is that it would never occur. How long would a manufacturing manager keep his job if he constantly built product, threw it away and built it again? Yet that happens on a daily basis to knowledge in product development organizations. Overcoming the urge to label this type of knowledge waste as "insanity," we will categorize it as:

Loss: Paying to create the same knowledge or solve the same problems time after time.

What Toyota effectively established with their Product Development System was one of the few truly effective knowledge management systems... a system with minimal knowledge waste... that pulls the knowledge flow through the Knowledge Value Stream into the Product Value Stream just as it is needed. Lean Knowledge Management.

Appendix II.B
Product Development Performance Assessment

Many people we talk to cannot believe that Toyota has four times the product development productivity as western companies. Think about it. Many of America and Europe's leading companies are the most successful in the world and they employ the best and brightest people, many of whom attended the best universities in the world. Clearly Toyota is well managed, but can they be four times better at product development than the best western companies, particularly western companies that are far more profitable than Toyota?

You be the judge.

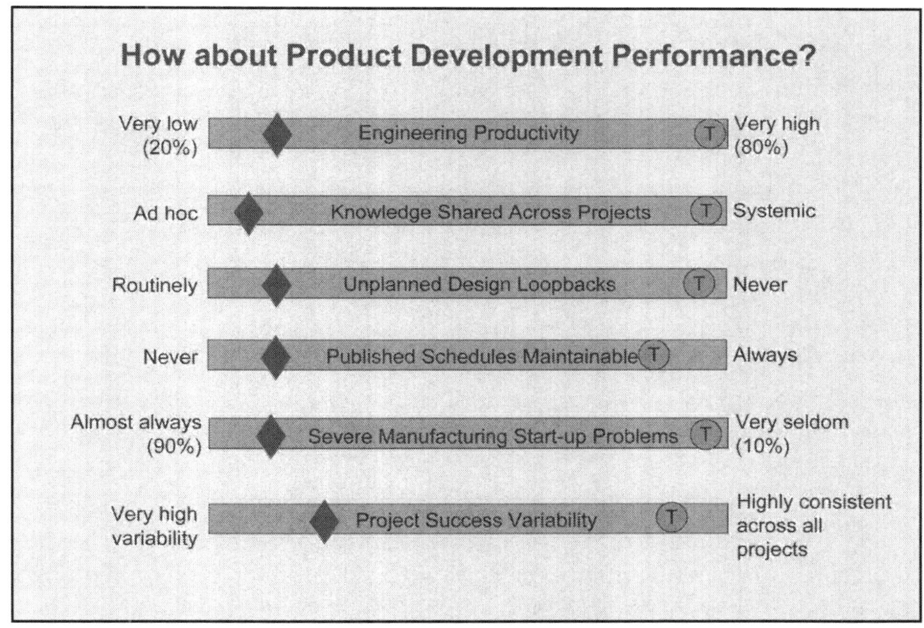

1. Engineering Productivity defined as the percent of time adding value for customers. How much time do your engineers spend on the following non-productive tasks:

- Completing compliance activities / metrics?
- Searching for information?
- Attending administrative task-based and accomplishment-based meetings reviews, and 'dog and pony' shows?

- Listening to project goals, updates, and status?
- Re-solving already solved problems?
- Re-learning the limits of product technology?
- Re-learning the limits of manufacturing and supplier capabilities?
- Re-learning what customers really want?
- Bringing new people up to speed?
- Fixing new-hire mistakes?

Over 80% of Toyota's engineering time, including both engineers and managers, is spent creating value for customers. In contrast, most engineers in western companies report 15-25% engineering time; most managers closer to 5%. Where does your company stand?

2. How well is your Knowledge Shared Across Projects?

- Do you fear the loss of knowledge through attrition / retirement?
- Is most project information stored in personal files or in heads of engineers?
- Is what was learned on prior projects only reused on a new project if the individual engineers from the prior project moved to the new one?
- Is known knowledge reinvented?
- Is the validity of available information suspect or is it not applicable such that it has to be recreated?
- Do problems solved for one product recur on other products?
- Is the knowledge required to make feasible design decisions visible?

At Toyota, all departments capture the knowledge needed to design products and manufacturing processes. Captured knowledge is reused across departments, platforms, product lines, and businesses. Toyota's knowledge management system identifies trustworthy knowledge so engineers know what knowledge can be trusted. New and existing technologies and processes are always tested to failure with sufficient prototypes to create trade-off curves or manufacturing rules. Trade-off curves are almost always robust enough for reuse on other current and future products.

However, the pace at which Toyota has built design centers and manufacturing factories around the world has stretched its capabilities.

3. How often do problems require Unplanned Loopbacks negating earlier design decisions?
- Are schedules padded with a buffer to accommodate unplanned design loopbacks?
- Is a single design concept defined early and if so, does it change during the course of product development?
- Do unplanned redesigns impact multiple product engineering and manufacturing areas?
- Do unplanned loopbacks cause confusion through miscommunication and timing?
- Do unplanned loopbacks cause schedules to be slipped?
- Do unplanned loopbacks continue into Production?
- Are early project reviews focused on educated / experience-based judgments and wishful thinking versus honest evaluation of hard data and test results?

Toyota avoids unplanned design loopbacks by testing the sets of possible design decisions before making those decisions. As a result, they effectively develop sets of feasible product designs from which a final design is selected. Toyota searches for innovation while carrying safe product designs. Weaker product designs are eliminated through analysis / testing until best design is found. Design almost always meets or exceeds quality goals on schedule.

4. Are the Published Schedules Maintainable?

- Are the first schedules communicated to customers consistently achieved?
- Are detailed task-based schedules at beginning of project still accurate at end?
- Do all members of the project team across all disciplines really understand the program details?
- How much effort is invested in updating task-based schedules?
- Are schedule slippages routine and expected?
- Are program reviews based upon tasks completed?
- Is an unplanned resource push with firefighting ever required to complete new products?
- Are resources usually available on schedule?
- Are next generation projects impacted by current project slippage?

At Toyota the initial schedules are essentially never missed. Features and functionality sometimes have to be traded off to meet schedule. A small planned resource push is sometimes required but unplanned resources are never required. Resources are always available on schedule and next generation projects are never impacted.

5. Are there normally severe manufacturing startup problems?

- Does Manufacturing experience serious problems with new products?
- Are customer shipments ever delayed because of manufacturing problems during the ramp?
- Are there lots of engineering changes and rework during the ramp?
- Does tooling get reworked and redesigned?
- Are cost overruns fairly routine?
- Is Manufacturing's role confined to reviewing product design alternatives and design ideas with regard to manufacturability and providing feedback?

At Toyota, Product Design Engineers understand most manufacturing capabilities due to years of working against Checksheets from Manufacturing Engineering. By virtue of those Checksheets being visible knowledge, Manufacturing Engineering input isn't just at review time . . . their inputs flow proactively into the product designs.

Manufacturing Engineering sets most final tolerances. Manufacturability is almost always proven before product design is finalized and serious manufacturing problems almost never occur in pilot production and never in production ramp.

6. Is there significant variability in business results across projects?

- Are project results predictable?
- Are new product projects ever canceled during product development?
- Where does your company rate in your industry on profit?
- Do program managers ever pad forecasts to help a project survive?
- Are your customers consistently satisfied with your new products when first delivered?

Toyota's business performance is unmatched. The company has added roughly $70 billion of organic growth in the last five years and made $14 billion of net profit last year. Individual products ROI is usually predictable.

We elected not to include the twenty-question Product Development Performance Assessment because experience has taught us that facilitation is usually required to obtain a meaningful, comparative score. However, we will be happy to send you a copy. Please contact us at:

http://www.TargetedConvergence.com

or e-mail us at:

Answers@TargetedConvergence.com

Michael Kennedy
Founder and CEO
Targeted Convergence Corporation (TCC)

Before TCC, I worked for Texas Instruments Defense Electronics for 31 years in product development, in manufacturing, in systems development — in both individual contributor and mid-level manager positions. I retired as a Senior Member, Technical Staff (SMTS) with a role of a leader in the creation and adoption of improved product development processes. My efforts helped enable TI to win the coveted Malcolm Baldrige award for process excellence.

I took an early retirement package in 1997 when TI sold the defense business to Raytheon. Why did I retire? After all, I was still enjoying my work. I retired because I had met Dr. Allen Ward and had learned about the Toyota Product Development System from him. It was fundamentally different from what I had believed and had been leading at TI. It also was fundamentally better and resolved problems naturally that our rigorous process approach seemed unable to resolve. Our system was built on detailed design processes to manage specifications and the ability to iterate designs to meet those specifications. The Toyota system was built on the premise of learning — what the customer interests are and how to build the knowledge to meet them. Products are simply the result of integrating the growing knowledge into a continuous rhythm of great products.

I wrote the first book, Product Development for the Lean Enterprise (Oaklea Press, 2003) while I was working jointly with Allen on the NCMS project where we met and on other joint efforts. The plan was that I was going to write a business novel that introduced the change problems and he was going to write a textbook that explained more detail. His tragic death in a plane crash cancelled the plans and we lost a great interpreter of the Toyota System. This book, which was posthumously published last year, showed his thinking at the time; unfortunately, that book did not include what I feel is his greatest contribution: the recognition of the LAMDA learning process as the foundation of their system.

So why did my coauthors and I write this book? It is one thing to understand what Toyota does and, logically, why it works. It is quite another to actually implement the fundamentals in a different company and in different cultures. We feel that it is now time to focus on implementation. That is what this book is about. All of the authors have extensive experience in product development and manufacturing. Our observations are different from those of academics, as often are our conclusions.

I hope you will find this enjoyable and helpful in planning the future of your companies.

Michael

Ed Minnock
Vice President, Business Development
Targeted Convergence Corporation (TCC)

Before TCC, I worked for Hewlett-Packard (HP) as a Vice President and General Manager with profit and loss responsibility for a $900 million dollar business. Prior to HP, I worked for small and start-up companies including some of the fastest growing in America.

I understand the pressure managers are under to meet financial commitments. Executive compensation is often based upon financial performance and investors reward companies that continually beat their estimates. Trust me. No manager wants to be the reason why financial commitments are missed.

As global competition has increased, it has become more difficult to deliver needed profit. Cost management has taken center stage. Many believe workforce cost reductions are an unavoidable element of responsible cost management in today's global economy. The low productivity of most organizations offers few other choices.

Now there is another choice, one that can put companies on the road to Toyota-like domination.

I first heard about Toyota Product Development from colleagues at HP who hired Dr. Allen Ward. The same colleagues encouraged me to read Mike Kennedy's first book, *Product Development for the Lean Enterprise.*

It all made intuitive sense; Toyota is so successful because Toyota's employees learn about customer needs and the technologies that can possibly meet customer needs faster than the competition. Still I was skeptical. How could a very large company achieve four times the product development productivity of most western companies? So I went to work with Mike Kennedy to find out.

It has been an awakening. Straight-forward and easy-to-learn practices such as LAMDA and Knowledge Briefs improve productivity immediately and empower people. The most pleasant surprise is the magnitude of achievements by leaders who have implemented a Learning-First Product Development System.

I hope this story and that the two case studies assist you on your journey.

Ed Minnock

J. Kent Harmon
Vice President, Training and Consulting Services
Targeted Convergence Corporation (TCC)

My personal journey to understanding and belief in the Toyota approach to product development was neither quick nor easy. For 22 years I had worked for Texas Instruments Semiconductor Division. The first ten years of my career were spent working my way up the engineering ranks to become a Product Development Manager for three product lines of computer chips. Along with the position came the responsibility for the revenue and profitability of those product lines.

In 1994, I was given an aggressive revenue goal for the product lines I managed. There was no room in the budget for additional headcount to develop more new products above those already planned. I had to make do with the resources I had and that meant we had to be more productive.

So my management team and I began a quest to discover and implement the best practices in product development. We searched out and experimented with a plethora of techniques from a wide range of disciplines: gated development processes, project management, queuing theory, quality function deployment, failure mode effects analysis and many others. We selected and deployed those that worked for us. Time-to-market dropped and engineering productivity increased.

Our successes were noticed and I was asked to deploy those best practices across 24 product development organizations in six countries, first as Co-leader of the New Product Development Methods Team and then as Director of R&D Effectiveness. With initiatives around product development processes, portfolio management, project management and metrics we increased schedule attainment by approximately 30% and reduced the average Time-to-Market by around 20%. These gains were not insignificant and offset the roughly five percent increase in overhead necessary to execute and sustain the processes. Overall, it was worth the effort.

When I met Michael Kennedy in the summer of 1994 I had left Texas

Instruments to pursue a private practice deploying product development best practices in other companies. Michael, of course, immediately challenged me as to whether the traditional best practices I was deploying were truly the best. He maintained that Toyota's approach as fundamentally better. This initiated a six month debate that was waged through email, by telephone, at conferences, and up and down the fairways of our local golf course.

From my perspective at the time, the traditional best practices were proven approaches. I had seen them deliver productivity improvement, although not on the factor of 4X which Michael claimed that Toyota enjoyed over the competition. I rather doubted the claim and suspected that any order of magnitude advantage Toyota had was derived more from institutionalized inefficiencies at their competitors than something special Toyota was doing. I also could not see how the Toyota practices increased the innovation rate. It seemed to me that it would actually stifle innovation.

Wanting to end the debate, I decided to put the Toyota principles to the test. I sat down in my home study and used the Toyota approach to design a subsystem of a simple product. The results were totally unexpected. The techniques worked, and they worked well. They almost totally eliminated all the issues we had struggled mightily with in the traditional gated product development processes. I could clearly see how Toyota, or any other company that practiced these techniques, would be tremendously more productive than those that didn't. And I could see how the principals could be used to focus innovation and make the innovation process more effective and efficient. I actually felt angry with myself. I had spent more than a decade studying, thinking, and working to make product development more productive and I had overlooked these simple yet powerful fundamentals . . . all of which are based on common sense.

Since then I have worked with Michael Kennedy to implement the basic principles of the Toyota product development system in dozens of research and product development organizations across the world. Each of those organizations was unique. They each faced different market challenges and each engaged different technologies to deliver value to those markets. And while they all differed in the details, they all shared a common need: to be more competitive in the marketplace they all needed to be more productive in product development. And along the journey with these organizations another common theme emerged —

one that I had never encountered in my work on traditional product development processes. The rank and file engineers were saying, "We should do this. It just makes sense."

There is one other common theme I have observed among organizations that are successfully taking the journey to Learning-First Product Development. They have visionary leaders at the helm. Ordinary management and cadres of process experts will not suffice. The reason why is simple. At the core of these powerful principles is the need to recognize that knowledge is the true value created by product development. Despite the fact that most companies are spending five to fifteen percent of their annual revenue to create this knowledge, there is no line item on the company's income statement that itemizes the cost of knowledge walking out the door, or the cost to recreate knowledge that can not be found, or the cost of solving the same problem time and again. Nor is there a line item for the revenue lost because the product didn't satisfy the customers' needs or the profit lost because the products developed were less than optimal. Generally Accepted Accounting Practices are great for counting the value after it is earned, but they will not reveal this lost productivity opportunity. It takes visionary leadership to understand the source of the value and to build the generating power.

J. Kent Harmon